God's Wrong
is Most of All

Also published by Kenneth Cragg

Semitism: The Whence and Whither
"How dear are your counsels"

The Weight in the Word
Prophethood: Biblical and Quranic

With God in Human Trust
Christian Faith and Contemporary Humanism
A MEETING OF MINDS

The Christian Jesus
Faith in the Finding

Faiths in Their Pronouns
Websites of Identity

Readings in the Qur'an
Selected and translated by Kenneth Cragg

A Certain Sympathy of Scriptures
Biblical and Quranic

Faith at Suicide
Lives Forfeit: Violent Religion – Human Despair

God's Wrong
is Most of All

DIVINE CAPACITY

Kenneth Cragg

sussex
ACADEMIC
PRESS
Brighton • Portland • Toronto

2 4 6 8 10 9 7 5 3

First published 2006, reprinted 2012, in Great Britain by
SUSSEX ACADEMIC PRESS
PO Box 139
Eastbourne BN24 9BP

and in the United States of America by
SUSSEX ACADEMIC PRESS
920 NE 58th Ave   Suite 300
Portland, Oregon 97213-3786

and in Canada by
SUSSEX ACADEMIC PRESS (CANADA)
8000 Bathurst Street, Unit 1, PO Box 30010, Vaughan, Ontario L4J 0C6

British Library Cataloguing in Publication Data
A CIP catalogue record for this book is available from the British Library.

Library of Congress Cataloging-in-Publication Data
Cragg, Kenneth.
God's wrong is most of all : divine capacity : per necessitatem
  Christianus / Kenneth Cragg.
  p. cm.
Includes bibliographical references and index.
ISBN 978-1-84519-152-8 (h/c : alk. paper);
ISBN 978-1-84519-140-5 (p/b : alk. paper)
  1. God—Omnipotence. 2. Providence and government of
God. I. Title.
BT133.C73 2006
231′.4—dc22
                                                        2005031336

MIX
Paper from
responsible sources
FSC
www.fsc.org   FSC® C013056

Typeset and designed by G&G Editorial, Brighton & Eastbourne
Printed by TJ International, Padstow, Cornwall
This book is printed on acid-free paper.

CONTENTS

CHAPTER SYNOPSES

Introduction

'Swear; swear!' – the wide incidence of oath-requiring and oath-taking tells the endless quest for verification, in hope to ensure it by the threat of perjury: honesty via 'the Name of God' in invocation of some moral ultimacy. Yet 'God's Name' is also ever blameworthy: hence the abiding question around any divine capacity to verify or be verified. What of a human suspicion of pointless chaos, threatening any doctrine of divine 'unity' such as Biblical, Semitic and Islamic 'covenant' theology purports to explore in nature and in history? Its ventures, its alleged findings, have long occasioned the resulting issues of language and vocabulary, of politics and power. Shouldering these, what of the role of 'will to faith'? What, too, of some 'wounded Name' inviting to emulation? Any 'divine capacity', whether for trust or blame, engages with sundry 'wrongs'.

1 God – Ever Blameworthy, Ever Oath-Worthy

The divine capacity alike for oath-reliance and inclusive blame leads to the question: What can the idea of 'omnipotence' mean? Then follows the cult of a Thomas Hardy and his kin concerning some 'blighted star', of a nevertheless sacramental earth. Paradox lurks in all such scepticisms which have no intimacy with any less 'blighted'. And how alert with benedictions this one proves. Theology, however, these days is put on the defensive. The means of verity prove as besetting as the need for it. Shakespeare's Richard III provides a telling example of the necessity of oath-reliance and yet of the wrongs that make it so far to seek, if no ultimate assurance avails on which to call. Where might it be?

< vi >

2 Shakespeare's Dramatic Mind and Art

The compelling power of Shakespeare's moral universe in the great tragedies will educate, but not dictate, the verdict we should reach about the depth of human perversity, or the strange ministry we find there of vicarious souls. The poetic force and dramatic intensity, as well as his private reticence, present the issue: Whence these hard hearts? Why these vulnerable selves? How the righting of these worlds? Things 'rotten in the State', 'insurrection' in 'the state of man', and 'God's wrong' are evident enough, unless an atheism absolves a non-identity. Yet, in that event, the very burden evaporates into a worse enigma.

3 Comprehending Divine Unity

Shakespeare has introduced us graphically to the theologian's concern for divine unity. This theme cannot be merely assertive, if mindless of a chaos, questioning the very case for a cosmos. Divine unity must be no mere matter of number as some simple discounting of plural idols – and the subtle ones, anyway, have a sophisticated perpetuity in the profits and powers and false worships of this world. Whatever we can truly mean by 'omnipotence', it must be a capacity for a sovereignty undefeated in the end. Even Islam can hardly stay content merely to say that 'God is One', *Allahu akbar*, and forebear to show satisfyingly how in this human world.

4 That Primal Suspicion

Maybe we are led to a 'primal suspicion', more than a final riddle – despair of a coherent confidence – given our 'dominion' in creaturely possession of the world. There may come some notion of a divine 'regret' about us, as 'the mistake of creation', or even 'a jealous god', regretting our stature and its threat alike to divine and human satisfaction. Or, via Nietzsche, perhaps we are 'beyond good and evil', pretenders to a ruinous usurpation, in defiance of ultimate sovereignty. Yet that distinction is only the more present when we will to flout it. We have only renewed the question of divine integrity. Suspicion withers: interrogation remains.

5 Divine Integrity in Human Covenant

A theological quest re-inserts itself. Long Semitic tradition found that integrity in the natural order, tutor of the sciences, nursery of the arts and arena of the sacramental. Jewry and Judaism came to privatize this 'dominion status' in a personal people and a particular land. The first Noahid 'covenant' became the Sinaitic. Islam disapproved that impulse, returning to a Noahid 'seedtime and harvest' and dependable 'signs'. Christian faith universalizd it away from Judaic form and norm, while receiving these as clues to *all* ethnic cultural identities as severally

< vii >

'peoples of God' called to a Judaic emulation of national 'servanthood'. 'Let God be God' requires, in parallel formula, 'Let man be man'.

6   *Divine Integrity in Christ*

The realm of nature thus received, however, is burdened by the reach of history. Here, where humanity distorts itself in inhumanity, any divine integrity needs historical credentials more taxing than those which a cosmic nature may afford. Where may they be found assuredly? Taking the Hebrew clue as to 'event as revelation' (Exodus and Exile) as being where 'knowledge of God' belonged, and – with it – the Messianic theme, Christian faith found that assurance made actual in Jesus as the Christ and that Christ, 'crucified'. In finding Him, it found – and founded – itself. It saw there, in that history, the sure credentials of God, both vulnerable and vicarious in Jesus being his Christ. It has survived all dissuasions to the contrary.

7   *Cares and 'Bewares' in the Trust of Doctrine*

That conclusiveness meant, and means, the trust of doctrine, of Gospel, of something 'given' only in order to be reported further. A 'Who has believed our report?' echoes from prophet to apostle, from pilgrim to saint. But the thing entrusted is to 'earthen vessels', so that 'God is wronged' when witness is flawed. This happens when its 'centre of gravity' is thought to be somehow reinforced by infallible institution, or inerrant Scripture, or sheer miracle, or spiritual pride. These presume to add some 'guarantee', as if to mean that divine perjury would supervene, whereby faith's centre would be betrayed as insufficient of itself. Divine fidelity has no need of extraneous guarantors.

8   *Versions of Vocabulary*

Looming large from Chapter 7 and its onus on personal faith around that faith's due warrant comes the vital trust of words, of language, analogy and metaphor. Many 'wrongings of God' transpire in the handling of deep and loaded themes like 'the blood that cleanses', 'the price of sin' and 'the Lamb of God'. The very word GOD is fraught with ambiguity, so that atheism also is liable to be a vacuous notion until we know what 'God' is being denied and why. The Pilate/Jesus encounter in John's Gospel is a classic example of the language hurdle, with its tangle around utterly incompatible meanings of the single word 'King'. An intelligent trading in words, on either side of communication, is the crux of meaning.

9   *The Necessary Ministries of Doubt*

All the foregoing around meaning, language, authority and converse indicates a vital place for doubt as ongoing interrogation. A true faith is

< viii >

no prescript for a closed mind. As with love, we only have 'guarantee' in the growing maturity of a relationship. Faith in heart and mind is as a mountain to a mountaineer, or – more modestly – a garden to a gardener. This chapter reviews how the very confirmation of faith came in its wrestling with what challenged it. The aftermath of the Cross was the most burdened of them all. And the most victorious. '*Whom* we have believed' takes care of all.

10   *Expediences of Politics*

Thus far the theme has left aside the mutual bearings of religious faith and political power. The Pilate/Caiaphas situation as the crux of Christian event had highlighted its presence. Long centuries of Islamic *Din* and *Dawlah* and of Christendom's Papacy and Empire or state religion, and Judaism's recent Zionist return to Davidism, all attest the lore and lure of the power nexus. Yet true faith must be uncoercive. The modern western mind can even see the secular state as a deep theological truth. While faith should not lust to control society, this does not exempt it from a lively role in citizens' ethics and the moral calling of power to divine account. In any event, law and power attain only a modicum of justice and common good. The rest – and these also – belong with the conscience religion can educate and sustain.

11   *An Honest Will to Faith*

A powerful logic thus far indicates what must be acknowledged as the necessary *will* to faith and its commitment. There has to be a will to believe, reciprocal to the will pereived, via nature and faith-history, behind all things. As in love, such will moves by an inward compulsion that is reciprocal (like the constraints of medium upon the artist or upon a musician's reliance on the instrument) and proceeds on credentials as having them be proved. Such 'will' is far from 'willful'. It knows and finds itself responsive. We have no option to be optionless. Unbelief, also, is an act of will rather than of mere mental dissuasion and academic negativity. This means more than pragmatic conjectures about the human psyche. It has to do with 'business in great waters' because mortal life is not passed in a harbour. 'There is a tide.' A soul may say: 'I knew that I was meant for Christ.'

12   *The Wounded Name and Its Kindred Servants*

But suppose the Christ-event we plead is mis-identified or over esteemed? – even though it chimes so far with the logic of this vulnerable/vicarious world. If we suffer *because of*, it may be possible to suffer redemptively *on behalf of*, unless as Nietzsche averred, Christianity has falsely glorified tears, griefs and wounds and thus enervated and saddled the will to power

< ix >

with pathos and cowardice. Paradox was always at the heart of life, as it is of faith. *Lex talionis*, retaliation, have ever been the bane of history. Society needs its sufferers who engage its bitter vulnerability as redeemers in a love that saves. It was always assumed that the crucified Messiah would have a collective discipleship, sharing the fellowship of His costly grace in their reproducing love.

Per
Necessitatem
Christianus

INTRODUCTION

I

'Swear! Swear! Swear! Swear!' – four times the troubled ghost of royal Hamlet senior calls from beneath the Elizabethan stage in Shakespeare's tragedy.[1] Why this imperious demand that a pledge shall somehow bind itself beyond its own sincere intent? The burden of verifying verity is everywhere present in human affairs. Yet how can an 'oath sworn' assure the situation since its very sanction, in the risk of perjury, remains at stake? The means we think can make truth-speaking the more dependable are only sought because truth's presence is darkly suspect. It is an odd sort of satisfaction that finds surer hope in the added factor of potential perjury. Can there be better trust in what is the less implicitly trustworthy?

The strange paradox here deepens inasmuch as traditional oath-taking has long been 'in the Name of God'. If that invocation has seen in God the utter trustworthiness to which all oaths might appeal, how comes it that the same 'Name' has been through long human story the eminently blame-worthy? Biblical theology and that theology in its Christian ultimacy[2] in their custody of that 'oath-worthy' Name are plainly at stake in its steady blameworthiness. The double burden is the opening care here of Chapter 1.

That Christian faith has a self-authenticating quality as 'possessing' the Name of God in its perpetual capacity to underwrite oaths taken 'in its Name', must also lay upon itself the reproach of His being the magnet of all blame. It becomes, at one and the same time, the theology of a supreme trust and of a dire mistrust. For it bears God's burdens in the very art of telling His integrity. Both are inherent in the same vocation.

< 1 >

Such is the theme of 'God's wrong most of all' alike on the negative count of sceptical accusation *and* of its positive corollary in the counter 'sanctifying' of the Name.[3] Hence our point of departure from the words in a Shakespearean context of desperate oath-proposing where honesty was most remote. Thus it is divine integrity which is perennially at issue in the trust-deeds of faith to which any theology witnesses. 'God's wrong' is for ever latent in how faith-custodians may disserve Him by their own ill-judgment.

For there are moods in contemporary agnosticism which think that Christian theology is perjured, that it swears to what it cannot hold, is guilty of 'bad faith'. Perhaps this ensues from the tradition by which so much oath-taking in all circles was by invocation of the divine Name. The immediate irony follows – where else? By what – or whose – truth may truth itself be pledged? Who arbitrates the arbiter?

This is why study of divine integrity begins with the dilemma in Chapter 2 of Shakespeare's Richard III, after Chapter 1 has pondered the inevitable query around all oathing, and 'God', for good or ill, its constant point and crux. Dark villain as Shakespeare's Richard was, his hope for credibility had no adequate sanction to which it might appeal. This irony, latent in all 'swearing' sought or given, is only the more underlined by the fact that God, as so steadily invoked in that role, is the uniquely inculpated object of all blame-laying in the human story – God as the foreground or hinterland of all weary repudiation of the universe as known to human griefs and tears. This paradox for Chapter 3 via Chapter 2 plainly leads to 'The Primal Suspicion' in its ultimate terms as outlined in Chapter 4. An inclusive 'Hath God said . . . ?' looms over all occasions of culture and society that dare to take reputed 'dominion' into mental and manual trust.[4]

But this 'authority' to be and to possess, and so to belong and become, needs to ask what theology and faith can ever mean by 'divine unity'. There can readily be misunderstanding here, as if faith in the 'oneness of God' meant a process of mere counting that did not arrive beyond 'one' as 'singular'. So much in God's alleged 'blameworthiness' derives from false notions of 'omnipotence', as being the supremacy of One who excludes all rivals in claim but fails to subdue all rivals in fact.[5]

II

Only then it becomes evident that all is a question of divine integrity and that Christian – or any other theological – faith's integrity can consist nowhere else. Chapter 5, therefore, moves into this theme, exploring the divine 'good faith' in the intendedness of the earth, which is the necessary corollary of Christian faith in its sacramental order befitting and enabling human tenancy. A serious and in no way complacent faith, it reads the world as having an architecture meant and made for human habitat by an inhabitant at once resilient and resourceful, intelligent and adaptable, with a capacity for endurance and an aptitude for patience, so that – like a mountain to a mountaineer – it excites and provokes us to achieve its mastery.

This reading of our habitat and of ourselves its custodians is the Biblical meaning of 'have thou dominion'. It sees natural history passing into economic history and both into cultural history. It is the hidden secret of what modern culture dubs 'the secular', understood as precisely this situation of things duly within our power, but not 'secularized' in the pretentious sense that they are no theme for reverence, gratitude and consecration. The bane of such radical misunderstandings of who, and where, and why we are, will be with us in sundry other contexts.

Chapter 5 then is pre-occupied with this defining theme and pursues it under the Biblical concept of 'covenant' known as granted and received. This bond between the divine and the human, between things sacred and mundane, is the ground-plan of a Christian sacramental order, where 'bread and wine' from the 'table' of the good earth and the human farm and orchard are the place of a hospitality which becomes thereby an inter-human society also, thanks to the gentle economy of God, alike 'on high' and lowly.

Human procreation is, of course, the guarantor, in double sense, of this situation of which the psalmist in Psalm 139 is the liveliest exponent.[6] The capacity to inaugurate our continuity is more and more entangled now in our competence to sustain the continuum.[7]

This sense of things, however, thus 'covenantal' and so, in turn, 'sacramental', is hotly disputed on many urgent grounds. The theme of an 'intending' creation for creaturehood is bitterly travestied – or so it would seem – by all that creaturely history has evidenced of deliberate perversity, corruption, conflict, tyranny and arrogance, on our human part. These have been darkly connived at, or not deterred, by religion itself in league with the angry politics of nation states and imperial power.

Human experience of dominion is either chronically self-deluded or all has grievously miscarried. There may, indeed, be a beneficent normalcy in nature, enabling a manifold technology, but what of nature's seemingly malevolent disasters sobering those visions of control and mastery? Some of these may duly prove amenable to precaution and correction, but the sense of threat abides and rankles in the soul.[8] The 'Where is God'? question will not rest.

Yet more deadly for equanimity with the theme of human creaturehood, as the divinely given 'architecture' of where we find ourselves, are the endless perversities with which recorded time has occupied and plagued it. Despair about human nature altogether reverses the celebra-

< 3 >

tion of the human dignity in the admiring eloquence of the Hebrew psalmist crying: 'What is man that you prize him so highly?' The rhetoric has to be all the other way and turn into lament: 'Better it were if they had never been!' History is too loaded with horrors ever to have been the project of an almighty sanity. If we mean to posit creation, creaturehood in its custody must be read as its damnation. How can we reasonably worship a God who has been so wanton with His world – a wanton-ness of which we humans are the bitter evidence?

Yet does not despair turn the tables on itself? There was the other psalmist who cried: 'Out of the depths have I called unto Thee, O Lord.' If 'prizing the human so highly', thus having the human the crux of divine policy for creation, is a divine wanton-ness *we* must reproach and accuse, are we not witnessing to the still more ultimate business God has with us? That 'depth' out of which God is 'accused' is our capacity for wrong and evil. The human cannot be the blight and bane of a good creation and not also be the theme and scene of a divine redemption. Humankind in a despair about themselves – translated into an indictment of God – are, by the same token, perceiving a divine liability for them. Our wrongs cannot be 'God's wrong', and not be also God's realm of counter-action. If we implicate Him in ourselves as a futile folly, we thereby engage Him in an answering onus to redeem both us and His creation.

That onus was the very substance of the Biblical Messiah, the Messiah of whose realization in history the New Testament faith believed itself possessed, and possessed in a 'Christ crucified'. Divine integrity in covenantal creation[9] passed into its necessary sequence in a Christhood that answered to the intention, and the frustration, of the first 'Let there be'. The Creator, with the summons of us humans into the 'good' of His intent and law, becomes – in one consistency – the Bearer of the burden of our wrong.[10] The meaning of creation, and the human dignity within it as also annals of despair, require the meaning and reality of redemption.

The Biblical story, as it issued into the self-awareness of Israel in the mind of the great prophets of the Exile, knew this future hope as the logic of the past, the prospect in the present. Chapter 6 here has to see it realized – as apostolic experience believed – in the ministry and Passion, the entire significance of Jesus as the Christ. There 'God's wrong is most of all' is present in a double sense. Historically 'suffered', taken and borne there, we see the representative wrong-doing of the age-long human scene, 'the sin of the world'. There was, in the same entire event, the discernible crisis-point of all those reproaches of God to which despair and futility have arrived from our human undoing of a good creation – an undoing we have then charged against divine wantonness in having made a flawed or foolish human scene.

The reach of a Christ crucified in the economy of God and of His good creation takes the full measure of theology with history, if either is honest with the other.

III

The deep Semitic sense of the created order as entrusted into a caring creaturehood on human part translates into a ruling sense of 'entrust-edness' on the part of 'God in Christ', confiding the Gospel of grace to the custody of a serving Church. The theme is central to the New Testament Letters, for they are the very instruments of its pursuit. Paul writes, for example, in 2 Corinthians 4.1: 'Seeing we have received this ministry, we faint not.' He would have his churches guarded by the worth and wonder of that which they guard. The Word that commissions must be the conscience that preserves.

Accordingly, in present context, Chapters 7, 8 and 9 are occupied with aspects of this theme. There are 'bewares' around the very 'cares' of Christian doctrine, lest faith-custody moves from the centre of gravity of the faith itself – out of a genuine anxiety for its 'prosperity'[11] – to lodge its security elsewhere. The form of such 'elsewhere' will likely be some 'absoluteness of authority', claimed to be vested in things textual or ritual, which have their due place only if never usurpers of truth they can only serve.

When the Bible, or authoritarian shapes of the Eucharist, are taken as validating the Christian reality, by dint of arrogating it in some exclusive way to their auspices, faith is then diverted from its real trust. For the trust it invites is then subtly changed, while the trust it recruits is in default.

If, in these ways, there is a sort of substitute confidence, the situation faith-wise might be likened to the offer of an oath to underwrite an other-wise dubious honesty by the added measure of potential perjury. Such an 'on-oath' device may have place in litigation: it surely has no place in the witness of faith about divine integrity.[12]

Might this situation, variously explored in Chapter 7, possibly come under the rubric of Paul in 2 Corinthians 4.2 where he writes: 'We do not use cunning'. The Greek word *panourgia* (*astutis* in Latin) has the meaning of that which employs subtlety to make its point, rather than 'great plainness of speech'.[13] Since 'God in Christ' makes historical 'the Christ in God' as 'the Word made flesh', the Bible, the Church, the ministry, the sacraments – being all instrumental to faith's expression – are no right claimants to annex its finality as their own. These have not put that faith 'on oath' as conceivably its better guarantors because *they* would never prove perfidious.

What faith is in itself, and with its ancillary servants in their due capacity, requires its own keen readiness for the ministries of doubt. This theme belongs with Chapter 9. An openness to query from without, as the necessary posture of authentic witness, means a lively ability to internalize what such query craves to learn or fears to trust. The faithful in these terms are no purveyors of the closed mind. Nor is faith commended by those who seem to be calling from a long way off.

Any such scenario for Christian faith in every arena of discourse across distance means the burdened business of words. Perhaps more heavily than any other religion, Christianity carries the onus of vocabulary, of uneasy translation into the mind-set and the speech patterns of today. Those 'letters of Hebrew, Greek and Latin', in the *titulus* over the Cross of Jesus, set their stamp on the early course of Christian faith and society.[14] Much in that mental structure no longer moves readily into the idiom of modern human society. In the inter-religious context of 'dialogue' the *non sequiturs* of language may be harsher still. 'Redemption', 'forgiveness', 'grace' and 'pardon' are words of non, or foreign, currency in a setting short on listening and deafened by its own raucousness.

Chapter 8 takes up the stakes here, heartened by the realization that hurdles are meant for leaping and that the very business present in obscurity is also present opportunity, inasmuch as misunderstanding kindles elucidation. The situation on the Gaza road in Acts 8, with a puzzled reader querying what Isaiah meant, invites the deacon into the chariot for a shared journey into comprehension. So it has still to be for an articulate faith that knows the loadedness of its task and can still find it exhilarating.

IV

Three other matters remain in an inclusive trust with the integrity of God, alike in the order of the cosmos and the meaning of the Christ. What of the political realm and the sanctions and sinews of power in the care of such custody? They can hardly be ignored, still less despised, yet can they ever be instinctively embraced? Does not the wielding of political power necessarily distort, corrupt or deprave the very business of religion and ask implicit forfeit of its own integrity and its ultimate task in the remaking of human nature? All that is at issue here can be usefully comprehended in Chapter 10 by reference to the dilemma of Pilate. This is the more apt by reason of the centrality of his role, as Procurator of Judea, in the Passion of Jesus. The faith as to 'God in Christ' was then intimately entwined with the 'sin of the world' in the very terms of political miscarriage, so that the integrity of politics had its place, with all else, in the necessity of redemption.

To arrive then at Chapter 11 is to realize that we have incurred an entire array of self-scrutinies, doctrinal, moral and spiritual. We may

< 6 >

begin to feel, with Robert Browning, 'how hard it is to be a Christian'. Being pusillanimous – though often charged on 'comfort-seeking' piety – is no part of being Christian in the contemporary scene. The odds are against its intention of heart, if not also against its logic of mind, its credentials in trust. It follows for Chapter 11 that there has to be a genuine *will* to faith. Issues that defy an easy consensus from society, or themes that vex the intelligence in their very fascination for the heart, must become, in some measure, the determination of the will. There was much indeed, philosophically, in William James' early 20th century exposition of 'the will to believe', if duly refined to the temper of the New Testament, apostolic, emulation of that quality of soul.

The motive in the will, however, is not reckless or impetuous. Like love, it knows there is a surrender to make, but, likewise with love also, it is discerning, obeys its reasons because it cherishes them. It is the task of Chapter 11 to take up this 'will to believe' in the twin concerns of both theology and the personal self. 'Has it your vote to be so if it can?' is the question it faces so that 'If it can' is proved and known, and becomes, like John Bunyan's 'sword of Goliath', the evidence in hand. Such faith it not a willful exclusion of doubt, as some malingerers assume and allege, but instead a gentle mastery of it in the glad pursuit of discipleship.

This very posture perhaps suggests there is one final charge to face, one that follows from its very nature and belongs with its utmost Christ-reliance and the divine insignia of the Incarnation and the Passion. Friedrich Nietzsche at the turn of the 20th century made himself its most vociferous accuser.[15] Christianity, he argued, was criminally flawed in its exaltation of the 'humble and the meek'. It enthroned weakness, suffering and abject docility and so forfeited or betrayed the majesty of power across the human scene. Or there were his near contemporaries like Thomas Hardy and D. H. Lawrence deploring the exalted image of the crucifix, the apparently incessant imagery of wounds and tears that Christianity presented to the world.

In identifying eternal sovereignty in these incongruous terms had Christian faith somehow glorified impossible paradox, so as to incur the unconcealed anger of Islam and the disdain of the classic Greek mind? Nor could day-to-day society tolerate such open contradiction of the norms of its own *homo lupus hominis* awareness of itself? Could 'the wounded Name' ever be the lot of some eternal mind, or 'long-suffering' be the clue to 'the mystery of things'?

Any suspicion that Christian doctrine had run away with itself was certainly at the heart of what it had intended to say. The charge that seemed most conclusively negative was at least where the great positive belonged. If Christian faith was about the very integrity of God it would need the utmost honesty in its own. The final point to remember would be that this 'wounded Name' would seek – and find – its kindred servants, each would be saying of themselves: *Per necessitatem Christianus.*

It has of late become popular for people to disclaim pretentiousness by remarking: 'We do not do God' – this, whether in deploring undue moralizing by politicians or despising the assurance of 'preachers' they dislike.

But what might 'doing God' truly mean in the divinely real where doing and being are ever one? Is there not a costliness for any righteous Lordship relating to the human scene and story – some *regnare servare* equation in the very meaning of 'Thou art in heaven?' Was an Isaiah over bold to have that sovereignty say: 'You made me your burden-bearer?'

'Capacity' we might say is a very capacious word. It is, say the dictionaries, 'the ability to take in and hold', to comprehend with mind and will and authority in mentally receiving and achieving power or grace. If that also defines to the full the arena of an honestly competent theology, it will be one rooted, on God's own behalf, in the depth of human experience, where 'God doing God' is most searchingly known and may, at length, come to be understood and loved as making us *per necessitatem Christiani.*

< 8 >

Chapter 1

GOD – EVER-BLAMEWORTHY, EVER OATH-WORTHY

I

There is a widely current, crudely naïve reproach of God which runs:

> God would if He could, but He can't, so He is not omnipotent.
> He could if He would, but He won't, so He is not loving.

It has a cogent brevity but forfeits a rational cogency and needs a wiser reflection. 'Almightiness', if we use the term, calls for sounder comprehension. The attitudes of a prevailing blame-culture do not sort well with a reverent or perceptive theology.

'He would if He could, He could if He would' makes a pleasant jingle but has nothing to do with the world of our human experience and our human liability. The double assumption of divine will and divine competence is being made, but only as a device whereby the one will cancel the other. The premise sets power and will at odds and so leaves the conclusion vacuous, inasmuch as neither belongs without the other. What is power that, for the argument, is said to be powerless (He can't)? What is love that is alleged to be loveless (He won't)? The double negative has somehow to get back to the viable meaning of the two positives it has assumed (He could, He would). For, in the absence of a viable meaning, they could never have framed the twin hypothesis.

One thing at stake is: What can 'omnipotence' truly mean? The point is central to Chapter 3's theme of 'divine Unity'. Here we need to dispel the popular notion of some 'ability to do anything', a notion both to include and exclude the 'impossible'. A weight so 'heavy' as never to be 'lifted' could by the same token never be 'weighed'. Divine 'omnipotence', by such criteria is altogether misconstrued.

< 9 >

> It never meant capacity to do anything and everything but power to achieve
> a universal purpose in all things . . . Its practical meaning is to assure us,
> not that God can do anything, but that certain things are possible for God.[1]

Conviction that this is so is the essential meaning of monotheism.[2] It is the confidence that underlies the sciences we humans pursue. These depend on the order of a cosmos human mind and hand can take into enterprise via the autonomy it bestows. As and when we pursue this liberty to be and belong, and can also kneel and wonder at the privilege, we find ourselves in the presence of an abiding sacrament and learn to disavow all angry denunciations of God.

To be sure, the impulse to these will persist, given how far also we set store by attendant harshness and perplexity that accompany our strange *imperium*. Need 'He can't' or 'He won't' cancel in our heart-esteem the capacities we exercise and then deplore a liable omnipotence that ought to have had things otherwise, when the way they are would better prompt a praise-culture, born of a good courage? Imaginary worlds require no engagement with venture, no occasion for attainment, no ministry to community.

Yet divine blameworthiness runs deep and cries loud, sometimes with more bravado than perception. 'Where looms the horror of the shade . . . I thank whatever gods there be for my unconquerable soul.'[3] Such deep enmity does not pause to wonder about a rationale of gratitude, its whence and whither. But W. E. Henley must be heard, if only to give the passion heed. A right theology wills no enforced silence on such feeling, seeing that its very occasions belong with what refutes it. As when another poet writes

> Out of the dark something complains . . . a thing creeps . . .
> Sleep, my darling . . . all safely in God's pocket,[4]

in a 'Cradle Song'. Is there an irony in re-assuring a nervous child with language that could be bitterly naïve? 'God's pocket' squares oddly with a world where so much is left by God's design to us and our capacities.

Among the most articulate and influential of voices for 'God-arraignment' was the poet-novelist Thomas Hardy. He was for his generation an arch-priest to an 'Almighty in the dock'. Truly he cherished village choirs and violins, deploring on this score the arrival of the church organ.[5] He cherished church architecture but had an animus like William Blake against all else ecclesiastical. Hardy saw the external world as indifferent to humans. Man's consciousness was, therefore, 'God's mistake. Our being brought to birth, untimely for us, was criminal in God. There was a prejudice against us, so that we must read the natural order around us as darkly dispossessed of all the positive features of any nature/humankind affinity. There was a mood to ban, on Hardy's part, glad sense

< 10 >

of partnership between fact and mind, between sight and insight, between the farm and the farmer. His taking this heavy agnostic stance was the more strange in one who truly characterized himself 'a man who noticed such things', as he cherished his Dorset and reported his keen sight so tellingly.

The 'blighted star' verdict on earthbound experience of this so tangible earth came, for him, from the fatedness which hung over all human emotions, private and social. Humans were so far, somehow, victims of themselves and it ought never to have been contrived – supposedly by God – to be that way. There was a crucial 'Nay' somehow lying athwart all human Yea's of yearning or aspiration or ambition, whereby all births, despite their inherent expectation and expectability, were in truth untimely.

It could not have been that Thomas Hardy drew this idea from the Qur'an's emphatic disavowal of it. Islamic Scripture ensures its readers that Allah 'did not create this world as if He were in jest', at play with a plaything. On the contrary, creation and us within it were 'in earnest', a thing of divine intention, never to be read – or taken – as 'in vain'.[6] Hardy sided with suspicion to the contrary. Any 'Let there be . . . ' of that 'serious' order was countered, for him, by what there is, as human story held it to his view. Thus he reached the celebrated conclusion to his *Tess of the D'Urbervilles* of 'divine sport', with the heroics grimly closed and the lessons, as Hardy saw them, no less powerfully inscribed in the literary legacy. For it might be said that Hardy had an uncanny capacity to make his point.

Oddly, in his comment on Robert Browning, Hardy claimed as his the 'neutral ground'. The two met each other frequently and Hardy wrote:

> How could smug Christian optimism (*sic*) worthy of a dissenting grocer find a place inside a man who was so vast a seer and feeler when on neutral ground?[7]

He wrote movingly lyrical poetry, later only as a consolation for the harsh reception of his novels. It was verse laden with the sinister and the miscarrying in human destiny. Charles Darwin's *The Origin of Species*, published when he was nineteen, confirmed or turned the bent of his mind while, earlier, Newman's *Apologia* to which he had resorted wistfully, left him unimpressed.

Apart from his sense of latent malignity in nature, Hardy was also acutely aware of the ravages of time and of history as a melancholy chronicle. Lingering memories of the fear of the doom of Napoleonic invasion underlay his epic poem *The Dynasts* with the choric 'Pities' to register, but not to heal, the crimes and toll of war. 'Time-born' man was 'time-torn', 'time worn'. He thought Wordsworth in his raptures was seeking pseudo

< 11 >

stimulation, while his American contemporary, Walt Whitman, was reproached for his gospel of humans 'transcending themselves' in mere gestures of the heroic. By contrast, there were days when he feared he was 'a spectre' hardly solid enough to impinge on his environment.

In his poem 'God-forgotten' he confronts God, not with human accusers, but his own enquiry for 'some answer to their cry'. Dialogue follows:

> The Earth? Sayest thou? The human race?
> By Me created? Sad its lot?
> Nay: I have no remembrance of such a place
> Such world I fashioned not . . .
>
> The earth of men – let me bethink me . . . Yea,
> I dimly do recall . . . It lost my interest from the first . . .

The deputation insists 'Lord, it existeth still', only to be told:

> Dark, then, its life'! For not a cry
> Of aught it bears do I hear now.
> Haply it died of doing as it durst?

There is other business anyway across a universe. Why should earth's race need to be heeded on 'their tainted ball'? Years later Hardy would follow with 'God's Education' and 'God's Funeral', where Stanza VI muses:

> O man-projected Figure, of late
> Imaged as we, thy knell who shall survive?
> Whence came it we were tempted to create
> One whom we can no longer keep alive?[8]

Hardy was scores of years ahead of A. N. Wilson and Richard Dawkins. We must kill theological hope by the device of agnostic despair. 'God's wrong is most of all'.

He had many antecedents, in David Hume, or the Shelley he so admired poetically, but his dire views of nature, of time and trusting faith, meant that even sexuality came under his dark scepticism. Though 'the human heart's resources' must be all we have, marriage – institutionalizing them – only entangled their dubious and fleeting benediction. Time cures hearts of tenderness he told in his own romances. *Jude the Obscure* shocked his readers with a portrayal of how warped, how tragic for both parties, marriage could prove. His novels are busy not only with strange, thwarting mischances but with intense personal problematics. Passionate women, like Bathsheba, fear themselves being overcome by the likes of Sergeant Troy and guilty about their fascination. Sue, with Jude, however, lacks all will to passion in a self-reservation of unfittedness for marriage and thus can only be ultimately withheld from Jude, to his great pain,

< 12 >

(while yet she 'marries' Phillotson). Hardy paints in Clym a maleness blighted by its intellectualism, and Angel one 'who, with more animalism, would have made a nobler man'. Matrimony seems only somehow an inhibiting convention of society, victimizing its human practice. The very sanctions of the institution of marriage would seem to mutilate the human experience or do violence in its social role.

The length in years and the art of letters and the range of influence with which Thomas Hardy was counsel and witness against God make him an arch-exemplar of the whole agnostic theme. Yet may there be a sense that he may have been greater than he knew? As we must see else-where, all the items of his 'burial' of God, whether nature, time, history or love and sexual exchange, find a glad reversal in the sacramental principle of all human life. At times he seems inveterate about his gloom. For even regret can die.[9] Yet a sympathy, as determined as his was latent, might read his persona and his pen as only honestly exploring and plumbing what easy believing might only evade and even a ripe theology only partly undertake. At least his measure of human loneliness knew how far it was self-caused . . . [10] 'One who, past doubtings all, waits in unhope', and at least 'waits', could reach what is 'past doubtings all' in the integrity of faith and know Hardy had been friend and mentor. We must see.

II

Thomas Hardy is one with a long sequence from Empedocles and Lucretius to Bertrand Russell in a varied animus against what is and has been, in the name of what might have been and never was. There is a very human irony between the facts of experience and a surmise from inexperience. What ostensibly they found from God somehow belonged to the God they never found. 'His wrong was most of all' because theirs should not have been otherwise so inexplicable, so absent from a remedy.

Thus Hardy always felt himself excluded from religious 'consolations'.

> That He who breathes All's Well to these
> > Breathes no All-Well's to me . . .
> While always I must feel as blind
> > To sights my brethren see,
> Why joys they've found I cannot find,
> > Abides a mystery.[11]

If, for Hardy, God 'existed', he could only be the theme of dark reproach. His near contemporary, A. E. Housman was of the same sceptical mind.

> Aye, look: high heaven and earth all from the prime foundation;
> All thoughts to rive the heart are here, and all are vain:

< 13 >

Horror and scorn and hate and fear and indignation –
Oh why did I awake? When shall I sleep again?[12]

A Nigerian, Chinua Achebe, musing on Umuahia's 'arrow', is kin to 'A Shropshire Lad', in this tradition of human disquiet as old as Homer in face of mysteries which, if they be 'divine', are at best inscrutable or at worst despicable.[13]

The hatchet fell from Ezeulu's hand and he slumped down on both knees beside the body. 'My son,' he cried. 'Ulu, where you there when this happened to me?' He hid his face on Okiba's chest.[14]

'Ulu' is the native term for God, the Theos of the Greeks and Deus of the Latins, Oduduwa of the Yoruba and Ngai of the Kikuyu, the 'somehow named' of all the peoples of the earth. Ezeulu promptly enquires where his deity was when tragedy struck. The question only deepens when the 'evil' is not from nature but from human kin. Why was Ulu not on his watch? Ezeulu is an Ibo-kind of Job, advised by his embittered wife to rise from cumulative sorrows to curse his YAHWEH and die.

In that dark emotion, Job is one with poets who have wished themselves unborn. One such – a rare breed from within Islam – was the poet-recluse from the Aleppo region of Syria in the 11th century, Abu-l-'Ala al-Ma'arri (973–1058). Despite his rich length of years he always deplored the burden of them. The toll of birth he was proud never to inflict on any and protested that his father (whom as an early orphan he never knew) should have abstained from fathering him. Smallpox in childhood marred him for ever and blindness condemned him to an 'imprisoned' life. The politics of his locale brought him little rest of mind and he savoured, but duly forsook, the cultural offerings and the mental trans-actions of 'Abbasid Baghdad in the heyday of those years. An inner generosity of spirit kept him sensitive and warm of heart, but the Qur'an's theme of 'returning to Allah' at life's end carried for him neither solace nor warrant. He preferred in honesty of mind to will his solitude as a kind of hermit from the world, its benefactor – as it were – in spite of himself in the excellence of his poetry and the power of his prose.[15]

He could have approved Louis MacNeice's notion about 'sub-poena-ing the universe', whose autobiography *The Strings are False* breathes a sad arraignment of the business of human living, where 'so-called altruism is merely a projection of egotism' and his society 'a nation of sexual frus-trates'. Even so, he asked whether 'man has to have sanction from outside himself'. If so, it was one no 'religion' could supply. He said that he and most of his friends 'regarded all persons who had any religious faith as museum specimens'.[16]

We are by now fully persuaded of the blameworthiness of God. A Victorian spokesman can be here the last of these undivine accusers.

Winwood Reade (1838–1875), three years before he died, published *The Martyrdom of Man*, a tirade against the human situation with at times a lyrical quality of passionate prose that fascinated many in his generation in a forfeiture of hope. It was a flowing indictment of nature and saw the universe as a vast death-dealing realm and the world a place where human aspirations 'buzzed like flies' in fruitless follies. Life could be compared to 'bottled sunshine' which death, the butler, would uncork.[17]

III

Theism and theology, it is evident, are made defendants in a burdened prosecution case. They should not complain but live more soberly, more ruggedly, with and for the world as thus direly envisaged by those who bring them to assize.

Yet at once there is a strange irony. It dwells in how this very court, this court of trial of belief, has for its own president the theme itself. The ultimately blameworthy is the evermore invoked. We have to pass to the abiding human impulse to verify their truths of word and deed, of ends and means, by passing 'under oath' with God the guarantor. He who, on the one hand, proves so abysmally delinquent must on the other underwrite all integrity as being supremely, omnipotently trustworthy.

We have to explore this strange anomaly as a prelude to a Shakespearean analysis (in Chapter 2) of the human wrong that makes the situation dire both ways, to be followed (Chapters 5 and 6) by the perceptions the theisms have of their engagement with divine vindication, as only realized in the human order of all that is obdurate.

It is useful to go to the same Shakespeare for a dark occasion of quest for the oath-witnessing facility God is held to afford, whether in corroboration of, or guilty substitute for, the good faith of humans.

His Tragedy of *Richard III* sees a loaded exchange between the devious Richard who announces himself in an opening scene as 'determined to be a villain',[18] and the widowed Queen Elizabeth whose daughter's hand in marriage he is seeking to obtain to further his own purposes. On every count of honour, it is a monstrous proposal. It affords the dramatist ample occasion for the lively art of repartee. Richard is already foresworn but his suit is pressing. He will overcome his ill-repute by a solemn oath. He offers 'my George, my Garter and my Crown' as guarantors whereby he can be trusted – the patron English saint of Palestinian birth, the knightly Order of Edward III's foundation and the very Crown of England itself at stake in him. The Queen rejects them all, as ever serving for the *bona fides* of so rank a wrongdoer. All three are 'profaned, dishonoured and usurped' in being so falsely cited. She goes on:

< 15 >

If something thou would'st swear to be believed
Swear then by something that thou hast not wronged.[19]

He offers 'by myself', 'by the world', and 'by my father's death'. This new trio have been exhausted already by Richard's perfidies. For has he not betrayed his very soul, darkly wronged the world and befouled his father's memory?

'Well then', he cries, 'I'll swear by God' – the ultimate resort. The Queen's counter-thrust is prompt and final: 'God's wrong is most of all', since all his villainies, in defiling all human worth, have defied God most of all. The weight of all God's long accusers rides upon her words but not with what she means by them. Of them she has no mind, in exonerating God from oath-witnessing for the likes of Richard. God whom he would invoke, Richard has the more maligned before and will again.

For such as Richard, in ethics there is no 'oath of last resort'. He is beyond all oath-proposing. He has exempted himself from any nexus with the integrity of God.[20]

Yet the very extremity of Richard's 'oath-worthlessness' only presses the question: 'Where else?' and the long tradition of 'falling back on God' as MacNeice's 'sanction outside himself' is deeply rooted in the human story. Even those we have reviewed, identifying 'God's wrong' more than man's or nature's, in and behind the absurdity or malignity they allege against Him, indirectly witness to an ultimate responsibility somehow there, if only to be urgently arraigned. They only have Him to accuse in a context that *should* be otherwise. The great Greek tragedians, Aeschylus and Sophocles, wanted to read the cosmic reality of evil as somehow party to the goodness that endured it, whereby alone its evil was known for the evil it was. Modern purveyors of the indictment of God have their anger only on the wistful ground of insisting 'it *ought* not thus to be'. Do they not, in measure, personify their accusation, inasmuch as in some mechanical universe they would only have the fact, and not the burden, of how 'it' proved to be? Only the liable can be morally accused. Talk of 'God's funeral' lacks the corpse for its own ceremony.[21]

Hence, behind all oath-seeking, all oath-making, is the human impulse to seek for satisfactory integrities in life and the instinct to locate the hope of them in 'swearing in the Name of God', the Name – we hope – dissemblers will fear to invoke. But is there not an awkward paradox here? What does such 'oathing' infer about human honesty *per se*? Why not the 'Yea' that is 'Yea', the 'Nay' that is 'Nay'? If an innate honesty is lacking may its absence not also undermine the oath? If perfidy ensues, are we the better served or the more deceived? To be sure, a legal sanction is added to the situation, but then that which needs to belong throughout is impugned as insufficient.

Doubtless, oath-taking has place on appointment to public office or entering into solemn trusts. It may then symbolize the entry into the charge concerned, which society's ceremonial inaugurates, both to reassure its public and fortify the recipient of trust for its discharge. Even in private realms the same may be due – witness Hamlet's father's ghost crying, from beneath the stage: 'Swear, swear . . . ' to steel his wavering son.

Yet it must follow that there may be selves so far foresworn already, like Shakespeare's Richard III, that 'God's Name' disowns all possible nexus. He may not seek heaven's patronage with hands so unclean. The very nature of transcendence would be impugned, as if 'suffering' his wickedness.[22] An ultimate 'good faith' where all sound oaths must go must be utterly antiseptic in itself. This steady feature of Shakespeare's drama we take further in Chapter 2. 'God's wrong most of all', as His reprobators allege in the very shape of things, would be undergone again by such 'taking of His Name in vain'.

The situation Shakespeare's Richard has us recognize only makes the more anomalous the fusion of the two elements examined in this chapter. If God, or the transcendent, shows such 'bad faith' over a malign and absurd earth, a human predicament so blameworthy, why should such deity be trusted to validate all human oaths and warrant their 'good faith'? Our will for 'binding words' appeals to some 'binding guardian' if not to be suspect as in tragic default concerning us. Such transcendence seems well within the bitter reach of cavil and reproach. Can all values there be safe, all confidence secure?

The irony is strange. The haven where we traditionally go to solemnize and pledge our own integrities, personal and social, where politicians swear their sacred trusts, is nevertheless the place where all our misgivings lodge concerning the tragic wrongs of history and the malfunctionings of nature's ways and means. There is and has long been this loaded contrast in the dual roles for God. Must we say that either the catalogue of blame disqualifies the guardian of our oaths, or that the secure address of these disowns and refutes the other?

The burden here is not lightened when the theme of divine 'omnipotence' supervenes, nor that of divine 'unity'. We will find in Chapters 3, 4 and 5 how the great theisms perceive it, how they bring divine 'oath-swearing' itself into the equation. Thus 'two immutable things that could not lie' – as Hebrews 6.17–18 has it – 'God's will to be Himself "on-oath" might avail to banish all blameworthiness on the one hand and dispel all misgivings on the other'. To these complexities we must come.

Meanwhile, one clear fact emerges from this dual fact of 'charge' and 'trust' concerning God. It is the fact of liability, or at least of human perception of it. Where the contrasted themes meet is in their assumption of 'unlimited responsibility' behind all else, some ground and principle inclusively 'chargeable' either way, to be indicted or to be

< 17 >

invoked, pilloried in 'bad faith' or revered in 'good'. Such is the 'either-or' of a quandary that takes rest in neither. Shakespeare's dramatic genius can teach us why.

< 18 >

Chapter 2

SHAKESPEARE'S DRAMATIC MIND AND ART

I

'There is essential difference between "Guilty creatures sitting at a play" and those sitting at a sermon.'[1] Noting this irony of an eminent Shakespearean scholar and having started with a Shakespearean oath-making, we take our theme further by the great poet's aid. Experience of his dark tragedies enacted leaves us in no doubt of their intense telling of 'God's wrong most of all' – a telling that compels engaging with his central characters 'perishing into reality'.

To be sure, we are in a theatre, not in a pew. The 'wrong' is the more surely there because its presentation admits no verbal moralizing and brings no prejudice of mind or dogma. To know Macbeth, Hamlet, Lear and Othello in the poetry of drama, the drama in its poetry, finds us required to live and think inside them. We are made to read the mystery of being human in its utmost reach as evil-prone and wrong-beset, yet with a universal sympathy and a measure of the sublime, utterly honest in allowing us no cheap illusion.[2] Shakespeare sets 'God's wrong' before us with an intensity that – being wholly dramatic in imagery and action in mutual deploy – requires us to take God's measure of the depth of what we witness. He fits that role the more in that, as we must assume, his playwright genius would surely dissent from it, lest we take him – impossibly – as a mere preacher. He reverses for us the old adage about the theatre-goer learning: 'To care and not to care', emerging 'with calm of mind, all passion spent'.[3] For here are passions that cannot be dismissed. They are ripe to command us unreservedly, as meanings from which there is no escape – which is only to say (since the dramatist may not in his art and task) that they belong with God and only in God can find their reckoning.

< 19 >

If this reads for some like a theological conclusion, the warrant stems from the very genius of the dramatist. The plays by their artistry forbid escape into indifference. They go where universal sympathies must be taken, lest we should evade the heights and depths of our own humanity. Shakespeare's tragedies make realists of us all, unless we mentally absent ourselves. Their realism commends us to God precisely by leaving the verdict to us alone.

Large if this claim seems to capacities for indifference, it is implicit in the double force of Shakespeare's art in the quality of the verbal and the visual concerting one impact. It presents us with a universe of the inner soul in 'horrible imaginings, where nothing is but what it seems', in the engrossing struggle between desire and dread. The critic with whom we began reads

> . . . reality such as might be discerned by an unerring and all-including intelligence which some of us might find it briefer and less cumbersome to call God.[4]

Her academic diffidence is well meant in avoiding to make a theologian of a dramatist. Few things are more cumbersome than some theologies. What she reads there can well suffice. Her brevity about measures of God in Shakespeare deserves enlarging in genuine openness to him and them together.

II

The misgivings we must have about 'theologizing' overmuch from Shakespeare are countered, however, by the actualities that belong to him and his career. As Hamlet tells his players, the business of the play is 'to hold a mirror up to nature' and 'show virtue (manhood) its own image'. He was himself actor as well as playwright and there was evident interchange between his products on the stage and the exuberant, clamorous and villainous audience of The Globe. He and they were fully 'Renaissance Elizabethans' with the zest of life. The times knew fullness, but not wholeness. Things were 'out of joint' as well as apt, like Falstaff, to be hilarious. The 'groundlings' had to be amused with witticisms but also silenced into awe and fear. The world of all, as the Sonnets of this same William told, was harassed in its very ardour with the old Grecian fear of death completing the ravages of time, of plague and imbecility. The stage itself, with its masks and curtains, its upper and its lower levels, its sundry ins and outs, was a parable, as Macbeth could say, of human life itself. It was out of the first Shakespearean realm of the comedies that the great tragedies emerged.

Their genesis, like their generation, knew the cosmos as the context but a chaos as its menace. The natural order, in its newly measured dimension by 'cosmology', housed that tantalizing 'piece of earth', the human self, 'master of infinite space' and 'quintessence of dust'. 'To be or not to be' was never – and always – 'a question', in that life, being no willed option, left an ever besetting one when reckoned by the deepest thoughts of mind, the dark impulses in the soul.

In this Shakespearean world, we are made to know how 'God's wrong is most of all'. The tuition turns on three interlocking elements in its portrayal. They are – a human universe of evil; its burdened implications about human nature; the weight of the vicarious in human society these impose. For all his instinctive taciturnity as the man he is in the art he pursues,[5] he does not hesitate to link all three with 'heaven' (*Hamlet*, Act III, Sc. 3, 36) 'O my offence is rank. It smells to heaven', cries Claudius, convicted by the speech of the Player-King. Yet he cannot pray, clinging to the gains of his murderous crime in possession of his crown and queen.

> Why, let the stricken deer go weep,
> The hart ungalled play,
> For some must watch, while some must sleep,
> So runs the world away'
>
> (Act III, Sc. 2, 259–62)

Hamlet's ribald commentary only sharpens the poignancy of unremitting sin. It belongs with more than the flux of politics or the rule of law. It is beyond what opportunism can explain, subterfuge condone or cunning attain. Something more than the device of 'the play within the play' has prompted a 'penitence' that vaguely seeks but cannot find a voice. Claudius admits a guilt he will only accentuate by a contrived exoneration, taking shape in still more dastardly designs against his nephew.

What worlds away this theatre is from the habitual usage, so often heard of late, about 'drawing a line under' this and that, so that we can conveniently 'move on' from what deserves to be interred in would-be ignorant neglect. Not here: Shakespeare's world has law and life and drama's language defer to ethics.

Nemesis is the stark theme in the saga of Macbeth, vividly enfolded in the swift sequences around the banquet scene and the loaded metaphors of blood and washing, of murdered sleep and haunted forfeit of it.[6] He sees a dagger hanging before him in the air, visible only to him who lately carried it. The vision signals to his soul the past he cannot shed, the future to which his deed condemns him. At length he accepts in defiance the logic of the inevitable, wading further into blood, tormented by the heirlessness of his wife's womb and his own grimly gotten crown. Shakespeare has no more telling narrative of 'the wages of sin', amply repaid in their proper currency. That ultimate defiance in Macbeth, which some have

< 21 >

seen as lifting him to Nietzschean heights, only the more advertises 'the exceeding sinfulness of sin'. The genius of the dramatist wants and thinks no 'Here ends the lesson'. It lives in drama alone. 'Guilty people' are on the very stage and, as Hamlet told the players, humans see their own image.

Hence that play's 'pith and moment' as a drama of revenge. The mode was familiar among Shakespeare's predecessors and rivals but *Hamlet* is different in the subtle complexity of the scenario – the fratricide, the incest, the usurpation, the time itself 'out of joint' and the darkly ruminative youthfulness of the central figure, so far haunted by revelations of the world, so far prone to fear insanity.

In having his Hamlet so charming, so enigmatic, so dogged by self-doubt, Shakespeare only the more underlines the heinous sinfulness he must confront. The father-ghost tells a hideous tale but that death should rise and demand beyond its generation the requital of its wrongs over-burdens a subsequent mortality too cruelly. Such though is the nature of murder that the dying cannot bury their death, nor murder close all accounts. In Shakespeare human sin is of this exacting *post-facto* nature. 'What's done cannot be undone' because – in the elusive phrase – wrong matters.[7] So the murdered King must rise and bind his son to take up the wrong, risen with him in unnerving claim.

The desperate task is fraught with other wrongs – 'things rotten in the state', the fate of the throne, the stake in the succession, 'the dread' not merely of 'something after death' but much of anguish, subterfuge, and guilt before death is reached. Does the ghost deceive? Is the mother truly this conniver? Why is he thus surrounded with veiled surveillance, arrases that hide informers, friends in pseudo 'love'? So does the drama advertise the reach of human wrong and tell a whole court's 'offence to heaven'.

It is thus that those who thronged to The Globe and Shakespeare saw and heard and learned and knew that there is 'reality' with an 'Ought' presiding over the human scene where all meaning holds and final values belong, whose 'wrong is most of all' when these are flouted or defied. Their world knew well the parable of its political order. That 'divine right of kings' they so revered held a dual sense. It not only warranted power in exercise: it ruled it in obligation. What was validly entrusted was not to be wantonly usurped. The self-accusation of Henry IV for having dethroned Richard II worried his soul and renewed itself in his son on the eve of Agincourt, brooding on 'the fault my father made in compassing the crown'. But, he pleads,

> I Richard's body have interred new
> And on it have bestowed more contrite tears,
>   . . . and I have built

Two chantries, where sad and solemn priests
Still sing for Richard's soul.[8]

This Henry has a livelier conscience than Claudius but the paradigm politic holds for all things mortal, as 'existence-warrants' only humanly possessed because they are divinely granted and, as such, accountable beyond themselves or their crude counsels of convenience and willfulness. There is a divine right of being no mortals can elude or morally disown, whereby meaning consists and truth controls. When there be wrong, it is God's most of all.

Nor, for Shakespearean tragedy, is this 'wrong' – as often in Christopher Marlowe – some 'Satanism' warring cosmically, the human realm apart. It stems willfully from the human bosom and those 'whisperers' the Qur'an finds there, prompting hate and suspicion, wile and guile in self-aggrandisement.[9]

Thus *Macbeth* 'entertains conjectures' and the pace of the narrative, its strange coincidences, carry them forward, while the imagery proposes how sinister they are. 'The blasted heath' is no more than the fitting milieu. The seething cauldron of three witches grimly intimates the brew inside his soul, its ingredients in the working tumult of his mind. 'Glamis, Cawdor, King . . . ' – a sequence half confirmed by the sudden promotion to the second, new occasion presented in the irony of Duncan's trustful guesthood in Macbeth's castle, the hasty letter to the lady of that house, ardent in her own ambition and quickly set to entrench conspiracy in a firm concert of their double minds. The spectacle overwhelms the audience with its tuition round the impulse of ambition, its grimly human challenge to the sacred principles of loyalty, of marriage, of captaincy, of hospitality. The witches have not inveighled Macbeth into extraneous wrong: they deciphered the dark already there and told in shadow the nemesis already brooding in the augury of one 'untimely born'. The entire *mise-en-scène* is dramatic disclosure of the name of the story.[10]

The battlements in *Hamlet* witness a similar pace of plot disclosure, serving to show unerringly the shape of 'wrong' as there in mortal terms, yet tragically beyond them in its full significance. The lonely sentry being replaced, the rumour of the untimely ghost, the counsel with the loyal friend – all preparing the ground for Hamlet's coming burden and the anguish in its realization. Then follows his own encounter, the solace – and anxiety – from even friendly interest in his mysterious secret, and the awful quandary in how to read it, bear with it and resolve it all alone. Skillfully, by dramatic verve and verbal artifice, Shakespeare has us share the fearful incidence of Hamlet's filial duty, his debate about its 'truth', his vacillation round a strategy, his very mastery of himself, and whatever be the 'one particular fault' that can confound all else.

In this travail of soul perplexity, his path is hedged around by human

< 23 >

devices of latent or express evil – the cunning crown-usurping murderer-king, his uncle; that tedious scheming 'counsellor' Polonius; their double-crossing the progress of his 'maiden love' for the 'fair Ophelia'; their sorry use of her as unwilling accomplice against him; the horror of his mother's marriage and its index to her mind and – perhaps – to the 'frailty' of all women; the very insubstantiality of all human nexus and the traumas of his banishment and untimely return to Denmark to learn the fearful how of Ophelia's demise – all these, being Hamlet's story, are Shakespeare's catalogue of human wrongings of another self, desperate 'insurrection' in 'the state of man'.

He will not say that 'God's wrong is most of all'. That he had already said in *Richard III*. The only 'Queen' in *Hamlet* is no Elizabeth of York.[11] Is there, truly, as some have argued, some underlying good, investing Shakespeare's tragic figures which their evils have only disrupted, somehow to compensate their tribulations? May it only be some resistance to despair that wants to think so? For amid all four, death and endings are unrelieved by credible hope, unless some slow return to normalcy suffices.

At least the truth is clear that wrongs, willful present wrongs, tell themselves in Shakespeare by every skill of stage-craft, every artistry of vocabulary, as crying for 'explanation' from more than chance, or circumstance, or mishap. They demand a diagnosis of perversity more ultimate than the legalities of law and order, subversive of more than the conventions of society. Thus, all needs a referent that takes the human further than itself, yet not beyond a human vocation with it. No referent is ultimate that has another beyond it. Life has many referents and philosophies try to find some hierarchy in them. But what can allow no further appeal beyond itself and have no cause or need of making one? Whether it is merely 'brevity' that calls such referent God, it is for more than convenience to say. This burden about God must probe the deeply Shakespearean issue of 'human nature'.

III

The king in *King Lear*, we might say, 'undaughters' by his curses those daughters of his patrimony and they, in turn, 'undaughter' him. His wife we never meet, the play being ominously patriarchal. Hence the hard question about 'whence in all nature those hard hearts?' Hence, too, the comment about Lear: 'He hath ever but slenderly known himself' (Act I, Sc. 1, 297). All four major tragedies confront us with the puzzle of human nature, even the concept in itself and the radical issue of its precarious exposure to the usages of society and the tenure of a physical body. How amenable are we to the régime of the demanding good, how susceptible to the corrupting blandishments and pressures of evil? These elements of the crisis of selfhood are clearly to the fore in *King Lear*.[12] Compared with *Hamlet* and *Macbeth*, its opening is wooden and jejune. How can an old king quit a throne with foolish avidity for love as 'quantity' to be professed in a loaded situation, so that Cordelia's plain (and disinheriting) reply is her honesty's only option?

Has this 'unnecessary' old age become so inured to the appetite of power that, even when ostensibly relinquishing the one, he still demands the satisfaction of the other, a menace to all in which he too long persists?

Indeed, he is irascible and exacting but need his vagaries plunge his two elder daughters into calculating harshness and mutual rivalry? Why should wrong so far multiply out of folly, and evil afford itself excuse from hate-augmented provocation? Why should magnanimity of mind avail in such as Kent and Edgar and not elsewhere, or Edmund not firmly surmount the stigma of his bastardy? Why should the contagion of evil spread so deadly far in the play's descent into hell and the fidelities so little influence its final ending?[13]

Is there, then, something incorrigible about human nature, some trend in selfhood towards easy capitulation to society's malignity, unless steadily resisted by a robust will to good? Is the costly *superbia* of Coriolanus only where his quarrel with Rome conveyed him, or Shylock only the sinister victim of the social merchandise of 'Gentiles', 'spitting on his Jewish gabardine'? 'More sinned against than sinning', to be sure, but what is it in selfhood either way, that makes for the comparative equation? The quotient cannot be only what we do: it must be in what we become[14] – which leaves us puzzlingly to explain the incidence of unconditional good and the lastingness of the insistent values by which it endures. Yet an unmitigated and inexcusable wrong is there.

In *Othello*, for example, there seems no reason in harsh circumstance why Iago should behave – and be – so malign, so cunning and willful in that malignity. The 'inward' that impels him tells a dire 'sinning, not sinned against', a sheer enmity out of a black heart, stooping to the plotted ruin of another man, making his own wife his unwitting tool. Othello, by contrast, has reason for a social stance that makes him prey to the guile by which he is ensnared into wild credulity – his 'service to the state', his prowess and repute, his foreign skin and his fine frame. His 'particular fault' is more a victim's than a villain's, the 'wrong' less of his heart than of his judgment until his ruin overwhelms his bride.[15]

The distinction Shylock's formula would make between guilt in act and things adverse that extenuate is one we can never neatly or justly allow. Yet, either way, the distinction between what we *do* and how we *are* abides. Even if the first extenuates, the second stays and worsens, if only for lack of restraint. Shylock needs to know that we are what we become and that we will become what we are. At length there is no exoneration. Thus the

< 25 >

problem of human nature rankles and, with it, the urgent issue of how redeemable we ever are and then how being so might happen and by what means.

For if, beyond ours or theirs (those others in the frame), 'God's wrong is most of all', the 'God-issue' becomes only the more puzzling, unless – like oft recurrent moods from Lucretius to this present generation – we repudiate it altogether in an escapist 'disbelieving in belief'. This the Shakespeare of these tragedies can never do. In each of them compellingly there is a moral universe of what ought to be and is not, of what is and ought not so to be. Lear will learn. The play on words is eloquent. The heath, the storms, his daughters and their maledictory wombs, may lead him to rage and curse, but they convey him to the end of his pomposity. They draw him from his first falsities to a saving knowledge of 'unaccommodated man' of whom he 'had ta'en too little thought'. The world that is symbolized by Edgar in the sub-plot, in Lear's story by Cordelia and Kent, is there as the measure of stability and truth, by which all things heinous are identified as such and manifestly shamed as vile – the things of Hamlet's 'cursed spite', fit only to be ousted by the good.

Shakespeare's world is always this way. No evil is consigned to fantasy or evaded in some Asian *maya*, or some *Lethe* of illusion. 'Will these hands ne'er be clean?' comes from the 'murdering of sleep' so that Lady Macbeth's conscience stays wide awake in Duncan's wakening to her husband's daggers and the 'breach of life'. 'If it were done when 'tis done . . . ' will never find it 'well', however 'quickly' brought to pass. Macbeth's final defiance, for all its brave will and words, only takes us where 'the end is known' as known it was from the beginning in its own school. If the stage at the end of *Hamlet* lies strewn with corpses, we do not wallow in the violence of melodrama: we see the casualties of a 'harsh world' where men 'draw their breath in pain to tell their story'. It is a tale of the willfulness of wrong and a world weary in its wounds.

Thus, and therefore, Shakespeare makes insistent the enquiry as to whether and where there can be redemption. Does Ophelia perish from the reality of Gertrude's guilt, only mediated via Hamlet's bitter entanglement in avenging the crime of Claudius, which crime sent his brother to a restless rest? What can issue from the triumph of the likes of Edmund and Cornwall over the now vindicated Cordelia and the utterly chastened Lear? Why is their quality, always there, now so costly reached, not crowned with celebration? What is the business of 'God's spies' which Lear proposes they could live to be, detecting the meaning of this unrelenting world?

If 'God's wrongs', in all 'the most', what then of 'God's rights' and of human 'rights' from Him? Ought not the depth of the one have the reach of the other? Shakespeare will not or may not say. His role as poet-drama-

< 26 >

tist is so well fulfilled as to withhold the verdict. Two emphases are all. For his task they suffice. There are these two – the grim reality of what humans do and are, and that what they are and do is against the grain of a moral universe. Neither would be what they are without that conjunction. 'God's wrong most of all' cannot be a negative register of sin without being also a positive index to the sovereign good it 'doth offend'.[16] But where, if anywhere, is His 'right' at grips with His 'wrong'? It seems to be nowhere in the climax of *King Lear*, the immolation of his old, 'unnecessary' age and of his only gentle daughter. There is nothing satisfactory in the final

> The oldest hath known most. We that are young
> Shall never see so much, nor live so long. (Act V, Sc. 1, 301–2)

It is laconic to the point of pathos. But were audiences and producers right for centuries in insisting on 'a happy ending'? There would be no 'righting' of the 'wrong'. Shakespeare knew the grimness of his vision and told it in the force of his entire art.

We may discern traces of 'redemption' in the gentler worlds of *The Winter's Tale* and *The Tempest*, but only at the cost of a certain wizardly and make belief. Leontes is at length rescued from his malignant jealousy and the usurpers rectified from their sin against Prospero. But this 'happiness is wand-contrived and convinces only with a ready suspension of disbelief about condign storms, magic islands, convenient winds and a handy shepherd. We are glad that Shakespeare reached that stage after his long, mysterious hiatus. For we need his quiet mood to savour a benigner world, given that defiant evil rules the tragedies.

IV

So is the tragic world only able to tell 'God's wrongs' and not discern 'God's rights' in their long righting? A sound theology, one we cannot fail to seek,[17] can reach toward a clue by honestly holding together both elements – the moral universe of the plays and their grimly mirrored wrong. It lies in the fact of the 'vicarious'. The victims of 'God's wrongs' are also 'injured' humans who carry the cost and pay the price of other humans' deeds and characters. They bear the brunt that belongs with a moral world. For only this incriminates the other. If all were bland neutrality no 'sufferers' would exist, but only the incidence of things. Nothing can be damnable if nothing is condemned.

What, therefore, emerges into utter clarity is that, given both, society is the perpetual arena of things vicarious. Humans make for wrongs as inflicted or incurred, the vicious and the victims in bitter mutuality, ongoings and undergoings, the harmers and the harmed. This situation is the very text of society. It is what Shakespeare's 'mirror' holds to view, showing us our own image, the concave and the convex of humanity in inhumanity.

Then the burning question follows – not 'whether' life is thus and, it would seem, irretrievably so but – 'how' the situation is taken, where alone it can be, by the injured and the made-victims. For, even beyond the mortal scene, wrong cannot be ignored. Avenging is the whole theme of Hamlet's crisis and the second part of *Macbeth* in defying it. How and why the 'righting' of the murderous usurpation, for those two murdered kings is 'God's wrong' even more, is plain enough. But how it might be 'righted' for Him as well as them when they are in their grave is the burden – for any theologian – of an eschatology. In Shakespeare, it is a mystery for ever unresolved, yet *not* one in its mortal sequel fit for irresolution. For this is what Hamlet and all Denmark, Malcolm and all Scotland, are missioned and minded never to allow. 'Murder will out' and 'mere anarchy' must not be 'loosed upon the world'.

With the living, the thing at stake can be less insoluble. Survivors can forgive and pray their non-avenging may draw the answering penitence which can grasp forgiveness – grasp it as given because they have grasped it as received. Then something like the *status quo ante* can return, but educated by the whole experience. In that event, the ill-used have been vicarious. They have borne the cost in the only terms that also 'bear its ill away'.[18]

They have been able to surmount the pressure of only two alternatives to such vicarious quality. The one could be a sullen, stoic clinging to the memory, a nursing of the injury in sustained resentment of its cost. Thus its entail remains alike with the evil-doer as guilty and with the sufferer as cherishing the wrong. The other is revenge, to retaliate, to get back against the other party. But then the enmity is only perpetuated, its first origins somehow justified – 'he took me for an enemy, let me prove to be one'. No 'evil then is overcome', for lack of good to do so, but if, instead, forgiveness in its double sense can be availing and availed, wrong has been 'righted' as neither avenging nor condoning could achieve.

The question follows, though our Shakespeare would never broach it, whether 'God's wrongs', being 'most of all', are anywhere so handled. Can divine omnipotence be known vicarious? This, the 'pith and moment' of a Christian theology, we must defer. It is no part of Shakespearean criticism.

Yet nothing emerges more compellingly from the technical mastery Shakespeare brought to the presentation of the human scene and story. His genius in that role – here only modestly explored – leaves us with one final observation. It is how inevitably vicarious are that scene and story known in collective terms. While it takes persons to forgive and be forgiven, the wrongs of structures, systems, nations, races, tribes and terri-

< 28 >

tories abound on every hand in poverty, injustice, tyranny, exploitation – 'guilty innocents' of contrived indifference on every hand. Too often, what can be done, by politics or ethics, brings only a modicum of correction and salvation. Being thus vicarious *de facto* all the time, how it might be so *de jure* must be the care of mind and will, 'God's wrong therein being most of all'.

< 29 >

Chapter 3

COMPREHENDING DIVINE UNITY

I

The human scene in Shakespeare's tragic universe must surely conduce the human spirit to atheism, so defiant of goodness is the perversity it betrays. How can Iago's malignity co-exist with a divine sovereignty akin to the Beatitudes of Jesus? There may be a certain blind heroism in Macbeth's last lonely bravado but it is only the greatness of accumulated guilt and crime, 'bloodied but unbowed'. Hamlet falls prey to a web of intrigue, perfidy and cunning, 'things rotten in the state of Denmark', more 'rotten' still in the 'pestilential vapours' of a sordid world brooding violently on itself.

What Shakespeare would have us believe was always as elusive as what he believed himself. Such was the reticent realism of his dramatic art. He cannot be commending unbelief. For there is a nobility, a strange wistfulness, in the perplexity itself, but somehow there would seem to be a counsel for an un-believing that gives itself to know the task of honest faith, if we would ever genuinely reach it. Such counsel 'holds the mirror up' in which theology may see its own thwarted features in their due contours. Shakespearean tragedy seems to deny any availing and prevailing moral order, unless we allow to the divine a strenuous evil antagonism. This might convey us to a somber dualism, pitting two irreconcilables against each other and making divine unity a fond and foolish dream.

So then, we must first concede that comprehending divine unity will be no complacent business for either soul or mind. Moreover, what is thus an issue for us humans *about* God is, by the same token an issue *for* and *within* God's own being. What for us humans interrogates divine unity in

< 30 >

wrong and sin spells defiance disputing it. If – re divine unity – would-be believers have to resolve a question, God no less has to overcome a contest. The stakes between belief and unbelief for us, are between sovereignty and usurpation for the divine order of being. The sense in which this must be so will be with us throughout these pages. How might 'God's wrong' ever be none at all?

It is easy enough to foreclose this theme and resolve the issue by bare assertion. Indubitably 'God is One'. The obvious exemplar of this assertive self-assured theology is classic Islam. Dualism and pluralism of worship are anathema. *Allahu akbar. La ilaha illa Huwa.* 'Greater is Allah. There is no deity but He.' 'He is exalted above all that ye associate.'[1] The familiar Islamic doctrine of *Tawhid* has been fully expounded but is timely here in present context, providing a steady foil to the Christian doctrine of divine unity which takes account of criteria Islam discounts, though they are emphatically present in the Qur'an. Those criteria have to do with human wrong.

A striking recent example of the Islamic dogma of unity and of the consequent gravamen against the Christian reading of a unitary theology comes in a narrative of personal conversion to Islam, which a late 20th century German diplomat has written out of ambassadorial experience in Algeria and Morocco and post conversion pilgrimage to Mecca.[2] His dismissive, negative aspersions on the Christian theme of divine Oneness provide useful insight on issues of profound contrast to which we must come. He sees in Islam 'a revelation of simplicity' in contrast to 'picturesque eclecticism'. He quotes a kindred spirit in a French writer, Jean Delumeau, writing in 1985 in *Ce que Je Crois.* As Christians hold,

> God is impotent (non-puissant), subservient . . . suffering in and with all those wretched people with whom Jesus identified. God suffers with us and more than we, under all the evil in this tormented world.

This, according to Hofmann, makes God an object of pity, whereas

> Islam's concept of God is undiluted, coherent and clear – One, indivisible, non-begotten, perfect, incomparable, sovereign, absolute, neither in need of perfection nor of His own creation, (who) guides through His prophets without need of Incarnation, pro-creation or self-sacrifice.[3]

The self-assurance of these strictures and of the theology that shapes them raises in vehemence points which in sobriety we must address in several contexts until Chapter 12.

The reckoning they require of us is best broached by exploring what, for any and every theism, we must call the 'God-and' situation. It is one from which the Qur'an is in no way exempt, though its involvement in detail is not here our concern.[4]

< 31 >

Within human experience, must we not conclude that the very word 'God' is a relational word? Like 'friend', or even 'rival' to be one is to have one. Unilateral friendship, solitary rivalry – these are contradictions in terms. 'In Him we live and move and *have our being.*' A right theology will be reverent enough to allow that there must be more to divine transcendence than the human relation. Yet, outside that relation there is neither knowledge nor relevance. 'Him with whom we have to do' is 'He who has to do with us' and no other. We are in this 'God and' situation of things mutual between Creator and creaturehood, between Lord and servant, between majesty and awe, between love divine and love human. There is no intelligent, no intelligible theology outside this mutuality.[5]

We cannot say that God is 'absolute' if we mean that He over-rides or violates this situation our theism believes to be of His own devising. Divine unity must be consistent with divine creation and custodian human creaturehood therein. It falls to Chapter 5 to explore the 'covenant' of human 'dominion', understood Biblically as the template of history and culture. There was the Noahid covenant of 'seedtime and harvest' normally ensured in the human habitat. This the Judaic mind narrowed and exceptionalized into the Sinaitic covenant which sealed that same territorial, ethnic assurance of livelihood and fulfilment in uniquely private terms, with the *confessio*: 'I (YAHWEH) will be your God and you (Israel) will be my people.'[6] The Christian 'covenant', told in 'bread and wine', by that very symbol, re-universalized things Noahid in a Gospel of grace that made 'all believers' fellow-heirs of things Sinaitic in open peoplehood to God. That story falls to Chapter 6.[7]

Such in the Biblical comprehension is the 'God and' situation where our experience of divine sovereignty and transcendence is everywhere within, never extraneous to, our human empire and privilege in custody of the natural order. All the Biblical themes of praise, gratitude, awe, reverence, wonder and joy – as so memorably celebrated, for example, by the likes of Thomas Traherne[8] – turn on what cannot be divine as not also human, nor human without being more surely divine. It is this reciprocity which must shape the doctrine and concept of divine unity. We may begin to see that it is not about mere number at all. Number has to do with units to be serially counted or deducted. These have to do with quantity, whereas divine/human mutuality in covenantal terms has to do with quality.

That vital distinction, however, has to be qualified in two areas. The one has to do with the attitude we have to natural phenomena. The other is the volition, volatile, vile, or virtuous, which we bring to the fulfilment of our creaturehood in mortal time and earthly place. The meaning of divine unity, for us, will be critically at stake in both, while eternally secure essentially in God. The course of thought on faith in unity has to take up both areas where the human situation 'enters deeply into God'.[9]

< 32 >

II

The covenantal Biblical concept of tenancy, trusteeship, fertility, trade, work and community, had all to do with natural phenomena – fields, mountains, rivers, wells, oases, habitats of every kind, tribes, neighbours, pathways and all things else reciprocal between the face of the earth and the hand of man. The issue always was whether these were chaotically sacrilized or sacramentally received. There could be no question of their mystery nor any respite from the anxiety they harboured when the elements failed and normal experience gave way to catastrophe.

Ignorance and frailty alike could demonize those features of experience and, as it were, deify phenomena so that the arena of dependence became a realm of placation, oblation, of symbol-shaping and idolatry. Such was the chronic problem of Muhammad's Mecca at the outset of his mission. Here was a numerical pluralism, reading life and its precarious scenario as tributary to fears and threats, a prey to daimons in nature's disorder.

Such pluralism might exist with belief in some over-all supremacy, in Mecca's case Allah over all.[10] For totality was more daunting, more awesome than any single daimon, the everywhere more menacing than the local haunt of risk.

Thus Islam's initial mission had to be emphatically dismissive of such fears, reassuringly hostile to this multiplicity of chaotic credences. There is only He, the One, the ever-controlling. The creed was necessarily stentorian, abolishing number, disowning this sacrilized scenario of nature's undeniable diversity and life's precarious tenure therein. Faith must be emphatically Unitarian. Because God was One, worship and belief had to be radically de-numbered. Only so, could phenomena be rightly understood by an imperative abolition of idolatry.

The urgency in the Islamic example was authentic and yet partial, insofar as it needed a theme of 'dissociation' in 'exalting' Allah above and beyond all those phenomena-dwelling daimons.[11] He must not be construed as in any sense a single-focus version of them. His sovereignty had to be the more remote in order to be the better obeyed. Such was the necessity the Qur'an perceived in the there-and-then setting.[12] There were, however, quite contrasting factors against this 'beyondness' in the territory of 'mercy', covenantal fidelity, and the gift of 'dominion' itself which Bible and Qur'an alike celebrated inside the abiding sovereignty that had bestowed them.

For these held the vital secret that countered and cancelled all notions of a chaos, the chaos that loosed the daimons that inspired the pluralism and imagined the idols. In its Arabian setting the Qur'an was profoundly Biblical in affirming things covenantal, when also enthron-

< 33 >

ing the solitary Lordship. 'Exalted be He!', was no formula for human experience in its intimate content.

In due time the sense of divine/human covenant fathered the ventures of a human science, moving from covenantal tenancy of a good earth that could thereby be perceived as a cosmos, to steadily growing mastery and control of its environment. Other factors not confessedly religious certainly also contributed and much turned historically on the development of facilities, mechanical and optic, tools and lens, whereby investigative exploitation could build cumulatively on its own successes. The Biblical/Christian sense of a 'God and' scenario underwrote the human possession of its meaning – whence painfully and hazardously the making of the modern world. There was even a mental contribution in the sheer sense of intelligibility from which the very niceties of theological subtlety drew their confidence.[13]

All proceeded this way as a corollary of divine unity, of a de-idolized, de-sacrilized world in which the human tenure was in genuine dominion, scientifically pursued but theologically under-written.[14] Then, however, a new issue arose by which the ever inviolate sovereignty of God was all the more at risk from the wrong, not of ignorance, but of sin. Namely, how the very lengths and liberties of human dominion, by some growing arrogance at their magnitude, induced a sense of elision of the divine in the sheer implantation of the human. Would the theme of partnership in privilege give way to 'there is only us' and 'man is all'? Was a happily de-sacrilized natural order, rid of inhibiting idols and phobias, as competently manageable, thereby also de-wondered, degraded, merely utilized? Would there not then be a deep inroad into the unity of God?

That this has largely happened is the evident fact of the contemporary world. The sense of its incidence goes far to explain the panic and alarm in forms of religious dogmatism in wild retaliation. These, however, only misread how risk-loaded the 'God and' situation has always been. They do nothing to restore its sanity, as if divine unity was fit only for assertion by violent partisans.

What our *imperium* needed to de-sacrilize in the name of God as One incurs a new idolatry of its own *superbia*, its gods of culture, race, commerce, and the nation state. These can only be subdued to their due legitimacy as occasions of conscience by the sacramental principle always present in the destiny of covenant. This 'minding as holy', ousting desecration by consecration, alone gives active meaning to the unity of God. Of Christian liturgy the Gospel story said: 'He was known of them (the disciples at Emmaus) in the breaking of the bread' (Luke 24.35). That was how the two told it to the others, with such urgency. It captures the 'God and' situation vividly and translates into the hallowing of all material things by their being taken up into – and realized as – a communion in holy things and, therefore, community in a hallowed world.

< 34 >

The traffic of the world may seem a far cry from such a perception of how the unity of God must have it mean and proceed. But such is the meaning of the sacramental order and 'minding for holy' the business of the commonplace. 'Letting God be God' happens in no lesser way. Chapter 5 has to take the point of a covenantal order further, after an intervening Chapter 4 has studied 'the primal suspicion' that calls in question the good faith of creation and Creator which, if it were warranted, would be 'the death of God' only in being the misprision of ourselves.

III

That suspicion demanded to be squarely faced, lest faith in the unity of God be some coward thing, afraid for its own credentials. Yet does it not lurk in sinister attendance on us humans all the while, urging us to a godless reading of our autonomy, untethering us from all moral and sacramental obligation? Need it be desolating to decide: 'There is only us: we are on our own'? We might even find it congenial, whether to our lethargy or to our pride.

In any event, it takes us to the second area earlier proposed, namely the will we bring to the 'God and' situation, as distinct from the cognizance we take of it in its presentation of phenomena to our comprehension and control. That was the problem of mastery; this is the pursuit of it. There we decipher in reason, here we determine in character. We encounter the nature of sin.

A naïve pluralism may people the phenomenal world with daimons and flout divine unity ignorantly: a deliberate self-will for wrong violates it sinfully. The 'God and' situation – as Shakespeare has it of 'the state of man' – 'suffers an insurrection'.[15] Divine sovereignty is then defied, whereas it was simply abused in pagan worship. The two might well coincide but the former is more heinous. How then does the divine respond to the human 'insurrection', defiling as it does both the related creaturehood and the divinely given purpose there?

It is here that the insistent assertion quoted from an incidental German source concerning a sublime indifference breaks down. A merely spectator Lordship makes all things vacuous by undoing the entire concept of an intending creation which, the Qur'an itself assures us, was never conceived as a 'plaything' or contrived 'in jest'.[16] Human sin cannot be of no matter to the God of a purposeful creation. A transcendent impervious to compassion would be incapable of any 'God and' situation. Only if the nexus were broken might its own onus be cancelled. We must know that the very vindication of omnipotence requires the dimensions of long suffering and pity which empty derision derides.

< 35 >

'Long' suffering, as we must say further in Chapter 12, has to do with 'reach' but how far and into what cost? The questions are not idle. It is the very faith in unity that is required to ask them. For if what has to be 'reached to' is not within competent 'reach' there is a denial of the unity of God. Even a cheap view of 'theodicy', tending to the reproach of God as in lapse of divine power or lack of will (either or both), crudely assumes as much. When, more reverently, we speak of divine 'compassion', what might 'com', as 'with and for', attain to mean? How would human perversity stretch the answer?

It is clear already, even in an Islam-style mood of theology instinctively shunning the question, that divine 'association' with the human situation incurs being vulnerable apart from any heinous measures of human perversity. If indeed, as the old Rabbis would say: 'The Lord is enthroned on the praises of His people,' when the praises languish and stay, where is the throne? 'Thou art worthy to receive . . . ' is the cry of John in Patmos. What then when the '*Gloria in excelsis*' is guiltily silent in human minds and wills and seemingly canceled *in profundis*?

There are clear implications of divine risk by us in the most absolutist theologies, so that it matters that *Allahu akbar* must be insistently affirmed, not in order to be true, but on behalf of ever being known so. Scriptures are via divine agencies that God must employ among human messengers. The Eternal does not address time except by reaching into it. What may be 'absolute' in the content has to mediatorial in the method. 'Treasure in earthen vessels' was how the apostolic Church saw its own worth within the worth of God.

It is clear that omnipotence can only be reconciled with creation and with human custody therein as a venture of deliberate condescension and consequent exposure to ensuing liabilities from which reality can concede no exoneration. For 'oneration' in positive intent is rooted there. Gibes about a deity sadly to be pitied, as if helplessly inadequate on earth if not in heaven, have no ring of truth in this cosmos of divine authority. Rather, they distort the sovereignty they should more searchingly explore to find the nature of omnipotence as self-expending love.

If it be said that compassionate omnipotence is paradox to refuse, it must be seen that there is paradox no less in its refusal, namely the paradox of a divine that has willed the human situation and found no answer to its evident perversity.

If we hold that limitation is anathema for omnipotence, it will not be so if that limitation is from within, in the nature of love as power suiting its real task. Divine self-limitation into the human 'association' we comprehend in our earthly habitation is already presently ours to acknowledge such. Is it not further consistent with itself in the 'reach' of its answer into our tragedy – the answer Christian faith discerns and learns in the incarnate and redeeming Christ, Lord of that ultimate *kenosis*?

< 36 >

Only so, that faith would hold, do we learn also the truth of divine unity, unity no longer anxious about number but told in the unfailing 'reach' of its 'long' suffering God in the ultimate doxology.

It was important to know divine unity this way in prelude to 'The Primal Suspicion' that calls into question the entire integrity of the divine/human situation, the radical innuendo that has to be radically refused and scorned. The sure assertion of divine integrity must duly follow, told in creation and Christology, as one inclusive drama. In that story this Chapter's duties will lengthen further, to be renewed again in Chapter 12. 'Let there be' and 'be there was and is' made the shout of creation to be greeted in answer with 'Let God be God!' The sequence of those two cries is the whole business of theology. Divine unity is not finally about number but about sovereignty.

Chapter 4

THAT PRIMAL SUSPICION

I

If there is, as here argued, the 'God and . . . ' situation whereby the theme of the divine belongs reciprocally to the meaning of the human, that very mutuality lands us squarely also in a 'God but . . . ' sequel. At the core of divine intention in the human and human response to the divine there dwells a dark suspicion. It lives in that paradisial question: 'Has God said . . . ?' It holds a sinister hint that there is a crippling caveat round the mandate to be and to possess, to occupy and replenish this waiting and amenable earth, this good and fruitful world. What is this something about an obedience which must circumscribe our supposed mastery? If we have been manumitted to a mastery, why is it summoned also into a submission?

What is this 'something God has said' which conditions: 'Be and reign' with a corollary: 'Be and obey'? Could it be that the Lord now has reservations, even a kind of jealousy, about the creaturehood He has so mysteriously contrived for His custodian? A sense of bad faith creeps into our experience of liberty. Misgiving breeds and broods over how genuine the possession is, hedged thus with 'but not . . . ' about its reach and its authority.

Al this seems to query the rubric which runs: 'If we can we may' – a line of thought which, for example, Oscar Wilde invoked in his oft repeated slogan: 'Only what is realized is right.' For the aesthete and the artist, art existed only to be pursued free of all inhibition,[1] being legitimate *per se*. None might say it nay. Should not selfhood enjoy this same self-warrant in all its realms of will and action?

What then of the competence studied in the previous chapter in its

< 38 >

Biblical delineaments of tenancy and privilege? Does not the very generosity of what is bestowed in our being 'associates' with God evoke a grudge on our part about expectation of our compliance with its *regnare qua servare*? We reign only in that we submit. The very garden of Eden conveys to the hard labour of the brow. The Bible shows a deep preoccupation with this burden, whereas Islam's theism seems ready for the sheer imperative, unready for debate around it, more minded to heed a command than examine a query.

To be sure, credentials for conviction cannot well be separated from credentials for obedience. Distinctions within theism will not be absolute, but reflection in the previous chapter on the meaning of divine unity illuminates the issue. We come to that suspicion about the 'God but . . . ' in the 'God and . . . ' only in the fullness of the theme that kindles it. 'Whom' the Qur'an calls 'your magnanimous Lord' is where all begins and ends.

Whether the situation prompts theists to interrogate good faith, there are non-theists everywhere who bitterly, or wistfully, press the question. Accusers of 'God's wrong' are popular and loud. Is the magnanimity a legend 'too good to be true'? What of the apparently malign dimension in its wake? The hard problem of evil in the world we experience – and its evident link with our own competence – might well engender this paradox of divine regret or scruple over the prowess and the stature bestowed so handsomely on humankind. 'Have I said . . . ?' might conceivably arise about the human scene with its 'Be and possess', making the vast risk a monumental mistake. Or so *we* might suppose on His behalf. What of God's 'bad faith' in response to ours?

Such a haunting dualism resulting has always told a menace for robust affirmations of unity. The bleaker forms of Asian Buddhism see snare and delusion in the mortal significance of human personhood. It is a fallacy to be transcended by attainment to non-being in what Sufi Muslims know as *fana'*, the passing away of the empirical self.

What haunts Biblical and Semitic theism is of a different order, whose anxiety is about misgivings that only exist because of the very grounds of confidence. The different premise is not that we are non-entities but that we might be fated captives. The Qur'an's several references of *zann*, or 'suspicion', concern only the suspect attitude between parties to Islamic situations in a context of armed belligerence and climate of *nifaq*, or hypocrisy.[2] Yet, political as these were, they deepened into more elemental reaches of good, or ill, will towards the core of faith. There was always the Qur'an's *la'alla*, the inclusive 'Perhaps' about human answer to the divine integrity pledged in the giving of *khilafah*, or 'trustedness' within the cosmos. Would humans bring that vital *tadabbur*, as intelligent reckoning with earth's meaning?[3] For such response lives by reassurance confirming the whole veritable human status and its summons into priv-

< 39 >

ilege Chapter 3 explored. The passages do not indulge some disquiet, they banish it.

These possible caveats about human meaning on a 'serious' earth, or the genuineness of human dominion, sustain no reasonable suspicion concerning our authenticity under God.

II

What stays more puzzling and disconcerting is the 'interdiction' in the Biblical narrative of Eden, forbidding 'the knowledge of good and evil', as radically exempted from all human access[4] What means this prohibition? Why should it seemingly contradict the mandate to be, and to possess and to subdue? Is there here some further hint of divine 'jealousy' about creaturehood possibly over-reaching itself, aspiring to 'be as gods' (Genesis 3.5) and so mounting some kind of challenge to the sole sovereignty of their Creator?

John Milton's Adam is described as

> . . . the master-work, the end
> Of all yet done: a creature . . . endu'd
> With sanctity of reason might . . . upright, with front serene
> Govern the rest, self-knowing, and from thence
> Magnanimous to correspond with heaven . . . [5]

'Self-knowing' suggests the clue to what otherwise perplexes in at once commissioning and restraining, endowing and forbidding.

This 'knowledge of good and evil' as a capacity withheld is best understood within that fusion of things only authentic in the reality of love – love as at once only realized as possession when surrendered in submission. The reach of liberty is the measure of responsibility. 'Knowledge' here cannot naïvely mean the competence to distinguish between benign and malign herbs, or to tell poisons from wholesomes. Nor is it the techniques that the sciences contrive and cultures enjoy. It can only mean the claim to pass from the status of creaturehood to some transcending of all moral accountability, a 'knowledge' that 'unknows' all liability to discriminate between moral contrasts and thus 'be as gods'. Knowing ourselves – in our very freedoms – still tributary to God and under His sovereign governance, as awareness of moral issues teaches, is at once our liberty and our loyalty, not one without the other.

> . . . Owe to thyself . . . thy obedience: therein stand,
> This was that caution giv'n thee . . . ordain'd thy will . . .
> Our voluntary service he requires,
> Not our necessitated . . . for how

< 40 >

> Can hearts, not free, be tri'd whether they serve
> Willing, or no . . . and can no other choose?

as Milton's Raphael explains to Adam.[6]

It seems clear that this paradox of a bestowal of relationship conditioned by its own content is the very nature and sanctity of love. It cannot be active without also being receptive. It accepts only to belong. What withholds 'the knowledge of good and evil' intends and awaits the practice of 'good against evil' on the part of an honest creatureliness that has understood the criteria of the good creation to which it is called. The lasting Biblical comment: 'And God saw that it was good' (Genesis 1.21) gives the lie to the contrary, precisely in proposing this cosmos for human domain where 'love would be the meaning', offered and received. For love always has this character of a mutuality that seeks and takes both ways in satisfying a common yearning. On the human side, it is pretension not freedom which is excluded: on the divine side transcendence not magnanimity which is reserved. That way, man is altogether 'let be', and God likewise on human part.

We confirm these great positives if we attend to the contrary case made by Friedrich Nietzsche's philosophy of 'beyond good and evil'. It was only logical that he should announce 'the death of God' in the same context. For the two stood in one. The claim that 'man-ness' in his 'super' sense should and could override the inter-human liabilities of compassion and humility and mutual acceptance, was – indeed – to 'kill off' the earth-meaning of divine Lordship. Nietzsche's 'trans-valuation of values' in the interest of due human self-assertion, of necessity limited to the aspiring few, abandoned duly human mutualities in life and society, precisely in jettisoning where, in God, those mutualities had their right esteem and warrant. The Biblical – and indeed Quranic – conviction that we do not have the fully human in the absence of the authentically divine was evident in Nietzsche's rejection of both. Yet, ironically, he thought he was pleading for 'a religion in which it was possible to love'. Had he not relinquished the only one there is?[7]

III

It is not only a Nietzsche who would have us stay with that wary query: 'Hath God said?' and keep a dubious scepticism about God's integrity. There is perpetual despair about the sanity of life, the intelligibility of the world and the authenticity of time. Honest religion cannot well be indifferent to the perennial incidence of suicide, nor be satisfied with the tradition 'of unsound mind' verdict in its wake. The quest for meaning is too urgent, too widespread, too faltering, for theists to discount. Life's

< 41 >

interdictions of good and inflictions of evil being so bitter, what knowledge has been forbidden us? We shall only learn 'love's meaning' when we have a mind for 'love's endeavour' and 'love's expense', as they are for us in God.[8]

For despite the fidelities we experience in the natural order and our mortal physicality with their redeemable consistencies, the loaded misgivings abound. Or musing on the reach of human credulity, so evident in religion at large, leaves many vigilant against the risk of repeating it. There is a contemporary bias in favour of agnostic reservations, having more to do with the commitment costs in discipline of life than with the faith's merits in the mind.

This situation is burdened by the tension between law and conscience, between public writ and private thought. When Milton in *Paradise Lost*, Book vii, told (line 217) of 'the omnific Word', he meant in context the sublime *Fiat* of creation, 'and the world unborn from chaos heard his Voice'. But then there was the 'let there be . . . ' of humans and further voice divine ensued, legislating, ordaining and restraining. From a place called Sinai the voice would command as well as commission the humans. How consistent, then, would be such theocratic ethics with the range of the dominion personal conscience must exercise? The question lies very close to that interdiction of 'knowledge of good and evil'.

One thing is clear, namely that the more absolute command controls (especially if somehow vested in 'institutions' of human authority – thrones, kingdoms, churches, powers, rulers) the less 'free' we are. The more 'free' we assert our private selves to be, the more responsible we become about 'good and evil'. There will be place, in Chapter 7, for the 'pitfalls' of 'custodians' who administer the divine and/or subject the human, in the interplay of public writ and personal conscience, of ecclesio-political magistracy and individual minding. Unless we are 'to give up all moral issues in despair', it is likely that many will opt for an agnostic neutrality about theological faith. Yet we cannot for ever elude what or whom has our loyalty, and where and why? Or how and why do things become 'good or evil'?

Inside these themes there has been, ever since the Stoics, an impulse to find between absolute commands or vetoes and free decision an area of *adiaphora*, matters of 'indifference', about which there could be a liberty not hostile to authority, where the latter's writ need not run and private light could find its way.

But should any such areas morally exist? Are they ever agreed? Moreover, the larger the claim from inner light, the larger must this category of things indifferent be – a situation which may well dissatisfy both authority and mind. Either way, on either count, the one thing not in doubt is the 'long-suffering' of God, if we have in mind Paul's counsel to his Ephesian readers: 'Grieve not the Holy Spirit of God' (4.30). For it is

< 42 >

vital to appreciate that what was being forbidden in the Edenic situation was on behalf of the attainments availing. 'Good he made thee, but to persevere, left it in thy power . . . Free in thine own arbitrament it lies . . . to stand or fall.'[9] The crisis in human experience belongs within the realization of the human meaning. These then must be the terms by which we learn the divine nature.

IV

It has to follow that all human moral judgments are critical for every conscience and for all society, with the contrast between 'good and evil' ever present and crucial, but that the ultimate security of this contrast rests within the sovereignty of God by whom it is never yielded into human mandate. It further follows that this situation is the very condition of our existence, our surest benediction. For it enables us to fulfil ourselves in the dignity and freedom of the moral will, precisely in binding that will to a tuition from which it cannot exempt itself, a school it may never escape. Only so could we be both responsible and responsive. To be 'beyond good and evil' is never the human experience. 'Between them' in the trust of selfhood we may always remain.

Is not this moral definition of our human world entirely corroborated by the nature of our mortal physicality and the created order of a deployable cosmos whose patterns defer to our custody, evaluate our honesty and lavishly afford our means? The neutrality of these patterns under our hands is what admits alike of our masteries and our vagaries. 'The primal suspicion' is a calumny exposed, once we appreciate the ethical reality. Yet accusers abound and their incidence, of whatever impulse, is a judgment on the whole universe. What queries personal meaning queries universal meaning. *Between* good and evil we will always be.

The Ulster poet, Louis MacNeice, grimly tells how, as if to illustrate this truth, he wanted to 'subpoena this universe'. But how, if he could only confront it by introspection? Whenever his Jewish wife, Mariette, was annoyed with him, she would recall that he was 'a Gentile'.[10] He was minded to count everyone with a religious faith 'wilfully deluded' and averred that most of his friends were of the same opinion. He held aloof from idealist causes of social hope, shunning the fascination Communism had for some of his poetic contemporaries at Oxford, like W. H. Auden, in those years.[11]

Such sombre outlook and the dejected rejection of any moral sanction outside the self – necessary as he thought it – may well have stemmed from the tensions in his native Ireland and, like Sartre, his French mental kinsman, the stresses of the European scene. He saw himself 'repressed' by his Episcopal father. Not even his evident poetic talent and his well

< 43 >

tuned classical scholarship sufficed to 'fulfil' him in the world. 'He never resolved the paradox of his uncommitment.'[12] Was this the crux of a haunting sense of gloom and an unreadiness to put it somehow to flight? Often akin in mood to Thomas Hardy, a sense of legitimate personhood eluded him. Poetry could relieve but not resolve this 'Let be what will be' in his private stance.

> Although we say we disbelieve, God comes in handy when we swear . . .
> We crave some emblem for despair . . . We need one Name to take in vain
> . . . That God exists we cannot know but need not care.[13]

Like Philip Larkin he found imagery in 'train journeys' and their dubious arrivals. Yet the fleeting moment belonged in no assured continuity.

MacNeice's rendering of 'the primal suspicion' was hardly an aggressive atheism. It betrayed an inclusive indecision of will, for which any militancy was hardly necessary and doubtless insubstantial anyway. Perhaps his most morbid mood told itself in his 1944 'Prayer before Birth', with its 'I am not yet born, console me', then 'forgive me', 'rehearse me in the parts that I must play'.[14] Could he have been reacting to Thomas Traherne's 'Salutation', where the 17th century poet ardently greets the prospect of nativity?[15] Traherne's call is 'Rejoice with me', as he surveys his limbs and esteems his faculties and wonders 'where they were hid from me so long' – 'I who nothing was!' For in Traherne's world the meaningfulness of one's existence belonged with the sacramental quality of all physical experience in the living order of an intelligible and sense-responsive world. Birth was then the threshold into welcome and into invitation.

MacNeice (1906–1963) and his earlier contemporary, A. E. Housman (1859–1936), would doubtless protest that their deep quarrel was not with that arena. For they were capable of the most eager response to their 'blue remembered hills'. The quarrel lay with the anguish of the human lot within them, where nettles grew on un-remembered graves and 'thresholds for salutation' led inexorably into darkened rooms of sexual frustration and the mingled claims of sheer finality, with its taunting blight on human aspiration. They belonged to a generation twice beset by the wasteful futility of war.

Yet might not a will and a mood like Traherne's have availed to counter the negatives that so captivated their poetic diction? For the passionate disquiets and the sacramental register of the world's Trahernes sprang from the same essential ground. Each alike turned on an obligatory goodness – in the one case for negation, in the other for salutation. Perhaps nowhere, in the English language, was that reproach more sharply sounded than in Housman's late poem, 'cursing . . .

Whatever brute or blackguard made the world.

'For a certainty,' he averred, 'we are not the first' protesting such a verdict. It was 'truth' there was 'iniquity on high'

> To cheat our sentenced souls of aught they crave
> . . . as you and I
> Fare on our long fool's errand to the grave.[16]

Housman, at least in these lines, is as close to blasphemy as any poet ever came. There is no misreading 'iniquity on high' except as 'God's wrong most of all' for this benighted earth and its forlorn denizens in mortal time.[17]

Yet an intriguing issue arises from the strange fact of literary pundits tilting at each other about the presence here of genuinely defiant disavowal of God and all things theological.[18] What could be clearer when Housman advises: 'Shoulder the sky, my lad . . . The troubles of our proud and angry dust, are from eternity'?[19] 'From eternity' the blame derives, to eternity the anger pointless goes.

The pause within the critics' quarrel about this 'God blackguard' language as 'blasphemous' has to do with whether 'pride and anger' as the exasperation of 'dust' validly sustain the defiance they want to utter. Are Housman – and indeed MacNeice too – asserting in the will what does not belong in the same absolute terms to the mind? For, in both poets, as with many of their kindred, a certain wistfulness is detectable beyond the passion of rejection. Is it only a mood that blasphemes, the more so in the vicinity of pride and 'dustiness'? The question in its implications emerges in Chapter 11. Meanwhile, the question stays whether blasphemies of willed intent are always and altogether blasphemies of the whole and rational soul? Even Thomas Hardy 'would go, hoping it might be so' at the appeal of rumours of belief.[20]

Was it only the accident of their generation that Louis MacNeice and A. E. Housman alike were drawn to religious themes, even when they were lyrically calling them into question.[21] If there were troubles from eternity, there were tears of eternity, and an instinct to associate them, if only in a sort of disbelieving in belief.[22] The elusiveness of faith answered to the sheer perplexity of things, but whether it could ever address them was for the will to decide. If the will to disbelieve was strong in both poets, it was finally on the will that the decision turned. It follows that the will to belief is always the arbiter beyond the ever tentative conclusions, the ever open occasions, of the mind as ever between good and evil.

MacNeice argued for more than poetry when he urged that 'to shun dogma is not to renounce belief', seeing that any 'faith in the value of living' must be 'a mystical faith'.[23] The very concept of dogma or, better, doctrine entails some *à priori*, an actual or potential warrant of authority by which to be convinced. That authority can only somehow be in 'the thing itself', the truth in its own recognizances. But what are these and

< 45 >

can the private self reasonably undertake their assessing, their legitimacy, their credentials? A deep reluctance here or a sense of frail capacity are then a frequent incentive to agnosticism, a scepticism of the mind. That posture however, and its latent honesty, cannot ignore or exclude the sheer business of living. Faced with the onus on the mind in the things of religion, many in the faiths-world will shift the centre of gravity of truth itself as such, to some warrant alleged to have it in dependable custody – a text, a Scripture, an establishment, a dependable custodian – whose warrant can somehow carry the onus for validity and be proxy for the faith-decision the mind is reluctant to incur, whether out of modesty or delay. But there is no exoneration or relief this way, seeing that the transfer of trust to some 'truth-keeper's' role, be it church or creed, does not escape the ever personal onus of verification.[24] It also suffers loss from the shift of the centre of gravity under which it now labours.

It follows that the task of faith-credence has to be taken up into the care of love's will, and faith – like life itself – become a matter of intent, of the set of the heart. This is in way to dismiss or despise the parallel role of the intelligence in the necessary scrutiny of what faith, as doctrine, offers and commends. It is to say that these very verbs, with their tribute to the mind's competence are also, and more, an invitation to the will of the soul.

Two poets taken at random bespeak the role of the will in the business, whether of faith or its negation. It is intense emotion and no patent rationality that cries of 'whatever brute or blackguard made the world'. When MacNeice, pre-born, appeals 'console me', rehearse me', he is soliciting pity, not arguing to a jury. His pleas are from the heart. They concern 'the parts that he must play. He fears the odds there will be in the script birth will set to his hand. From the passion where the mind broods on the enigmas of belief, the will must proceed with the open ends of love. Maybe Housman's 'land of lost content' – in either sense of that word – can be found 'the land of will's intent'.[25]

V

If thus the thrust of grim anger from the passion of the heart and the enigmatic logic is always an open question, we are brought back to how 'the primal suspicion' incurs, by its very premise, suspicion of itself. Like all 'atheism' it has first to pre-suppose what it is at pains to deny. Perhaps this is the reason why certain minds, at least in modern times, express a complete unconcern about belief and unbelief either way. Thus Thomas Mann, exploring out of his own impulses the saga of *Joseph and His Brothers*, interrogates himself as to:

< 46 >

> Belief, unbelief? I hardly know one from the other. I really couldn't say if I considered myself a believer or an unbeliever. I have the deepest doubt or scepticism towards both positions.[26]

This 'negative incapability'[27] is plainly a posture of the will. It cannot be a conclusion of the intelligence. For it proposes the impossibility of inclusive doubt. In a sense far beyond Descartes' 'I cannot doubt that I am doubting,' Mann's comment adds up to a meaninglessness of all meaning. One cannot be sceptical about *all* alternative 'positions', except in the willful luxury of idle emotion. For the business of living persists and, with it, the necessity to pursue some mental option. Even a willed abeyance of 'position', whether as a gesture of rebellion or despair, will entail some reasoned task of mind, at least if one is *compos mentis* enough to profess a scepticism either way.

Something of the same compulsion to decide can be argued in the reverse direction, namely that faith itself, even ardent faith, may stem from a determination of the will to be believing. Writing in *The Poetry of W. B. Yeats*, Louis MacNeice claimed that his Irish contemporary 'faked his beliefs because he so much wanted to believe'.[28] Exercise of will in such terms is a very frequent phenomenon, not least in sharply dogmatic credulities or convictions. When it occurs, the honesty and integrity of faith are at risk. But the element of will in belief is only the more evident.

It follows from both situations – whether the nonchalance of a Thomas Mann or the desirousness of faith attributed to W. B. Yeats – that there is a necessary confluence of will and mind in any and every believing situation in religion. Therefore it must be so likewise in any and every encounter with the pros and cons about 'the primal suspicion'. Any vindication of 'the love of God' and, therein, of the integrity of 'the good earth', will require the same unison of soul-will with honest mind. Truth, like a garden, only avails to be itself in the care of love, while the love that cares is intelligent and aptly skilled. These will corroborate each other, the love developing the skill and the skill exercising the love.

Perhaps this is the reason why the instinct of New Testament writing and benediction was always to couple together 'the knowledge and love of God', so that neither would be had without the other. For 'love of God' is both a subjective and an objective genitive – ours *for* God responsive to the love *in* God.

Yet the onus abides whereby the will that is emotive cares assiduously for the minding that 'knows'.

Ought we then to conclude that 'God has indeed said . . . ' concerning the non-violation, at our will, of that 'beyondness' in divine care of the contrast between 'good and evil'? For so ordaining it should remain is the very ensuring of the cosmos in which we realize ourselves, for good or ill. The things conditional for our dignity are also conditional for our

< 47 >

humility. The limits of our self-authority are the credentials of our self-fulfilment. We are truly human by virtue of the inviolate divine sovereignty. The dominion we inherit is from a transcendence it loves and knows in its own submission. 'O God! Not gods' is what we humans cry when our humanity is right. 'Knowledge as love and love as knowledge' are the ground and reason why.

Yet still pretension otherwise abounds. Our cultures overween, our sciences exult, our prides persist and so, with them, our accusations seek out a guilty transcendence we will reproach. 'The primal suspicion' holds some in thrall, unless it is overtaken by an ache-exempt indifference. Thus the faith of the theist will always be engrossed in the 'justification of God'. Its resource can only be in mind and heart together, mind in its will to love and heart in its will to know.

Two succeeding chapters must take up that task in study, first of our habitat in nature and the case-making of its character and, through these, the Christian criteria of 'God in Christ', such Christology being where the good faith of creation may be most adequately identified.

Chapter 5 will need to renew aspects of the present one because of its own perspective of divine vindication. The issues in divine reproach and divine integrity belong together. How deeply they reach conveys the argument to the *per necessitatem Christianus* of Chapter 6. It is one that requires and engenders all else that must follow, of 'pitfalls', 'word-meanings' and other measures of faith.

< 48 >

Chapter 5

Divine Integrity in Human Covenant

I

It is well to realize that the problem of evil only exists inside the question of God. In an unintended, and therefore pointless world, wrong would simply happen but it would not puzzle, nor perplex. It could evoke neither anger nor anguish. Only a universe somehow meant for human cognizance and wrought for mortal tenancy and rational, moral human 'dominion' could ever come to be counted reprehensible. Only the human presence and the human privilege allow any logic about divine reproach. Conversely, has not the enigma of wrong and evil been the prime source of the will to atheism?[1] If it is this 'here-we-are-ness' about us humans that underwrites that 'God is', then only because we and God belong together here is there any point in disputing the way things are and still less in bitterly accusing them.

We noted earlier how absolute and imperative was Islam's espousal of divine unity. Factors urgent in its repudiation of plural worships and idolatrous superstition made it less than adequately alert to the issue of divine unity as more than a matter of number, in negation of plurality – witness the very shape of the Creed: 'There is not . . . except . . . ' While there is no doubt of its register of *zulm* and wrong, the Qur'an broadly saw these as doing violence to a numerical oneness. Thus it did not undertake the heavy burden of Allah's unity as mastering all defiance, in terms more radical than denunciation. Men, as pivotal verses said, did not 'measure Allah with a true measure'. 'Right measure' had been the deep concern of Biblical theism. Islam relied on a divine inscrutability where the desperate weight of the mystery of human wrong was not allowed to arise for the human mind. Allah was quite assertively, 'over all things omnipotent' with a manner of omnipotence needing no strategy of human relatedness in long-suffering and patience.[2] Its perception of the human predicament was content with the sufficiency of command, guidance, direction, exhortation and law as a moral 'thus it shall be', the moral *fiat* of Allah's religion feasibly in place. As we have seen, its account of human wrong in Chapter 3 was only sharing the Biblical parallel in more prosaic terms. In being 'resolute for divine unity', it did not concede that divine unity concealed any issue around divine integrity. What 'God had said' imperatively in law and holy writ dealt decisively with that sinister: 'Hath God said?' of a surreptitious Satan.[3]

Thus the unity of God took adequate care of the authority of God. The one could be seen as entirely secure in the other, whereas in the Biblical scenario the issue of the latter went far, in Satanic terms, into the reality of the other. Wrong presented a genuine challenge to divine sovereignty. Humanity was the crux of the issue between them, seeing that humans were uniquely the sphere of divine enlistment and so, in turn, the crucial realm of Satanic cunning in intervention. So much is plain and clear in the case thus far. We have to recognize that 'the primal suspicion' *does* mean that a divine integrity is at stake in the avowed 'goodness' of the creation and its purposeful entrustment to human hands and their capacity for its custody in culture and civilization.

II

This theme of God's 'good faith' with us – so far implicit in our very response to it – exists for faith in two related realms of its incidence, namely nature and history, or place and time. The Christian Bible finds them both present in terms over which we can write 'Emmanuel', 'God with us'. It is a 'with' that means 'for', as quite banishing that 'primal suspicion' in the evident vindication of passionate 'good faith'.[4] In either case, this 'Emmanuel' is the more emphatic, the more assured to us, precisely because it has faced – and faced down – the awesome implications of any alleged 'bad faith'.

The first of these 'Emmanuels' in the natural order is the theme of this chapter, namely 'covenant with the human via the Hebraic'. The second, differently in nature and in history, is that of 'the Christ in grace' – to follow in Chapter 6. There is a vital logic from the first into the second. It is a logic which turns on the meaning of the 'us' in that 'Emmanuel', whether particular, or embracing all. That central issue about the will to faith comes in Chapter 11. In these three chapters the focus is squarely on 'God's wrong most of all' in ever belonging with us.

The immediate theme has to be the 'human via the Hebraic' in the foregoing summary. It concerns the crucial Biblical sense of 'covenant',

< 50 >

made particular – though being potentially human-at-large – by the idio-
syncratic reading of Hebrew history,[5] where what belongs in all geography
is exceptionalized for theology. In pondering how the physical, temporal
factor in the human story could be so sharply 'interiorized' for theology,
it is crucial to appreciate how strongly identity mattered in the ancient
world.[6]

Jewry and Judaism have long insisted that God is known and served in
'minute particulars', whether the colour and measure of the fringe on
the *tallit*, or prayer-shawl, in synagogue worship or the timing of Sabbath
eve and the safeguards of its celebration. Theirs is by long usage a most
meticulous religion.[7]

The same instinct for divine immediacy informs its whole story,
binding YAHWEH, the very 'Lord of hosts',[8] with the rigour of a defining
specialism, opting for an explicit people, choosing a specific place and
enshrining in His purposes a unique story, an expressly distinguishing
history, that yields an ever distinctive Scripture. Ben Sirach,
Ecclesiasticus, lets personified 'Wisdom' explain:

> . . . I looked for a home, in whose territory was I to settle?
> Then the Creator of the universe laid a command upon me;
> My Creator decreed where I should dwell.
> He said: 'Make your home in Jacob, find your heritage in Israel.'
> And so I came to be established in Zion.
> Thus He settled me in the city He loved
> And gave me authority in Jerusalem.
> I took root among the people whom the Lord had honoured
> By choosing them to be His special possession.[9]

Ben Sirach's 'privileging of the privileged' in these downright terms
engendered and perpetuates large problems. For it had to co-exist with
the countering assurance: 'Every people and nation were under my sway.'
It was a particularity for ever in the context of some universal, yet for ever
exempting and exempted from the whole, in which alone the universal
consists. For the divine and the human situation is never geographically
or ethnically confined.

That Biblical *mise-en-scène* of YAHWEH's oath-swearing was always at odds
with itself over the universal/particular paradox it for ever enshrined. It
would be unduly bold to say that such ethnically directed oath does
'wrong to God', but the conjecture is necessary, if only implicit, in a
complete Biblical integrity.[10] It is bold because the assurance of divine
covenanting is rooted in the Biblical tradition and, through the concept
of 'Messiah', was historically the source of a Christian universalism which
fulfilled it. Yet, prior to that perceived, received and ever disputed fulfilment, the incidence of 'election' by 'covenant' created a deeply
ambivalent relation of everything Jewish to the generality of humankind.

< 51 >

What of God's belonging outside the Judaic perimeter of His 'sworn' people-adoption?

Did it somehow compromise the theme of creation, of procreation readily proceeding, by divine fiat of 'male and female' in the Genesis scenario, and the world-wide distribution of all these thus 'commissioned' peoples to the ends of the earth? It was seen and somehow held to have 'narrowed' the nature-sworn features of Genesis 1, 2 and 8 into people-sworn singular terms with Abraham 'and his seed', so that the Bible essentially begins with that founding patriarch and with his right-affirming traverse of the destined land. Inevitably then the question presses as to the relation between 'that bow in the cloud', 'the seedtime and harvest' pledged to *all* peoples and the one enpeopled land 'flowing with milk and honey' in its – and their – distinctiveness.

We might draw a careful analogy from a Shakespearean scene.[11] Portia, the puzzled wife of Brutus in *Julius Caesar*, entreats him about his preoccupations. Might a non-Jew likewise enquire of God:

> . . . Am I . . .
> But as it were in sort of limitation?
> . . . Dwell I but in the suburbs
> Of your good pleasure?[12]

Her plea is solicitous and gentle. Emotions run deep concerning the meaning of what strains relationship, conveys one party to disquiet concerning the other's mind, which – being elsewhere – stirs misgiving. It fears incipient rejection and rightly so, seeing that 'Love your neighbour as yourself' translates into 'he/she is as you are', making 'one and the same humanity'. That one humanity includes Jewry. Shakespeare has Shylock eloquently invoke it when, in the criminally 'Gentile' Venice of Bassanio, a single humanity was his plea of last – and first – resort. 'Hath not a Jew eyes . . . ?' affirms one human neighbourhood, so that 'Who is my neighbour?' may have no racial limits.[13] 'I am as you are' all must say to the other, since 'neighbourhood' earth-wise is singular.

Being 'in the suburbs' – or worse – of the divine mind has always been the menace, either way, of the Jew/'Gentile' differential, 'in sort of limitation' the habit of society.

III

This means that we have to study what is at stake in Judaic particularity of race and place in God's economy on two levels. We might describe them as historical and geographical, the better to see how 'God's wrong' might be seen 'worst of all' in how they eventuated as duly divine 'swearing'. If thereby Biblical loyalty is strained, it is only that it might be truly upheld.

For it presents a situation in which query is the necessary shape of vindication and dubiety the condition of faith-discernment.

Historically, the fact of 'covenant' meant a Judaic attitude to other peoples in terms of their presence as inimical or beneficial: Edom against Israel, or Joseph and the Egypt of his near Pharaonic role there, the later Rameses and Moses, or Nehemiah and the benign Cyrus. The pattern would be continuous from Samson and his Philistines to the Maccabees against the Seleucids, the Zealots against their Rome.

Peoples and powers were always assessed relationally to things and fortunes Judaic. For long this meant a deep measure of self-congratulation via the perennial alibi of 'them that hate us'. An implicit self-approval could be drawn from the belief that ills and evils were always from elsewhere, until at length, with the great Amos, the 'inimical' to Israel/Judea in the heathen powers could be read as condign divine retribution on the 'oath-bestowed' 'people of YAHWEH. Then, by the same token, Amos was able to discern migrations among such peoples in something like 'exodus' terms, so that all history had to be seen as governed by divine ethics that embraced all nations and could belong punitively with 'chosen people' and not only with their good fortune. These deep issues in developing comprehension of what YAHWEH was 'sworn to', as Jewry's abiding mentor, emerged as their long and precarious education.

There is no less a fascinating study in the geographical interest of the Hebrew Bible. For all the exclusive stress on 'the land', its being duly 'dwelt' by its due people, there is – especially in the eighth and following century prophets – a lively celebration of 'the ends of the earth' and of 'the isles waiting for YAHWEH's law'. One might stay to wonder how much Ezekiel knew of the 'isles' that are now Indonesia or the Maldives, when his survey of the commerce of Tyre across the seas spurred him to assurance of her doom.[14]

Always there was the same ambivalence about the geographical as of the historical, a wondering wistfulness for the remote, the distant and the strange and yet a will to subdue all else to the sovereignty of the magnanimity they alone possessed. It was never – except in the dire pain of exile – a 'we will go to them'. It was always that 'they will flow to us', to seek, enquire, learn and recognize. It is this which made exile so fraught a dimension in the Hebrew reaction to geography.

Whether history then, or geography, in the prepossessions of the Biblical mind in the long centuries and sundry scenes from Abraham to Malachi, 'the oath which YAHWEH swore to our fathers' was ever their anchor, alike in memory and travail. Before exploring how risk-prone in both time and story their chosen status was, it is well to linger over the whole concept of the divine in oath-making relation.

There are almost three hundred 'swearing' occasions in the Pentateuch and through the rest of the Hebrew Canon, with the

< 53 >

YAHWEH/Jewry model ordaining similar fidelities between His people in their social relations. Qoheleth counsels 'keeping the king's command' having 'regard to the oath of God' (Ecclesiastes 8.2). Oaths contrast with 'cursings' which invoke ill, while 'to swear' is to ensure the good in the will as duly the good in the deed.

Earlier, Chapter 1 noted the paradox of oath-taking among humans as somehow reinforcing an honesty which ought to be already there in the first place, while implying a lack of honesty in offering the extra of an oath. That devising of better assurance among us mortals might be justified for legal reasons and on occasions of public role-taking. Such necessity can hardly apply to God, still less the implication of misgiving in the absence of an oath undertaken. Surely a divine integrity is reliable enough without the added factor of an equally unthinkable perjury, thus needlessly present. It must seem a strange vagary for an eternal mind to reach into the realm of mortal time by proffering an oath.

Yet, throughout the Hebrew text, the 'oath YAHWEH swore' frames the narrative of 'the fathers', to be cherished, memorialized and ritualized 'through all the generations' as heir to it.

Explanation is given in the most purposely Judaic writing in the New Testament. Men 'swear by something greater', as we saw in Richard III, to make their fallibility dependable. God's oath could only ever be within Himself, adding – as it were – announced truth to essential truth, so that 'by two immutables' the humans in the meaning might be the more assured (Hebrews 6.16–18).

This explanation of the incomprehensible is plainly meant in and for our human situation. God accepts a 'necessity' only necessitous by dint of His strategy with us.[15] Thus He makes Himself vulnerable to us by a readiness to be chargeable to our misgivings, answerable to our fears for His good faith with us, fortifying us by consideration for our frailty of heart.

Seen this way, it could almost be as if the divine will to oath and pledge and re-assuring promise anticipates the whole logic of the Incarnation and of 'God in Christ', stooping to our condition.

Thus, while the force of an oath is superfluous because divine integrity is inherent, oath-willingness is present for the better benediction of the slow of mind, the heavy of heart. The implications here for the temper of all religious authority and of those who wield it, to which we must come in other chapters, are evident enough. Our yearning is to have all values secure from the wastes of time and the corruption of the years.

Understanding in this way the oath-made, the oath-received, in the Biblical, Judaic tradition returns us to the study of its Hebrew story, with the stimulus of knowing that the logic in it was wholly humanitarian.[16] Such study, however, does well to take note at once of a strange anomaly in the oath-situation between YAHWEH and His people. It is the more note-

< 54 >

worthy in that it belongs to the event in which that situation was most signally experienced.

For, in the theophany of Exodus 3 where Moses finds himself summoned to liberate his people from tyranny in Egypt and – dubious or fearing within – enquires concerning 'God's 'Name', he is only elusively re-assured. In that daunting scenario he is asking for some guarantee. None will be given. There is no 'swearing' that ensures the result but only a summons to trust what alone the event as lived through will vindicate.[17] The reply from the bush that burned is no enigma, as 'I am that I am' would be. Such a word would never motivate a craven people called into a heavy risk. 'I will be there, as who there I will be' is surely the meaning. It belongs with the God of Exodus that only Exodus will 'prove' who He is. The hazard must be run as the only context of the knowing.[18]

Was it not somehow this way for Abraham even with the 'oath-swearing'? For, as the New Testament has it, 'he went forth not knowing whither he went' (Hebrews 11.8). Even 'covenants' are in the active proving and their 'sworn-ness' a concession to human frailty.

These considerations pose the ever pressing question whether this Hebraic covenant was immutable or conditional, irrefragable or rescindable. Seeing that, in any event, it is participatory, must it not be both, by any paradox of what inter-engages the divine and the human? Do not the two elements inter-establish it? The fidelity partners into the human, the Judaic, privilege it confers. The one is indeed beyond all change of mind (Romans 11.29) but that mind has willed the means of human frailty and will not, therefore, be exempt from these. Only on that paradox can the hope of vindication turn – a point vital to the authenticity of Messianic hope and Messianic fact.

The soul of the Hebrew Bible was endlessly troubled by this situation. It was implicit in the Isaian – and later – analogy of 'the vineyard of the Lord of hosts', standing as it did alike for the territory as 'land', and for the 'people' as 'His pleasant plant'. Thus the covenantal standing was subject to two interrogations, the one concerning the generality of nature, 'lands at large and their nations', the other the exacting perplexity and pain of exile.

YAHWEH's care for particularity in 'His people', within His other, Noahid covenant did not fail to sustain the ecologies worldwide. Indeed the rain that fell on Judah watered no less the land of Edom, while 'the waters of Israel' were kin to the 'rivers of Damascus', despite the disdain of Naaman the Syrian for their inferior esteem. We noted earlier how Hebrew psalmody splendidly celebrated a fertility it knew to belong beyond its own borders and summoned 'all people that on earth do well' to join its music. There neither was, nor could be, any particular escape

< 55 >

from the identity of their landscape with habitats everywhere. To separate was never to isolate the particular. Exceptionality needed that by which alone it knew itself – the human whole.

This paradox became an anguish when this human equation presented itself to Jewry in Assyrian or Chaldean shape, as predator and scourge, when 'other' humans surged aggressively from 'the waters of Babylon' to invade and cruelly subdue the Hebrew lands and captivate their people. It was then that the divine stake in their particularity would demonstrate the paradox of the divine/human participation. It would disclose, in one history, the divinely Messianic and the humanly wayward.

Whereas before, the significance of other peoples argued Jewish exoneration, now – thanks to readers of the mind of YAHWEH like Amos, Hosea, Isaiah and Jeremiah – it argued a new meaning in divine fidelity via the 'guilt measure' of 'His people' in the very logic of events. What might, to the mind of some Elijah or psalmist, be 'God's wrong (doing) most of all' in the disaster of exile, came to be experienced as the utmost spiritual, ethical shape of divine loyalty. The Messianic dimension in the very heart of God could be discerned in the new measure of fidelity that would be learned in the 'disenlandisment' of a still unforsaken people. The YAHWEH who had 'carried them' in Exodus, still did so in sin-requital and – beyond – in the lessons which only exile could teach and which restoration would seal. This sense of the 'Messianic' as the very form of covenant participation was still, for the most part, strictly confined to the particular, yet held not only the promise but the clue to how 'covenant' might become inclusive of all peoples. That history belongs to Chapter 6.

Thus, in adversity when ignorance might charge God with 'wrong' in the sundering of land and people, a larger integrity, both with covenant and people, was effectively at work. Would a never exiled Jewry ever have realized the divine 'Name' in its Messianic reach of compassion and redemption? Only in that education of their sorrows would the further discovery ensue, whereby that experience might at length equip their people-privilege to fulfil itself in the universal inclusion, as implicit there from the outset. The divine integrity was present in a historical patience which conveyed Hebraic self-awareness through a long cycle from self-congratulation to self-abasement, from a self-esteeming to a self- deploring privilege, from the dignity of difference to the humility of guilt.

In the school of 'acquaintance with grief', via the tuition of the great prophetic tradition of the eighth and seventh centuries, there transpired an intense personalizing in the inward heart of what had earlier been a corporate, collective awareness. 'Covenant' itself was somehow interiorized, as if 'newly' in the private heart and not only in the body social. That new personalism had a profound impact on the whole Messianic concept, and the shape of the expectation that looked for it, whether in 'the house-

< 56 >

hold of God' or in the wideness of the world. There would have to be, in reckoning with Messianic hope, new criteria for Messianic credentials.

IV

Perhaps, then, we may borrow for the entire exilic experience in Hebrew story the words given to Moses at the burning bush and know that 'God had been there as whom there He had been'. In the one, as Buber insisted, there had been 'the right of YAHWEH to be selective' in the dramatic 'election' of the Exodus. YAHWEH, in the same integrity, would have the right to be so in the drama of adversity. Covenant was still participatory, the divine persistent in the human so awry in itself, so prescient in its prophets.

Always, however, the latent issue remained. In election and in covenant, in the status of being YAHWEH's and YAHWEH being theirs, the Hebrew mind and conscience knew – we might say autonomously and exceptionally – what all peoples and lands knew commonly, in terms that were undiscriminating between them, except in the incidental terms of climate, flora and fauna, the sundry accidents of geography, landscape, terrain and economic yield. To be sure, these factors varied enormously and any folk could well salute or deplore the way their lot was cast. Not all could happily congratulate themselves with local 'milk and honey'. Nevertheless all are comprised within a single – not otherwise distinguishable – human and created order. Thus the long Biblical tradition of 'special relationship' must be understood inside a single, and uniform creation. Habitats may vary widely: habitation is one and the same.

Could it be that the intensity of Hebraic reading of 'difference' had its roots in its very human cherishing of history? Yet even migrations anywhere, as Amos noted (9.7) might be known as under the divine hand, while the writer in Judges 11.24, in the mouth of Jephthah, seems to allow that Chemosh had bestowed the land of Moab on the Moabite people. Later, there was the Jewish tradition that the 'option' Israel had accepted had been erstwhile offered to others, only to be by them rejected. Could other races, then, have been somehow likewise 'chosen'? The Biblical tradition, according to the Deuteronomist, was firmly 'You only have I known of all the kindreds of the earth.'

Even so, it seems consistent with the Biblical doctrine of creation that God – even 'the God of Israel' – has only 'chosen peoples' in the plural. Whatever the *de facto* partialities in its incidence there is a *de jure* impartiality in its structure. Whether primitive or technological, the sciences that exploit the natural order do not ethnically, religiously or feasibly discriminate between places and cultures in their processes. 'Rainfalls', as Jesus noted, avail alike for 'the just and the unjust', since their 'heav-

< 57 >

enly Father' is *teleios*, 'inclusive' in His benisons. Is there, then, a residual issue about divine integrity inside its sure vindication in the Hebraic terms we studied? It is vital to recognize that Biblically all human experience is 'privileged' and none exceptionally so. There must, therefore, be some point where divine integrity in the historical, ethnic covenant consorts truly with that in the universal order of creation.

During the centuries, there came, it would seem, a lively awareness that there might be a problematic around this 'private amity' between God and this people. Might it be mistaken for some divine favouritism? This fear would seem to be evident when the Deuteronomist wrote:

> The Lord did not set his love upon you, nor choose you, because ye were more in number than any people: for ye were the fewest of all people. (7.7)

The case-making went on to explain the role of the divine 'oath', 'sworn to the fathers' and on that ground to interdict all communion with surrounding peoples in response to that divine fidelity 'keeping covenant and mercy with them that love him'. The form of the apologia seems to sustain a certain perplexity arising from inevitable contact with those other peoples, as well perhaps of the bearing of their own creation faith.

This point concerning international significance, with its careful modesty in 'election', was reinforced by a still deeper aspect of the status it conferred, namely the destiny of 'Israel my servant'. The exceptionality had its great warrant in its instrumentality. 'Showing forth' the praise of the Lord and exemplifying 'peoplehood to God' – these were the sure grounds for the dignity of destiny and the destiny of dignity. With Hosea, Amos and their peers, this note became ever more prominent in the dual sense of both honour unique and reproach severe. When the travail of exile supervened, it was the 'servant status' which intimated to Isaian minds the vocation of a suffering Messiah. As we must see in Chapter 6, the entire New Testament faith concerning 'God in Christ' was altogether indebted to that discerning of the Messianic theme. It was a development central to any assurance about a divine integrity.

For the very force of 'the Israel my servant' theme implied another issue. If there was something exemplary in the role of Israel this way, for whom was it meant and could these be moved, called or bidden to respond? If such people-service was so vital in the economy of God, would it always have to be unilaterally recruited and exceptionally fulfilled? Might some other people, some 'alien' nation, have vocation similarly even if less crucially? Could others covet the dignity?

Here, however, the exceptional still seemed to find a sure perpetuation, in that the very model it afforded would need never to forego itself in order to be forever available. There could be no other 'Israels' lest being 'the Israel' should thereby lose its unique relevance to the poten-

< 58 >

tial attainment. YAHWEH's integrity, as the Deuteronomist declared, was immutably committed to that 'oath-made bond', His 'swearing to their fathers'. YAHWEH's fidelity would stay with the one ethnicity of defining intent.

That there is a gnawing problem here is not in doubt, if we are to hold with the Biblical doctrine of creation. The twin form of a discernible apologia, namely 'fewness' and 'ministry', suggests its presence. It would be possible – as much else in Hebrew Scripture does – to have the problem of 'election' rest with the dogma of a divine inscrutability, with some *Dixit/Fiat* of the sovereign mind – 'He has said, Thus it is.'

Yet does that, can that satisfy an honest theology or our steady experience of an un-differentiating actual human economy, a global inter-realism? Must not the 'sworn' destiny of the 'chosen of YAHWEH' be duly realized, truly irrefragable as 'oath', in terms of its altogether real *historical* eventuation, by its dramatic tuition, in an 'all nations' destiny? Have not many 'oath-swearings' been duly fulfilled in terms that required their own release, as with a pedagogue when an education is complete?[19] If we – as it were – concede that God 'keeps His own counsel' beyond all human interrogation, we can then no longer ask ourselves: 'Shall not the judge of all the earth do right?'

Furthermore, unless held realized by historical fruition, the insistent 'sworn-ness of the oath' proves liable to perverse claiming on the part of heinous minds. 'Chosen status' has been a heady wine to vain pretenders, exceptionalizing their own peoples and their cultures in nefarious terms. The phenomenon has been a dire affliction upon the Jewish people themselves, for the obvious reason that a false exponent will hate the veritable one.[20]

That negative point altogether apart, was there not, at the heart of Hebraic covenant, awareness of positive destiny to fulfil itself in terms which attained its 'oath-character' by achieving its necessarily universal end? Integrity on God's part itself meant that intention, in the very impulse to its original occasion, whether in the tribal ethos of those 'fathers', or the 'amazing' drama of that Exodus.[21] Read that way, the divine 'immutability' abides in an interiorization of the experience in the Hebrew soul, as a bond never rescinded in being a pledge historically made good. Such is the Christian theology of the New Testament in its entire debt – in such terms – to the Hebrew-told fidelity of this 'Lord of hosts'. We have reached, but only via Abraham, Moses and their kin, 'the knowledge of the mystery of Christ' with Jewish peoplehood in its secret.

When Hebrew religious genius came to its fullness in the great prophetic tradition, it had one supreme quality and, because of it, was under one urgent necessity. They came together in the Messianic theme. The first lay in its sense of the particular, the historical, the concrete in the 'immediacy' of the divine way with them. The second was that the

< 59 >

logic of these in their Hebraic incidence in time and land and story should enlarge to take in the universal, the human inclusion. The God who had been ready to be greeted and served as tribal, prizing 'His people so highly', meant – by the same token – to prize a whole humanity in 'the Word made flesh'. The clue of 'presence among' and 'action for' in the one testament meant the universal reach in the other. For, otherwise, where would be the 'benediction of all nations'? The original warrant for the exceptionality lay in its final, urgent vindication.

< 60 >

Chapter 6

Divine Integrity in Christ

I

The study of theology, we have argued, always finds itself in a 'God and . . . ' situation. This is not because the divine has no reach or relevance beyond the space and time of humans. It is that only there is the divine encountered. Infinitude must surely come within our contemplation: it cannot come within our cognizance, nor explicitly inform our worship.

This is so because – for Biblical faith – this 'God and . . . ' situation is understood as the theme of divine 'oath-sworn' concerning it, a pledge whereby experience of its meaning is held to be the making good of an unfailing promise, whether about land, or people, or time, or history, or – as needs must be – all these in one. Such is the Biblical scenario, about the natural order in Noahid terms of 'seedtime and harvest', that is, the economies and cultures via the agronomies of all peoples in their lands, and in Mosaic, Siniatic terms of exclusive Jewish destiny as 'chosen people'.

Thanks only, but crucially, to this perception of a divine 'pledged-ness' towards us humans there transpired – by an innate logic – a 'God but . . .' situation. Only what had been 'sworn' could be intelligibly accused. A God who made promises might thereby be readily arraigned. There could be no viable complaint about 'the way things are', in the absence of some dependable intention concerning why 'things are' at all. Finding them so manifestly slanted in their incidence, their logic and their lively evidences towards the human need and mind, some 'covenan-tal' theology could well suggest itself to alert beneficiaries, tribes and nations, inhabitants and denizens. The dependabilities of science could indicate an oath-readiness in God.[1] Peasants in all countries dwell thus

< 61 >

far in 'lands of promise'. Hence the 'God but . . . ' situation, when draught, or rancour, or distrust supervened to interrogate with blame a suspect divine aegis and breathe the 'Hath God said?' of reproach.

Assessments of diving 'oath-fidelity' would be more loaded and exacting, by dint of their very terms in the sphere of the Siniatic, than of the Noahid. For they concerned a particular ethnic history – a history which might itself be entangled with issues arising from seeming historical miscarriage. Even the legitimacy of its very particularity might beset its people's relations with their human neighbours and haunt their perception of themselves. The more that covenant emphasized the 'servant role', the more the question there of seeming miscarriage would invite the agnostic around and within its realm.

So much we have seen in the previous chapter in the burden of Hebraic identity borne by Hebrew prophethood, in the anguish of land-forfeiture and exile. For YAHWEH's oath-worthiness had been so far tied into 'the prosperity of His servant'[2] ensured alone in place and corporate fact, in tenancy and destiny.

As in the realm of universal nature and all territorial agronomy, so also in the sphere of a singular ethnic history, the proof would be in the ongoing. Had there been no 'oath-sworn', there could be no self-interrogation, no urgent historical assize. For what thus judged them implicitly also judged their Lord. The burning question of their own Hebraic 'salvation' from national miscarriage was also the burning question of how and whether their 'servant' capacity would be realized *vis-à-vis* the human whole.

It was the dynamic of the divine 'oath' that set the question: its outworking in history which made its answer crucial to divine authenticity in its very making. From that necessity came the Messiah and Messianic hope, both educated by the tragic history to anticipate the central role of suffering in their essential character. Only the deeply vulnerable had ever proved the redemptive – the vulnerable that could 'bear away' because it truly 'bore' the evil.

If God was 'covenant-minded and 'covenant-bound' toward the human situation and – historically so via the Hebrew factor and its 'prosperity' – two issues were bound to emerge by the logic of the previous chapter. They had to do with how programmed divine intent, via its Messianic action, would be achieved. Would its achieving have an inclusively human scope or stay strictly within a Hebrew orbit? If the latter, how would its inclusive relevance, as the Abrahamic 'benediction of all nations',[3] come to pass? If the former, would those nations at large be eligible to aspire to be like Jewry, as agents of divine ministry and be instrumentally 'chosen peoples', never as 'originals' but hopefully as emulators? Might some 'church' think or find itself taking a diversity of ethnic identities, hitherto excluded, into divine employ?

< 62 >

II

Such were the issues found emerging around divine integrity, as rooted in oath-liability, at the close of the preceding chapter. They were certainly more than latent, often deeply articulate, in the concern of Hebrew psalmody about 'the ends of the earth' for His possession, and the reach of Hebrew prophethood for a 'salvation' that had 'all nations doing Him service'.

It is true that for generations, from Samson with his Philistines to Ezekiel with his fulminations against Tyre, the Hebrew genius saw all 'other peoples' as inimical to themselves and often, thus, a factor in self-exoneration, the blame attaching elsewhere. Yet ethnic diversity, not to say the martial power it could deploy, constrained the Hebrew mind to face the perplexity – on their premises – about the human manifold.

Furthermore, that Noahid covenant concerning tenancy of the good earth was only theirs in belonging to others. Might the evenhandedness[4] God showed in geographical ecology extend at length to the historical where, supremely, Hebrew 'chosen-ness' belonged?

When the moralism of the great prophets, and the education of bitter exile and novel experience at the ministering hands of 'heathen' powers, set puzzling questions for exceptionality,[5] one inherent feature remained. If there was to be a revised cognizance of the human other, of ethnic and cultural diversity, it must be that 'they' came enquiringly to Jewry rather than that Jewry went to 'them'. Zechariah, prophet of the return after exile, sees 'them' coming in very deferential style to reach the hem of Jewish garment, saying: 'We will go with you' (8.23). We will come to you was the cry and the impulse in what came to know itself as 'the New Testament'.

It transpired in, and as, the conviction that the original, constitutive 'God and His people' order was – by its own inner logic and bias[6] – destined to pass into an inclusive peoplehood of faith, one open to all who willed to come, in response to a personal register of its accessibility and of the content to which such access would convey them. What it held for them came to be defined as 'God in Christ reconciling the world'.

The story of how it happened so has to use this language of 'came to be defined . . . '. For it was the story of two inter-acting dimensions of an entirely inter-validating quality.[7] The one was the Jesus of his Galilee/Jerusalem history, the other was his 'reception' – he and his story – in the cognizance of a wholly Jewish discipleship that came to reckon duly with the evidences as leading to their faith-decision on their import.

It is vital to have clearly in place for the understanding of Christianity this unison between the 'event' Jesus was via his life and ministry *and* the taking of these into the loving evaluation, the reading definition, human

< 63 >

heart and mind came to because of them. The term that locked both elements in one was 'the Christ' – that whom this Jesus had been, that whom all human hope awaited, as hope *per se* had been nurtured, puzzled, revised and anguished in long Jewish tradition of 'Messiah'.

There was, in Christian origin, this 'being' of the Christ, dramatically thus in the Jesus of the story *and* his 'being' so believed as 'Christ' by a discipleship acceding to him in that meaning – not the one without the other. Christianity lives by the conviction that he did not 'miscue' them in the faith they found, nor did they 'misconstrue' him in finding it so. There was an inherent mutuality between Master and disciples, between a Christ actual and a Christ confessional, 'to be and to be known to be' by the corroboration between enactment and comprehension. The Messianic could only ever be either in being conclusively both.

One could say that this necessary counter-partnering of event and conviction was anticipated in the haunting Messianic appeal in Isaiah 53.1: 'Who has believed our report and to whom is the arm of the Lord revealed?' 'Report' – soon to become in New Testament terms 'the tradition' – means exactly 'that which has come to our ears' and, therefore, 'that which we are having to say'; it is 'news' in dual sense as both heard and told. 'The arm of the Lord', a Messianic term, is the Christ event, the enacted significance of Jesus. Those who bear the tidings are those who have perceived the event. They are 'witnesses', on double count of 'having seen' and 'having understood' their seeing, so that it becomes, further, an 'inseeing' or 'insight'. A faith that drew from a history could only come that way.

The same point is explicit when we ponder the Johannine Prologue of how 'the Word became flesh and pitched a tent among us'. As 'flesh', i.e. in 'body', as 'life' in time and place, 'the Word' conveyed meaning via biography. What God was saying lived a human life. But what 'the Word' was saying, being 'worded', had to be known, as all words are, as meant for lips and only carrying on them. Hence meaning for uttering and uttering of meaning. Is there not the same point in the First Letter of John: 'That which we have seen and heard, we declare . . . '? (1 John 1.1). So we have the confessional Church from the historical Jesus as only mutually explanatory. We have to carry the unison further into the theme of a 'Messiah', once crucified and world-wide.

III

It was evident enough in Chapter 5 how many questions waited on the nature of Jewish expectation. Who and how would be this central figure on whom everything rested? Was 'he' an individual at all, of perhaps – somehow – the nation itself, if only once for all in its proper temper, such

< 64 >

as 'keeping a perfect Sabbath'. 'Israel, my servant' was an ambivalent identity, if the role was collective rather than singular. For how could 'the nation' be its own emancipator when the nation was the very measure of the need? 'The whole head is sick: the whole heart faint', an Isaiah had cried. 'The arm of the Lord' could hardly be the collective people. The shepherd imagery was always singular.

In the crucial Who and How?' quandary as to his identity, there were two quite incompatible clues – the one political and martial, the other prophetic and tragic. They had nothing in common, except in being 'in the frame', though even then in quite contrasted currency, the one belligerent, the other never strident. They differed totally over the Messianic task because they differed entirely about the human situation 'he' would resolve.

Judea in the years of Jesus' ministry, and well before and after, was occupied territory under Roman imperial power. By the lights of Jewish zealotry, the Messianic task was the land's riddance of that heathen presence, its folk's liberation from that alien yoke by the realization of Jewish monarchy in some David *revididus*. This assertive mind had its representatives, albeit consorting there with quisling tax-gatherers of Roman sympathy, among Jesus' disciples. It would seem that those expectations coloured their allegiance to him, however tense the combination. Their personal presence indicates the sort of option they thought they had in him.[8]

It was evidently one for which Jesus might be – or become – minded. According to the three Gospels, its gist had been with him in the desert watch when, at the outset of his ministry, 'trial' Messiahships had presented themselves. Beyond the lure of ostentatious miracle, or the popular pull of economic plenty, lay the alliance with the corrupting cult of power whereby 'kingdom might be his'. This had been rejected but – rejected 'for a season' – dogged the situation throughout in the 'trials' where those disciples had been 'with him' (Luke 22.28) variously musing on what might, or should, eventuate.

Throughout, and increasingly as time moved, there was for Jesus – if not compellingly for them – that other 'counsel', the imagery that stemmed from the supreme Messianic map-reading that came from the tradition of Hebrew prophethood. There 'the Lord's anointed' was 'a man of sorrows', a vulnerable figure who, at deep cost, carried the evils by which society defiled itself and, only so doing, ensured that truth did not succumb, nor guilt extinguish hope. 'Not by might, nor by power, but by My spirit,' had 'said the Lord of hosts' (Zechariah 4.6.)

Had anyone thus far made the vital link between Messianic meaning and the haunting figure of the 'marred image' and 'acquaintance with grief'? Prophethood had been silent during four centuries of Seleucid and Maccabean authority, but that mysterious one was 'My servant' too,

< 65 >

bearing the title that also designed 'the extolled' who would be 'very high'. Yet how could that eminence be, without the power dimension only political sovereignty could ensure? There would have to be strange paradox, if ever a Messiah of that tragic order were to be identified, either by its true and only 'designate', or by the discerning recruits he would need for his validity. For, however personal Messiahship would prove to be, there was no doubt of its ultimately corporate realization in the world of history – something like a recruited and recruiting church.

Had Jesus not somehow left himself no other choice than this by the options he had discarded in the desert, if he continued to dismiss them in the ministry? That corporate dimension, so finally requisite, was already embryonic in his band of disciples, though they would only ever shape into it in sequence to his own Passion as their inauguration.

If either their 'enchurching' and his 'redeeming' sorrow were to come to pass, were not the antecedents already present in the Galilean story? Must we not set the Messianic issue, the burden of its resolving, squarely within that companionship between the ever-lonely, never solitary, Jesus of the Gospels and his intimate, if motley, disciples?

That it preoccupied both him and them is evident enough, despite the long puzzlement of exegetes about a reticence concerning it.[9] Before Messiahship could be 'proclaimed' – if by mere 'loud voice' it ever could be – it required to be defined. Public claim could only violate private reality and delude popular credulity.

Hence it follows that the most articulate occasion, prior to the Last Supper, on which the theme was explicitly broached between Jesus and the disciples, was on the occasion of a remote retreat from the throngs in Galilee and the avid in Jerusalem,[10] to the borders of the Hermon foothills in Caesarea Philippi, well out of earshot of the rabble or the roguish or the ruthless.

'Whom do they say that I am?' 'Whom do you say that I am?' The questions came in a necessary sequence because answers were genuinely at stake. That there were among them disparate ideas about him is evident enough – and variant notions of hope in their discipleships, as a retinue of uncertain zealots and reformed servants of Rome. How were their motives responding to the experiences of his ministry? More important still, what might that ministry be suggesting as to a Messianic destiny, definitively his and derivatively theirs?

What clues might there be to resolve that perplexity? Most urgently of all, were the constraints thus far beginning to resemble the travail of those superb prophets from whose stories 'the suffering servant' figure had derived? Did the 'trials' of ministry, the things that befall because of it, fit into their pattern? Was the logic out of Galilee reading like that of an Hosea grieving over an errant society, or a Jeremiah at odds with an arrogant establishment that had no mind for his witness?

< 66 >

These were the questions waiting on that Caesarea–Philippi rendezvous with 'the future of a past'. By that time it was clear enough that Jesus faced adversity on many sides. While it is true that 'common people heard him gladly', and that he was no Jeremiah who 'sat alone because of Thy hand' (Mark 6.20 and 12.37, Jeremiah 15.17), yet there were gathering issues between his ministry and his society and gathering crowds, and rumbling murmurs attending them. There was the vexed question of the Sabbath, 'made for man', made for his rest and perspective, but not as if 'man was made for sabbaths' by a tyranny of legal severity of the letter. Behind that was the sharp question of 'authority', the right 'to say such things'. With these went that practice of intimacy with 'his Father', the *Abba* of his language, and his extending of its range to all and sundry – so different from the self-pre-occupations of traditional Jewry and the inviolable difference they had from 'Gentiles'. 'Your heavenly Father knows . . . ' 'cares . . . ' 'numbers your hairs . . . ' 'forgives . . . ' did not square easily with 'Israel Thy people' or 'what the fathers said'.

It may well be that the actualities of ministry were tied in Jesus' mind into the suffering matrix of great prophethoods. The questions in Matthew 16.13 and 15 tell how heavy with things Messianic retrospect was, the future would be. They were evidently necessary in the pre-occupations both of Jesus' leadership and their discipleship. The implication in 'one of the prophets' could hardly be plainer, together with the allusion to John the Baptist and the coupling of the enigmatic identity; 'Son of Man'.

Everything so direly latent in the exchange emerged, but only into radical conflict, by the terms of Simon Peter's response: 'Thou art the Christ . . . ' – meant in the confused measure of their predilections but needing immediate corrective by Jesus, in ardent disavowal of what he knew those to be. A Messianic *confessio* had been given voice in a momentous encounter and, for that very reason, had to be radically disowned. 'I am not the Messiah you think I am.'[11] 'The Son of Man must suffer . . . ' Already being implicitly 'rejected', he will become explicitly so, in something like the tragic progression depicted in the parable of the vineyard and the husbandmen. When they returned south from Caesarea–Philippi to the customary scene, that single moment had caught the hidden drama of what had already been and of what would transpire to be. The ministry had gathered momentum and its disciples embarked on a journey into still more ultimate confusion and distress.

How should a reverent theology understand what, at climax, was for him 'the cup my Father gives me' and the resolve: 'Shall I not drink it'? That ' . . . or one of the prophets' was – we might say – a destiny about a theodicy, a justification of God in an evil situation. Their vocation to suffer, as they read and accepted it, was no wild death wish, but the assertion of divine righteousness and truth the fact of human wrong, was

< 67 >

grievously flouting and defying. Doing so was inherently costly but their readiness for this ensured that those 'things of God' did not succumb. They lived on to bless the human future. Only in thus *not* being 'overcome of evil', could evil be 'overcome by good'. 'For transgressions' they were 'stricken', whence society would learn 'with their stripes we were healed', 'they carried our iniquities'.

There was nothing artificial here – arbitrary, contrived, legal or fictional – but only the inherent quality of what suffers *from* wrongs done by its capacity to suffer *on behalf of* them. So, by bearing was to 'bear away', and release forgiveness and have evil 'quite undone', not in its guilty incidence but in the entail it would otherwise have darkly kept.

Inasmuch as this lexicon of suffering had passed from its prophet exemplars into the image and visage of 'the suffering servant', it had every occasion to be the clue to Jesus' mind, in the onus of his quest for the meaning and the fashion of 'Messiah'. That, arguably, would be the more so in the light of the gravitation of his public ministry towards a climax 'like the prophets'. Might events and precedents, time and trust, be converging to the like finale?

Enigmas remain, not least about the significance of the Palm Sunday entry into Jerusalem and its strange anti-climax by nightfall on the Mount of Olives. We need always to keep within the reckonings of scholarship the verdict the Church actually reached and founded itself in doing so. To this we have yet to come. Earlier, due stress was laid on how a once-for-all personal Messiah would anticipate corporate fulfilment.

On both counts, we reach the 'Upper Room', 'the Last Supper' and 'the bread and wine'. Jesus and his disciples are together, symbolically in the meaning of the Passover, the sealing in Exodus of the covenant with Moses. He 'desired' to celebrate it 'before I suffer'. He talks of a 'new covenant in his blood', that not of a sacrificial, ceremonial 'lamb', but as of 'the Lamb of God bearing . . . the sin of the world'.[12] Only a 'parting' in view made any 'remembrance' necessary. For Jesus – in their immediate context and for the rest of their mortal days – was altogether unforgettable. The meaning of the 'bread and wine' could not have been about 'whether' in memory, but only about 'how' in worship, not 'whether' a memorializing community would ensue but 'what' their sacrament would celebrate as 'new in the kingdom of God'.

By those tokens, not simply as the 'teacher', the 'parable-izer' or the itinerant healer, he was the sufferer, the one crucified, the Master from, not Galilee alone, but through the Gethsemane to which Galilee conveyed him – and conveyed him because of the shape of the human scene through which he passed. The Lord of the Church would care liturgically for the shape of its mind, but in perpetuation of the summation of his meaning in his Cross.[13] Only that would gather all the other aspects of his 'enfleshing of the Word'. 'This is my body given for you: this is my

< 68 >

blood which is shed for you'. 'Take . . . and divide it among yourselves'. So doing, it can only recruit you to its imitation, its redemptive drama, its policy in the world. How to the world it will belong, will require you to relate.

This it transpired to do through the mystery of the Resurrection, the emptiness of a tomb and the mission of the disciples. Whereas a rite of remembrance that saluted teaching might have sanctioned a coterie of admiration, 'this' other 'in remembrance' would forever underwrite how alone 'the Christ' had accomplished 'Christhood' and how, so doing, had assured to us 'the knowledge and love of God', of 'God in this Christ of His'.

From that first Eucharist, explaining and possessing his Passion, its 'I am among you as he that serves' would become: 'I am among you as you who serve.' The ruling *servare* word had its root in 'My servant, the Messiah'. That figure with that role of Christhood had issued from within the exclusive covenant of 'YAHWEH with His people' as their vicissitudes had 'learned' them. It was the shape of the Self-consistency of God with them. It would need to pass into the inclusive peoplehood of a corporate Messiahship, bonded in His Name from all peoples. In both, their sequence would be the assurance of the integrity of God.

IV

'Behold I and the children whom God hath given me,' which Hebrews 2.13 cites from Isaiah 8.18,[14] captures this explicit sequence between 'the One Christ' and 'the many Christians' – drastic as the grim *non sequiturs* are which have to be studied in the chapter following. Those 'children' in the case of the crucified Jesus, as bonded in that Upper Room and from Galilee called to be 'with him' as disciples, were further called to a perpetuation of his significance across the world, in 'word and sacrament', in life and ministry, in act and fact. Messiah must needs have such 'zealotry' to express his own in 'the zeal of his house', but only in the terms he showed.

That it should be so corporately, and in world-open terms, came from its own inner logic as this belonged with the integrity of God – 'the God of Abraham' in whom 'all kindreds of the earth' could 'congratulate themselves.' *How* it came to be so is the fascinating theme of the New Testament, one that explains its very existence as a document,[15] as a text with 'Gospels' about a history and 'Letters' guiding a community, neither necessary but from the other.

The textual reality, turning on the circumstantial actuality, is no less exacting for scholarly duty than the Christology they tell. Yet the sequence from 'us' to 'you', from 'Jew' to 'Gentile', from first locale to

< 69 >

wide world, in truth happened, and happened inside the integrity of God, whose 'wrong would have been most of all' had it not so occurred. For 'chosen people' could only be a cherished privacy in long being a purposive one, until the very cherishing achieved the purposing and translated its wide 'intention' into fact. Doing so would for ever perpetuate the defining status as inseparable, historically and essentially, from the end in view.[16]

The story of how a wholly Jewish apostolate, in loving fee to Jesus as the Christ, attained this destiny and greeted it as such, is the birth story of the Christian Church and the burden of the New Testament writings. It was a story with as many 'loose ends' for meticulous scrutiny, as the Jesus-history from which it sprang. For the faith it would satisfy means to see in faith what it must know with love. 'Too right to be false' is then a sounder formula than 'too suspect to be true'.

Scholarship has issues from – if not at issue with – the development in the Book of Acts which, anyway is only 'the acts of some apostles'.[17] Who were those 'Hellenized Jews in the story of the martyrdom of Stephen and who those anonymous folk of Cyprus and Cyrene who took the initiative of going to the 'Gentiles'? That they did so independently of the mother Church in Jerusalem is obvious enough. Could they have been sensing a kind of 'you also' thrust in the very quality of the faith they took? Did they learn a warrant there to have their faith like the open arms of a Jesus crucified and so embrace all who heeded their word? How then could they withhold its reach from all but Jewish born?

Perhaps it was in the nature of a revision so radical of an ancient mindset that it could only happen by a voluntary, risky, tentative, anonymous development, outside the orbit of office, convention and established tradition. Yet it was no surrender of historic privilege but, instead, a new accessibility of 'peoplehood to God'. Pioneers, indeed, they were, but they did not think or speak of 'supersession'. The verdict about them and their vision from the body of Jewry was still to come. It was not theirs to know that, at length, after long brooding, it would be adverse or that a majority in the nation would disavow it as any destiny of theirs.

Meanwhile, there were all the official misgivings or apprehensions of disloyalty that innovation kindles. There was fear for the sanctity and dignity of law at risk with 'lesser breeds'. There was the instinctive suspicion conservatism always has lest something be done for the first time. There was the tenacity by which a cherished *status quo* defends its sacred life.

Thus 'when tidings of these things came to the Church in Jerusalem' there was alarm and hesitation. There were divided counsels, anxious competing pros and cons. It was not that Jewry was immured within itself in total incommunicado. There were 'proselytes' on every hand, enquirers, would-be adherents, even Roman centurions who 'loved their

< 70 >

nation' and built for them synagogues. Greek culture had entered far into learned and popular Jewry, not to say also Latin with long Roman occupation recruiting its local agents. Jewish hierarchy was dealing every day with Roman power.

But exclusive peoplehood, apart from its long Abrahamic and post-Exodus mystique, was guarded by unique birth and sanctioned by the ritual of circumcision. While other tribes had the latter, only Jewish circumcision carried a separatist significance so emphatic. As 'the mark in the flesh', its necessity had long been the sharp deterrent for those numerous 'proselytes' pondering its costly way of access into Jewry. If its demanding was to be lifted, how would the vital integrity of things Hebraic be safeguarded against an in-flooding of those 'Gentiles'? It was not a hurdle that could be lowered. It was a crucial either/or.

But if the sanctions of Jewishness were utterly at stake, so also were the dimensions of the Gospel. Either those over-eager 'men of Cyrene', innovative Africans, must be reined in, or must be known and approved as veritable pioneers by grace of the Holy Spirit. The mind of the evolving community must be decided by the founding Church in Jerusalem. There is only the narrative of Luke to sketch the story and how tantalizing are his limitations, requiring us to read alertly between many lines.

That, prior to the Council in Jerusalem, there were two main personal factors seems not in doubt, namely the Apostles Peter and Paul, the one a salient representative of the faith's natal tradition from its origin in Galilee to its climax in Jerusalem, the other epitomizing in himself the elements of the thing at issue.[18]

Whatever the vintage of its sources, the experience of Peter according to Luke's record in Acts 10 and 11 fits closely the logic of the men of Cyrene. He is obviously – at Joppa – sharing in extended mission, lodged with the practitioner of a dubious trade – not to mention the noxious smells at 'Simon the tanner's'. The plea from Cornelius at Caesarea is authentic 'proselyte' timbre, both in its deference and its yearning. Dreams had not seldom been a source of impulse. Cornelius is alert to 'who is who, and where'. He has enough confidence to initiate a plea.

Similarly, all the aspects of Peter's reaction fit the wider setting. He has an immediate sense of darksome compromise and, faced with a concrete situation, his instinct holds the customary word ready: 'Lord, I have never . . . ' to ward off the impossible. To make a journey needing an overnight stay, even to enter 'Gentile' domesticity – these are ineligible temptations. Luke's words are eloquent even in their sheer simplicity. The messenger 'continued knocking' – as what he stood for had been doing for decades.

Moreover, even Peter's noon-hour slumbers had their canny point. This was the Phoenician shore. Those linen sails he saw, of Egyptian manufacture, were not the bed-sheets of slumberland. They belonged

< 71 >

with vessels, ships, riding off-shore on that harbourless coast. Ships meant cargoes, cargoes spelled bizarre countries far away, with their exotic products and their alien cultures, fit to coincide with the knocking on the door.[19] The issue it posed – 'to go or to refuse' – captured the whole theme before the nascent Church.

This Galilean apostle was sage in his decision. He would go, re-assured by his own dream. A dream could equally avail for either party, token of their human bond. But he would go with friends to share the risk, to witness his handling, to be party to its outcome for better later inquisition than had he been alone. The old Hebraic order had its right in the very procedure by which it might be modified. It was all a cumulative transaction, doing justice in its process to all aspects of its content. The travel traversed the stakes, the coming in *chez* Cornelius entered on to the evidences. An incipient 'Gentile' faith was there already, thanks to unnamed bringers of the Cyrene vintage. Peter's destiny was to register how genuine they were, so that he could move from the tentativeness with which he came into the baptism he arrived to administer. 'Who was he', he asked himself 'that he should withstand God?' – a man no longer debating with himself over the unthinkable.

Luke has surely distilled the great theme into a single episode. It would be likewise in his reporting of the other central apostle, with an even more telling sifting of the implications.

V

The Saul/Paul conversion may hold points of query for the historian, especially about his links with Gamaliel and the martyrdom of Stephen. There are few for the theologian, seeing that his experience on the Damascus road had within itself the essence of all issues. It is well that we attend to it closely and to what the voice from heaven did *not* say. Saul's zealotry against reports of the nascent faith exactly captures the Judaic reasons behind the crucifixion itself. Its points at issue are those that ranged between Jesus and his hearers, to culminate in his rejection. They perpetuate the heart of Christhood as the Church, by its very genesis in doing so, had identified as the Christ-meaning, the meaning in the event he suffered.

Thus Paul's change of heart and direction turned essentially on that meaning being authenticated alike in history and in faith. The Christian community Saul was veto-ing so fiercely was right about Jesus as the Christ, about the Christ as in Jesus. So much was explicit in what he heard. A cry from heaven in such heeding ears as Saul's, crying: 'I am Christ' would have evoked wonder, but no surprise, adoration but no prostrating crisis. Was not 'Christ', the 'Christ' of due expectation, supposed to be

< 72 >

'riding on the clouds of power'? What was utterly shattering was that the voice said: 'I am Jesus . . . ' the very one 'you persecute'. This 'Jesus/Messiah' identity was the very crux of Saul's persecuting fervour as demanding to be angrily denied. Saul was being contradicted, disowned, in the essence of his mission. The Cross which he violently saw as only ever – and vilely – 'unMessianic' was vindicated on the highest authority in the contrary sense. His entire cast of mind was halted as decisively as his journey. He had been interrogated about his persecution of the Church, as the crux of his disdain for the crucified Jesus. Both had to terminate in surrender to the reality that either had in the other, Jesus and his people.

The 'pricks' metaphor plainly captures this situation. He was urging with them the beast he was riding. They told his zeal. Yet that zeal, while goading him, was troubling his conscience. The drama should not mislead us, so that we miss the build-up that all such crises undergo. Vehemence often arises from self-doubt, when it must steel itself against fears that will might falter. Resolution needs to fortify itself. The more the urgency, the more the insistent anxiety. There had been that Stephen with his strange serenity, addressing his heavenly Jesus as guardian of his dying spirit. There had been the sheer persistence of the misguided community Saul harassed. Was that recent crucifixion somehow also haunting his calculations? It is well not to think the drama of the journey the full measure of the story. Learning, then and ever, to address this same Jesus, the Jesus of Stephen and the 'Church', as 'lord' would be the defining of his personality, and also the emerging of the ensuing credal words: 'Our Lord Jesus Christ'.[20] That 'Lordship' was 'Messianic' because this 'Messiah-story' was the storied identity of the Lord.[21]

We realize that Saul/Paul experienced the elements – in far different vein – of Peter's more prosaic journey to Cornelius, namely the pro-'Gentile' implications of this Christhood wherein 'Jesus was Lord'. Tradition has them both finally in Rome, the ultimate symbol – in that century – of attaining to be 'worldwide'.[22] Peter's Joppa–Caesarea–Rome travel story, we might say, was less resoundingly fulfilled than Paul's Damascus–Jerusalem–Antioch–Troas–Illyricum–Rome saga, but both translated in fact and image the world-wide-ness of the Cross.

If authentic Messiah had been this Messiah-Jesus' way, then the Jewry-centred Messiahships of political power, or apocalyptic intervention, or Essene deservings, in being 'not taken', were decisively annulled. A 'Jesus crucified' could 'draw all to himself'. This redemption, in those terms and of that compassionate order, could enfold 'all according to their need'.[23]

Then could be foreseen the ultimate 'consolation of Israel' of which, according to Luke, old Simeon had sung on Jesus' 'presentation in the Temple'. In final Messianic recognition, he would be – in that order –

< 73 >

'light to lighten the Gentiles' and therein, and ever, 'the glory of his people Israel.[24]

The Book of Acts leaves Peter and all other apostles behind – apart from the vital Council in Jerusalem – and focuses thereafter on the 'Gentile' vocation of Paul alone. Apostolic Church history is bereaved thereby, except for what may be deciphered from the Letters. But deficiency, in this sense, in the New Testament admits, to advantage, of a deep – if only symbolic – emphasis. It is the link in the personality of Paul, the now 'singular' narrative figure, of two essential issues in the entire theme of Christianity and its fruition from a founding 'chosen' peoplehood in Jewry.

Those two issues are its essential roots in the explicit ministry of Jesus *and* its warrant therefrom to be worldwide in its reach and sympathy. For two things came together in this Paul. The one was his personal absence from the Galilean company with Jesus and thus any acquaintance directly with that ministry, and so in turn his warrant to be apostolic, having not been disciple. The other is his sense of vocation to 'the nations'. Since it was vital that 'this Galilee, via this Cross' was going to the world, what was more apposite than that there should be a personality caring with their linkage in a single vocation?

This awareness is clearly present in his lasting concern to make good that absence, lest it be taken to disqualify his whole apostolate. What better than that a single biography would make good the lack, as the very context of achieving the mission? Thus he might embody in his own story the unity of 'Jesus as the Christ', whose 'acquaintance with grief' he too, Paul, had come to understand by his own 'acquaintance with grief' en route to Damascus. For such his journey had been in the shattering of his old self in discovery of the suffering Jesus.

Thus he would know the antecedents of the Cross via the crisis through which he went, the crisis that had ensued for him because of what that Cross authenticated. 'Have not I seen the Lord?' he protested in his Letters. His acquaintance with the Galilean had come through his learning the crucified. He had reversed the education of the twelve disciples in thus acceding to their number.

It is strange that some New Testament scholarship has argued that Paul had little interest in the narrated Jesus of the Gospels. For the notion is bizarre. What he wrote in 1 Corinthians 13 is a portraiture of the Beatitudes. 'Remember the words of the Lord Jesus' was his bidding to the elders of Ephesus (Acts 20.35). There are other citations, notably on food taboos and moral discernment. His very conversion had made good his absence in person from the ministerial scene that had informed the Cross on which it turned.

VI

If, thanks to Luke's concentration of the history, Paul's story and person enshrine the 'Gentile' inclusion in Christ, they certainly articulate, with characteristic fervour, the Jewish soul-searching that inclusion caused. Hence doubtless the malignity with which some Jewish scholarship has lambasted him as the arch-traitor. How passionately he strove, in Romans, Galatians and elsewhere, to reconcile that mandatory inclusion and his mission for it, with the ongoing 'chosen-ness' of his kindred people. He is to be cherished more for the zeal in which he wrestled with that reconciliation than the details he reached.

Once, he averred, 'the fullness of the Gentiles had been gathered', there could be a mass 'obedience' of Jewry to Christ. Both foresights have had long, long occasion for proof. Had that inclusion only really been for the time being, and not the abiding quality of an open Gospel? Would the notion of 'mass access' ride with the necessity of personal faith? Then in Galatians he made strange play with the Hagar story, reversing the precedences.[25] Was the idea of 'the wild vine grafted' into the true one adequate imagery when John (15) would be saying that Jesus alone was 'the true vine'.[26]

Perhaps it is wiser to read Paul's resolutions for his burdens of heart as evidence more of his sincerity than of their adequacy, and fall back on the enduring sense of 'I know whom I have believed', and am convinced of his capacity to keep all of me and mine he has in trust (2 Timothy 1.12). Paul could preface his Jew/Gentile 'negotiation' with that emerging formula of credal tradition: 'This is a faithful saying . . . ' His Christ Jesus came into the world to save 'undifferentiated' sinners.

Then, and ever, that is the final theme – divine integrity in 'Jesus as the Christ, as the Christ in God'. Abrahamic, Mosaic covenant would keep a defining faith with itself in bringing to pass a destiny for all peoples. These would bring their own 'birth', irrespective of what ethnicity had already shaped and potentially recruit the shaping into a vocation like to Israel's. They too could be a 'hallowing folk in a hallowed land', in the meaning of the sacramental situation enabled by their education in the Incarnate Christ.

Only with disciples in an Upper Room, against the memory of prior Passover, was any 'new' testament enacted. 'New Testament' came to mean two actualities. The one was that sealed in 'bread and wine', the other was the document which has this name.[27] There is an eloquence in the dual sense of the 'New Testament' term. For it came to pass as a text (of Gospels and Letters) only through and for the world mission of its other meaning. Only spreading community needed to go back to be informed on Galilee and Jesus. Only lapsing generations needed their

< 75 >

historians. The twin factors of widening ranks, and 'old disciples' passing, generated texts to educate the first and make literary the failing memories of the other. Hence the book we know. *It* came to pass (the document) only because it (the word) was world-seeking. The knowing was only in the going. The going was the school of the knowing. The covenant in 'bread and wine' became – only so – the text of things agreed, as thus the double evidence and credential of what those things were.[28]

This Christian textuality is sadly circumscribed by Mediterranean shores. The confining context, within Greek and Roman culture, is a drastic limitation for a Scripture intending the world. There is so much else we would dearly love to know, for better possession of what is there as ours. Does this somehow now mean that divine integrity is in doubt? It could so mean, the Holy Spirit apart.

What then suffices is that the New Testament in its givenness and by virtue of its nature as that 'going/knowing' thing, yields us precedents, like the Council in Jerusalem, from which we can responsibly derive guidance for our contemporary mind. Thus it requires to be a co-operating Scripture and asks of us a kinship of soul, with examples of this situation in Chapters 8 and 9. The text will not suffice us without our task because of it. That task will not lack for want of what we see it lacks. For we believe in 'the Spirit of truth' working by love.

Peter (1. 4.19) said we had 'a faithful Creator'. He and all co-writers witness to a faithful Christ, proven in the faithful Jesus, and 'one Lord Jesus Christ' the index to 'the faith-keeping God', blessed for evermore.

If, thus, there is no doubt of the divine integrity, there is the greater urgency in minding the pitfalls of those testaments' custodians.

< 76 >

Chapter 7

CARES AND 'BEWARES' IN THE TRUST OF DOCTRINE

I

'Knowledge as love and love as knowledge' was the double descriptive of Christian faith which emerged in Chapters 4 and 5 and had exposition in Chapter 6. 'Love' and 'Knowledge' as together the centre and circumference of faith dwell in the personal soul but belong in community, as both inner conviction and corporate fellowship. The self where they abide abides in them, as the inwardness of confession shares the outwardness of a witnessing society.

It is the genius of authentic faith to identify its centre of gravity around which it coheres within, and by which it is weighed without, the terms in which it possesses its meaning and offers its relevance to the world.[1]

Inasmuch as love can be disparate and knowledge contentious, there has always been in religion a tendency and a temptation to let this *raison d'être* as love and knowledge be overtaken or usurped by some protective custody or other that moves the criteria of its authenticity and changes the feel of its integrity. The point was anticipated earlier. The task of this chapter is to search the sundry forms this subtle situation may take and thus put in jeopardy both the content and the discipline of believing.

That truth in human care will always be at risk is evident enough. The more precious the truth's content the more precarious its security. Paul seemed well aware of things at risk when he linked the essential fabric of Christian faith with the frailty of its apostolate. Its origin was in 'the God who commanded the light to shine out of darkness . . . ' the initiation of an intelligible order of nature that would yield the sacramental principle of human privilege to possess, consecrate and celebrate via the arts and

< 77 >

sciences of a grateful reverence as thus entrusted. This has been the constant theme of these pages.

But that same divine intention in the human scene and story ' . . . shined in our hearts to give the light of the knowledge of the glory of God' and that glory 'as in a face – the face of Christ'. That divine redemptive cognizance of human wrong as vitiating the divine enterprise with us, fulfilled the God of creation as the 'God in Christ', the first 'Word' corroborated in 'the Word made flesh', informing in love and knowledge the minds and hearts of answering faith.

That sequence through creation to Incarnation and the Passion could not fail to pass into human care and ministry. To these it gave being; to these it was entrusted. Paul named it 'this treasure', *thesaurus,* had 'in earthen vessels', mere 'pots of clay', fragile and fallible.[2] He had found a defining paradox for the unison of faith and custody, the gist of belief and the risk of witness.

What 'earthen vessels' did he have in mind? Perhaps the hazards of his perilous life-style and the several limitations of his own physique. Or they may have been the frailties of will, the lapses of behaviour, in the sundry churches for which his travels cared and his letter writing handled. For, as he told them, these dispersed communities were, in their turn, faith's 'letters' to the world (2 Corinthians 3.2–3).

It is more likely that he meant the vocabulary of faith explored in the chapter following, the miscarriages of meaning that can readily arise in the transactions of language. 'A pitcher broken at the fountain' as Ecclesiastes noted (12.6) is no less a tragedy of laden words than of human old age, when their weight they can no longer carry or they must get currency in new scenes. Was it this sense of things precarious that wanted the 'treasure' term about the transit, as well as about the content, as in the usage 'precious' where the two combine.

The two come together in the faith-trust that is discipleship and the faith-trust that is apostolate. In a strange way the two roles were the very making of the New Testament document, in the Gospel narrative of their recruitment and the epistolary pastoral action of their dispersion across the Mediterranean world. In dual custodianship of the founding memory and the extending mission, the ministry of Jesus cherished the ministry of the Church and either story engaged the other. It is the 'treasure' in this charge we are set to esteem and explore, with due attention to the centuries-long pitfalls into which it has strayed. When so doing, 'God's wrong has been most of all, 'seeing that things wondrously divine were committed to 'vessels' so humanly fragile.

II

For present purposes the hazards of fallibility, institutional and spiritual, have to do with anxieties or dilemmas latent in the nature of custody itself. Learning to appreciate how susceptible the trust of truth can be to safeguards assumed to preserve, commend or underwrite it better than that truth itself, until it is almost at the mercy of sanction other than its own, is urgent on every side. Exempting the invocation of political power (the theme to occupy Chapter 10) these risks in custody would seem to occur in four identifiable ways in which the 'treasure' suffers the 'earthenness' of well intentioned 'vessels' in the usages they follow or the exigencies under which they act.

The four might be described as authority lapsing into authoritarianism in which Christian faith acquires a sanction, even a *raison d'être*, other than its own dimension as the self-defining of 'God in Christ'. Or, secondly, there is the coveting of near magical 'mystery', as if the narrative of 'God in Christ' was a story whose clues needed to be miraculous. Other 'vessels', in the third place, come to see the celebration of faith resolved into an elation of soul that reaches for highly emotional charisma, as authenticating a Christian identity. Fourthly there are those who virtually surrender any 'knowledge and love of God' – that pivotal New Testament phrase – by resort to some 'cloud of unknowing' which disowns the sacramental order of sense experience in the natural world and the clarity of 'knowledge and love' as ours 'in the face of Christ'.

This quadrangle we have to survey in surer detail, conceding that the 'essence' of any religion, or what we are calling here its centre of gravity, are liable to debate and contention. But if custodians are not to be found 'taking God's Name in vain' they must 'know whom they have believed'.[3] 'God's wrong' as explicit in certain forms of worship, or implicit in certain notions of mind, is clearly present in the 'guilt' warning in that third of the Ten Commandments. It abides in the still deeper meaning of the apostolic cry: 'Grieve not the Holy Spirit . . . '[4]

Just as an earthenware pitcher can break into shards, so the theological mind may suspect its own fragility and want a stouter receptacle in which to encase itself, some carrier of tougher fibre than itself. This very imagery suggests the urge for the infallible Church. But suppose the 'earthen' was the right custodian and the Christian mind never intended to know or claim 'infallibility'. The apostolic imagery was apt enough then, need it cease to be so now?

Nowhere perhaps was the will to be attaining to the infallible more painstakingly told than in the story of John Henry Newman. His misgivings about the validity of Anglican Orders and his careful exploration of 'apostolical development' led him to conclude that God must have

< 79 >

committed His otherwise precarious Gospel to an institution so authoritative that the Christian believer could then be gladly rid of the onus of 'private judgment' and take all 'validation' from the writ of the Church on which such *magisterium* had been laid. Divine providence could not have failed to 'house' the faith reliably in such institutional guarantor, the sure deliverer from the tribulations and perplexities of the personal task. The poet, G. M. Hopkins, pleaded the same logic.

Thus the centre of gravity of 'God in Christ' was subtly shifted to the Church of a due guardianship. Faith would no longer be where it most belonged, that is in the 'fullness of Christ', but rather in its custody elsewhere. Moreover, any Newman cast of mind in this situation had in no way escaped from the onus of private judgment. For just as the credentials of 'the fullness of Christ' required to be searched by responsive belief, so also did those of the now-authorizing institution. There would still need to be a persuaded-ness about either and, far from being reduced, that obligation in respect of an infallible or indefectible society would be greatly increased. There would still remain the question: Why trust the trustee? And the quandary: Who or what will ensure the surety?

Admittedly, honest faith had large liabilities to sift deep issues to resolve in any faith-receiving of that 'fullness of Christ' via its scriptural mediation through story and text, through tradition and *kerugma*. But those burdens for honesty became far greater when they concerned the long vicissitudes of the church centuries, its entanglements with human frailty and political intrigue. Was the Newman-mind really saying that faith, either way, could be so infallibly verified as to leave, by its very nature, no necessary element of courage to believe? Was it rightly instinctive to faith to seek, to want, to demand guarantee whereby the role of venture, even of risk, would be altogether excluded from its enterprise?

That situation was not one that could dispense with communicating, mediating and conveying factors. It might be well for piety to sing: 'Simply to Thy Cross I cling,' but honestly doing so entailed and engaged much more. What Cross? How 'clinging'? Whether 'simply'? Any implicit faith needs explicit debts and inward logic. The 'believe and trust' directive means both in their true duality – not 'believing' what asks no action, nor 'trusting' what needs no grounds, but – as with genuine love – a sure confidence and an active surrender.[5]

When the faith-authority apt to that situation, not content with that warrant, hardens into authoritarianism it usurps the kindred trust of commendation. It risks ceasing to be the kind of authority that *deserves* hearing in liberty, that merits credence by its deference to the autonomy it addresses in the hearer.

As, or if, it does so override its authentic quality does it not seriously diminish the role of the Holy Spirit in the truth-faith relation? The question is resisted by those who espouse organs of infallibility and firmly insist

< 80 >

that what categorically 'defends' dogmatic faith has been reached by entire dependence on that Holy Spirit. The authority that duly becomes authoritarian is held to have rightly become so by the guidance, and now with the sanction, of the Spirit of God. Yet how, then, is the activity of the Holy Spirit ensured within the personal soul and conscience of the individual? That the Spirit's writ runs freely there, no less than in some corporate mind, is surely explicit in the mandate to 'abide with us for ever'?

To be sure, rank individualism of judgment has no place in the reaching of the corporate mind, the onus in a *consensus fidelium.* But may not the utterly authoritarian church improperly curtail both the academic liberty of scholars and the spiritual integrity of the faithful? Has it not in fact notoriously done so over many centuries? Perhaps there is a problem with the current sense of 'defence', rather than the original Latin one, if it suggests a fugitive and fragile thing that needs protection crucially – protection as distinct from due and alert trusteeship. The latter will be vigilantly aware of a protective scrutiny for all that might distort, impugn or malign it in an ever changing, ever perplexing world. Yet it must ultimately rely on what we may well characterize as the self-sufficing resourcefulness of the truth itself. Christian faith is a voyage, before it can be a harbour, and only a haven in being ever a discipleship.

There is a similar infringement of personal conscience and of spiritual integrity, on the part of those who absolutize the due role of a custodian Scripture, a sacred textuality which guarantees itself. The authoritarian that is beyond 'justly due authority' occurs no less unhappily with a canonical Scripture than with an infallible church. The lust for inerrancy is the same. It is an attitude which rides roughshod over many tasks and the mind and duties of the heart. It covets the same respite from personal liability, alike for the fact and for the content of faith, that characterizes the will to an utter church-security.

A little reflection should make it clear that there were many hazards and problematics in the Bible's contriving to be the cluster of books which we now handle and revere. Did not the collections, 'Old and New', come to be by human decision? To be sure, their being *thus* gathered did not endow them with their 'inspiration'. It recognized it. Yet something at least of their authority, their currency, turned and turns on much decision which might so easily have eventuated otherwise.

In the very texts we now study, of the great Hebrew prophets, as of the historical narratives, there are strenuous questions around their vicissitudes, their minting and editing, their reading, their textual shape and their exegetical study. It would be entirely false to their genius and their genesis to treat them like infallible railway guides to which we go for unequivocal information. Are they not more truly 'oracles of God' to which we go for that they mean – and go aware of the constant issue

< 81 >

between what we take them to mean and what we hear them say? It is an axiom of the Holy Spirit that Holy Scripture does not consort with sleeping partners or transact with closed or lazy minds. Holy Writ is no telephone directory in which we 'look up' numbers, as if their truth was mathematical.

This would be evident enough, were we not sometimes afraid of the quest they require or impatient for our certified conclusions. An alert humility is even more urgent in relation to the New Testament, where our ultimate confidence lies in how closely its documentary formation marched with the missionary expansion of the Church, so that it yields sufficient precedents for every generation from the decisiveness of its own. But it only yields these to studious wrestling with its whole scenario. Why these miscellaneous Epistles? What does Galatian fieriness have to teach us now, or the 'idol-meats' issue in Corinth? How is the collection of Letters 'sufficient' for us (the Anglican term) when this Scripture is intended for a world-wide Church and they are all sent around the Mediterranean?

Then the Gospels – why four of them? What of their vintage, their partial consensus, their mutual differences and the aegis under which they transpired and the fortunes of their being finalized as we know them? What also of their inter-relation and especially of the distinctive standpoint of the Fourth? How may the theology they yield engage with the history they narrate, so that our faith's Christology is honest with its scholarship?

Clearly their intelligent possession has to grapple with the many duties of such scholarship and with the impressive fact that no other literature in the world has been so productive of intricate investigation stored in multitudinous volumes.

At the gravity centre of such duty is the crucial fact of Christian faith's distinction between 'the Word made flesh' and the words made Scripture. For the one is master of the other. The written conveys us to the Incarnate Word, the person, ministry and Passion of Jesus as the Christ and so of Christ, this Jesus way, being the very index to God. In the desert tests of Jesus the formula: 'It is written' could have insidious, even demonic, import, only properly resisted by a more discerning 'it is also written'.[6] The contemporary Scripture cite-r has to be no less discerning. There is no safe refuge in an uncaring literalism. The Gospel of John can be read as a study of how literally misguided text-users could be when 'they searched the Scriptures' while not 'coming to Jesus'.

Belonging to the very centre of gravity in the Gospels was the Messianic theme and its bearing on the course and climax of Jesus' ministry and its perpetuation, for example, in the Damascus road vision of Saul/Paul as a decisive event in the making of the primitive Church.[7] Aspects concerned us elsewhere in these pages. Lively faith has to be ready for

< 82 >

loose ends and tentative conclusions, when issues may not honestly be finalized. But its liveliness knows that this necessary posture in no way leaves it insecure or dubious, held as it remains by the centre that holds. Thus the Bible-user cannot afford to be like the driver of a 'berlin', a cab with the driver's seat partitioned off from his passengers and their willed-for destination. There are endless non-textual questions also to speak their way to the Bible-lover from an exasperated or bewildered world of unbelieving curiosity or hostility.

For such there are frequent stumbling blocks in the habit of metaphor and analogy faith custody deploys. These concern us later, but it is well to measure how our familiarity trades usages that only breed contempt in strangers to their alien imagery. That strangeness is one the insider needs pains to register. It means that our 'earthen-ness' with 'vessels' is more brittle than it ever was for the apostles with their Hebraic ancestry and their Grecian circulation.

The New Testament Letter to 'the Hebrews', of un-identified author-ship, exemplifies the art of 'sitting where others sit' in concern to be intelligible across whatever impedes by, instead, recruiting it to serve. The writer's anxiety was for his Jewish readers, apprehensive about things they cherished apparently imperiled. Accordingly, he maximized the logic of their preservation newly appreciated in its transforming loyalty. This very quality, which makes the Letter oddly resourceful for us now, was precisely its fidelity then in the task of being comprehensible. That asset in the faith as told must be the aspiration of the faithful telling.

Occasion for both in one in the 'treasure' world of 'God in Christ' is thus perpetual and strenuous. It is most surely ours when 'earthen vessels' carry the heart of preciousness itself, whose meaning is ill-served if counter-weighed by an authoritarianism uncongenial to its own humility, its gentle honesty and its capacity of patience.

Perhaps the ultimate query about idle, routine Bible-citing is that it supposes there is no ministry remaining for an active Holy Spirit or the promise of His guiding left negligible. Or, from fear of that openness, He may by contrast be too willfully, perversely invoked. There is danger, of course, in the 'liberty' where the Spirit moves. But if that is apt enough for the Spirit, how not congenial to us? The Holy Spirit has His own – if vulnerable – safeguards in consensus, patience, gentleness and 'the bond of peace'.[8] We do well to seek and love and serve the authority that has no lust to be authoritarian.

III

The second pitfall of faith-custody was earlier characterized as a tempta-tion – in effect – to handle the admitted 'mystery' of faith as if it were a

< 83 >

detective story[9] we could factually resolve, or a ritual over which we could preside, on behalf of a memory we must perpetuate. By either means, do we contrive what may subtly part us from the nature of faith and do 'God wrong most of all'?

To write this way is to interrogate, not to deny, the assumptions involved, our context being care for 'God's wrongs' arguably present, either at the central sacrament of faith or in the faith's narrative as text. The former is more readily explored.

It has to do with the long tradition of belief and liturgy known as 'transubstantiation', unknown to the New Testament but firmly held for centuries of Christendom. Yet, as a dimension of Christian worship, it would seem to be conceptually obsolete, theologically invalid and emotionally naïve. For it misreads the nature of matter, compromises sacrament and ill-serves devotion.

Do physicists still understand a 'substance' in which matter carries 'accidents' accessible to sight, touch, taste and measure which, however, can never be known by these senses because they, the senses, impede the penetration that might reach it? Is not matter an unimaginable whirl of atoms where no 'substance' can belong? Or belong in terms that admit of sense-perception or solid definition? This riddle apart, what avails from thinking or believing that its normally persisting 'attributes' have been dispossessed and re-possessed by another *de facto* substance? Does not the concept almost suggest a device of magic calculated to excite a consoling but deceptive satisfaction?

Perhaps the trouble can be located in (some) grammars' distinction – one English cannot make[10] – between a nominal and a verbal sentence? All turns on that elusive verb 'is'. *Yusufu najjarun* means 'Joseph is a carpenter' in Arabic. No verb occurs. No 'is' is needed. Apposition suffices. 'This photograph my father' employs no 'transubstantiation'. Perhaps a sacrament also, at no cost in veracity, can be of this order, so that we might say: 'What the Lord doth make it, that I receive and take it.'[11] The words of Jesus' institution would have been a nominal sentence in his Aramaic. That being so, the concept of the 'accidents' of bread and wine abiding but belonging to actual 'flesh and blood' would be grammatically needless as well as physically untenable.

Furthermore, the entire sacramental situation is at risk by the notion of an explicit point at which a miracle occurs – the more so if this point is isolated and saluted by a ringing of bells or other timed acts. These suggest a climax in what is a sustained encounter with meaning via an entire liturgy with its sequences, its doctrinal logic and its devotional intent. If climax there be, it must surely lie in the partaking, the receiving as a rite in meal, a meal as rite, explicit in the very terms of food and drink.[12] Participation is crucial, consensual in community, personal and private in conviction and gathered into the shape of centuries at

< 84 >

worship.[13] Only in this fullness is the situation duly sacramental, as inclusive 'memory' of its first night narrative with that night's perpetual significance thus canonically enacted to keep Christ's own command. 'This do in remembrance . . . ' needs rigorously to educate and control our practice. 'God's wrong' is at issue otherwise.

The urge to find a spectacle rather than a sacrament is further marked by the practice of 'Veneration', when the Host, elevated in procession is entirely the one and in no way the other, if – indeed – the Eucharist is a meal in which receiving faith is vividly meant in an actual receiving of the elements. How the sacramental situation is made to cease when response is only visual is carefully expounded in O. C. Quick's *The Christian Sacraments.* He writes:

> The consecrated bread may only be identified with the Lord's body within the outward and visible context of the Eucharistic rite.[14]

There has been endless musing on the 'Real' in the 'Presence', whether magical, or mechanical, or merely symbolic. 'My God and is Thy table spread?' needs to subdue them all to the central pledge: 'There am I in the midst of you.'

A vindication of a devotional exercise that is visual has been made by John MacQuarrie who claims that, since the 'Presence' is *visible* only to the eye of faith, and that there is no empirical verification of what 'Consecration' achieves, the *eye* of faith may verily see things beyond the physico-chemical. Thus Veneration is legitimate and, indeed, desirable. The elements are still among His people.[15] 'Adoration', thus, quite distorts the due relation between objective and subjective, the communicant withdrawing the one and isolating the other. A 'presence' that can be localized in a box and, as such, revered, is not 'a communion of the body', either societal or personal.

Subtle and interminable as are the controversies in sacramental things, their nature in history and devotion is the primary issue for theological integrity.[16] Two other considerations are important. One is the sad diminishment of 'priestliness' when it is virtually centred in one liturgical act. The other is a susceptibility to superstition in devout circles. The two have much in common.

Things 'priestly' belong in far wider realms than liturgy, as liturgy itself tells them when it issues into the self-giving of the priest as pastor, shepherd, preacher, self-foregoing lover of souls. Such issue is ever present for communicants themselves, their 'here we offer and present . . . our souls and bodies . . . a living sacrifice'. What of George Herbert's 'priest to the Temple' or John Keats' 'moving waters at their priestlike task'? Or a radical communist, the French poet Henri Barbussi, 'aware from the start of the priestly possibilities for the writer in a secularizing society', as one sensing – in his gifts – 'the great benefit of language'.[17] Thus poets,

< 85 >

artists, authors – not to say housewives, mothers, parents, teachers – no less than clergy, may 'priestlify' their tasks and bents and doings as truly sacramental things. 'All may of Thee partake'. There belongs a perennial 'eucharist' of hallowing and receiving and endless 'consecrations' of the moment, the season, the context or the crisis. Is there not a forfeiture of liturgy itself, if the priestly action is unduly localized in time or form or ritual setting, unless these affirm and energize their wider truth?

Comparably, are communicants, devotedly at Mass, beguiled into a potential superstition, if minded to attend a miracle, a mystery somehow tangible and saluted *in eventu*? Will the 'Presence' be truly 'real' in its own genuine terms of awe and wonder, unless perceived, received and conceived in its right totality as its first history, its theological entirety, have told it? However we interpret the concept and authority of 'symbol' and the intention of a 'rite', any sense of sheer 'miracle' will disqualify all piety around them, unduly exalt and mystify the 'office' that presides and impoverish the devotion that awaits it. It is evident that many abuses by the unduly credulous of pretentious agencies have ensued. These in turn have grievously provoked a correcting zealotry ready to mire all in calumny and venom. It would seem the strangest irony that 'Holy Communion' should have long engendered the most unholy antithesis of its meaning and intent. A church historian, in sombre mood, might resemble the fabled artist who, asked what he was painting, answered: 'What emerges.'[18]

Even so, might not some other historian raise a counter plea? Dark and sinister perversions have indeed 'emerged' in history around the Eucharist of faith. But what of the evident tenacity, the long perpetuation of devout belief in its miracle-veracity? Is there not a case for letting piety cherish what – to the sophisticated – must seem a foolish indulgence in illusion? Does not religious meaning rightly assimilate emotional demands? If old Immanuel Kant could observe of his simple-minded gardener, 'Lampe needs his God', may not like communicants be allowed their genuine conviction? If the function of faith is to impress the soul with assurance and its consolation, maybe its liturgies should afford them, be it only dishonestly to the mind-set of unfeeling critics. Who or what should finalize that argument? We must allow its presence. Maybe God's grace and forbearance are so far out of reach that 'God's wrong' – as else-where also – will let it be so. Yet 'wrong' it will remain, since to 'love with all the mind' is urgent too.[19]

IV

The other dimension of custodian temptation to which we pass is doctrinal, not liturgical, and has to do with sheer 'miracle' in a different realm of faith. It is vital to see the Virgin Birth of Jesus, and His resur-rection as leaving an 'empty tomb', in the meaning, prior to both, of the Incarnation of the Word. Scrutinized outside this context, they become items of extra-rational belief, articles of perhaps ingenious substantia-tion. Only in 'the Word made flesh' does the Christian credalist assess aright these two events of faith. Otherwise, he invokes some supernatural which no faithless enquiry can comprehend, no scientist establish.

It must first be clear that neither virginal nativity nor resurrection were verifiable in fact apart from their significance in faith. Could the facts of Mary's pregnancy with Jesus ever be historically ascertained, just as the vacating of the sepulchre was never optically witnessed? In the first case, the human witness and the actual factors are not, and never were, probe-able in inquisitorial terms, seeing that Mary's virginity had no mention in Jesus' teaching nor in early Christian mission to the world. It would be pointless to try to interrogate how it might have been factually proved by explanation. For was it not of faith's needing, on the ground of faith's Messianic reading of the Messiah-ship of Jesus, as the great theme of its evangel concerning his Cross? Thus it would be congruent with faith's attained fullness – a fullness attained on quite other grounds than Mary and virginity. Those then would be its only grounds, grounds in no sense standing in a sheer quality as 'miracle' but altogether based elsewhere in faith's own inner necessity. These, we have to say, took it out of bare historical reference, as a 'sign' for faith alone, a conviction corroborative of faith formed on other fact. To have the Virgin Birth sustain the Incarnation is to reverse the role of either. It is also to ignore the disavowal of the pure 'miraculous', unrelated vitally outside itself, in Jesus' response during 'trial' in the desert.

Minds not content with this perception of virginal nativity may want impulsively to ask: 'But did it really happen?' Maybe we should answer: 'Yes, indeed,' for those whose will for that dimension requires them so to hold, while others may be allowed to see it significantly congruent with the ultimate 'historical' in Jesus as the Christ, and He 'the Christ in God'. These 'others' are no less responsible to truth but, being so, do not see themselves as analysts of evidence, but as disciples of meaning for whom the ultimate is Christ in God.

Then, for all, with or without more historicity than His, the signifi-cance of virgin birth abides,

> That Fatherhood in Son-like deed
> And birth to low estate
> Consents our motherhood to need,
> All mothers consecrate.

is a comprehension fit to preface all else in Christian faith. Mary's *Magnificat*, whatever its Lukan provenance, is a hymn of celebration and

< 87 >

surrender for all travail in God's Kingdom.[20] Reading, in 'all generations', the norm of Mary's vocation has taught all ministry to respond with: 'Be it unto me according to Thy word.' Annunciations are perennial.

That divine action moves through human means has been ever the signature of the Holy Spirit. 'The Holy Spirit and us . . . ' as the Council wrote from Jerusalem concerning what 'seemed good' in apostolic mission. The Virgin Birth was thus ever an event in faith, in ever recurrent implication for discipleship. It could denote how, while the human was there recruited, the initiative was always God's. Jesus and the consequential Gospel would be known for no finite enterprise but had its authorship within the very being of God. The womb of Mary could be understood as receiving the creative word which, in New Testament faith, was one with the first 'Let Us make in our own image . . . ' whereby humanness had first become to be.[21]

It is important to Christian faith in virgin birth that these precious meanings belong to Mary alone. No other shares *her* 'annunciation' nor her role. These do not require or validate her own 'immaculate conception', nor its doctrinal extension to a preceding generation. Be it *unto me* according to Thy word' was the answer of her prayer. Those elaborations would jeopardize the very meanings they assume to enlarge.

Moreover, with the supposition of her 'perpetual virginity', they seriously imperil the vital Christian place for the sacramental dimension of all responsibly sexual experience. Her bearing Christ's Sonship as a virgin mother does not imply some inherent blemish, either in the action of intercourse or in the sanctity of the womb. To believe it did would violate the entire Biblical doctrine of creation and the human mandate of 'priesthood' in procreation, the most mysterious privilege of all. Sadly the meanings of virgin birth in the Gospel have too often been read as somehow voiding that privilege as ineligible in the theme of the divine economy. That would be to see a wholly negative rationale and darkly miss or cancel the deeply positive meanings.

Doubtless what is at issue here entails the contingent theme of 'original sin', which 'immaculacy' is thought to by-pass, as if – too crudely put – there needs be a sterilizing of divine nativity from its infection.[22] The corrective of the aberrations of either doctrine is relevant in the other. 'Born of the Virgin Mary', so promptly followed by 'suffered under Pontius Pilate', is the credal confession where, we might say, 'God's right is most of all' – the right of initiative, the right to instrument and the right in love's *kenosis*. Those two clauses, despite the strange gap of silence between them, must be held closely together.

< 88 >

V

Do we not need to possess a similar theology relating to the empty tomb? As with the Virgin Birth, factual, historical investigation, if ever possible, could not explain its 'emptiness'. Possible mis-identification of the place, some filching of a corpse,[23] a legend necessary to the disciples' mind-set[24] – all these conjectures have been advanced. None can now, or ever, be detectively pursued, proved or disproved. Perhaps its emptiness is not that sort of fact.

Then, of what sort otherwise? Is not the answer comparable as with nativity through Mary? It becomes factual for faith in the full and primal context of faith's actual experience, and not otherwise or as a proof-theme in itself.

As with Mary at the outset and with Resurrection in the climax, Christian faith is affirming divine initiative into and through a human Incarnation – a divine action/activity which fulfils and historicizes divine grace. How, we must ask, is Incarnation ended, concluded, completed? Every instinct will be to say 'Never'.[25] But 'never' is a word quite inapplicable to what is said to have occurred 'in time', what is known as being an 'advent', a 'coming', an 'inhabiting'. All these are events which must need ensue in place and time. Except perhaps in memory or legacy, they cannot be 'eternal'. For they are 'events'. Yet, in the meaning of Christ's Incarnation, they are eternal.

How, then, as event (singular) partaking of eternity for *that* and all time's sake, are they concluded, ended, known as done? John's Gospel is alive with the theme of 'going away' and 'abiding for ever' – an 'expediency' in the one, an assurance of the other. How is this situation to happen? The birth of Jesus is not 'undone' because 'He abides with us for ever'. Yet, in the very worth and intention of the Incarnation, He dies. He would not be incarnate otherwise: He is 'the lamb slain from the foundation of the world' (Ephesians 1.4, cf. Revelation 13.8). That death is our redemption's price and climax.

And also 'He is buried'. This clause has always been vital for Christian faith.[26] There, in time-terms, is where the Incarnation ends. Yet, in its being from eternity, it never ends.

Are we not, therefore, in faith and its honesty, aware in Resurrection and Ascension of a frontier both Christ and faith are crossing, whereby what was (and is) eventful in time returns into eternity, taking there all its time-told story to be henceforth eternity's own 'exegesis' of itself?[27] In this way, the New Testament often conflates Resurrection and Ascension as one and the same. The 'forty days' between, with all their symbolic reference, enclose the education of the disciples in this unison of an 'undoing' and an 'ongoing' of Incarnation.

< 89 >

How urgent that education was arises from how dire the crucifixion had been, how devastating their failure during it. Hence, surely, the strange, educative overlap of old familiar scenes and tokens of unfamiliar mystery and awe. An omni-presence is overtaking the familiar presence but in the same, congenial, habitual terms of the incarnational narrative – walks by the wayside, meals on the shore, sessions round a table, the olive slopes, the hillside and the boat. The 'Do not cling to me' of John 20.17, with its explanation: 'I am not yet ascended . . . ' is surely of this context. Immediacy must become memory and memory the ever present shape of faith in its correspondence with eternity.

Does not the emptiness of the tomb belong exactly with this historic progress into faith – an Incarnation that has reached its redemptive climax as its temporal completion *and* its eternal perpetuation as the time-told deed of God? Occupied, that sepulchre would give the lie to all and make Christ-believers 'of all men most pathetic'. Vacated it tells faith's total story. That faith is neither proved nor shaken by queries over 'who moved the stone?' or how, or why or where? Its becoming vacant was never eye-witnessed that it might be the more faith-confessed. That faith does not consist in uneasily conceding 'miracle' but in understanding divine Incarnation and how 'the Word made flesh' passes from that 'flesh' condition only to be for ever what its 'today' in time had shown it – 'the day of salvation', the long, short 'Now' of 'the accepted time', the more assuredly 'accepted' by the sign of an open grave. 'They beheld where He was laid' . . . 'He is not here'.

We must discern this same unison in the story of the Ascension, as employing in spatial terms this frontier, this 'from, with and into' of the exalted Christ. Visual, corporeal departure is consistent with the 'where' of here-and-now: 'a cloud receiving him' marks whither – beyond mortal sight – he goes. It is a going into sovereignty and symbolic rest. Departure passes into Lordship where it had always been and would abidingly remain – abidingly both there and here.

Without this education, this way, how could the Church have known itself? That thus it came to know itself vindicates the way it happened. The empty tomb had its place in both, but not because mere archaeology had somehow proved it so. Faith's referentials are within itself. Faith is responsive to what informs and kindles it. Can faith and history be otherwise?

VI

There was, it was suggested earlier, a third shape in which faith's meanings might be ill-served as God-Meant and God-informed, namely by resolving into an elation of emotion that meant to celebrate them. This magnifies what are termed *charismata*, or evidence of 'gifts of the Spirit',

< 90 >

by which validity is proved and joyfully indulged. It diminishes the problematics of doctrine we have reviewed and, by the same token, can be scant on intellectual responsibility, the emotional experience being the conclusive thing. It is liable to become an exclusifying thing whose danger lies in the satisfaction of a personal possession. It desires to 'love the Lord with all the soul', but is in danger, both intimate and liturgical, of doing so in abeyance of 'loving Him with all the mind and strength'.

The New Testament notes the phenomenon as present in the early Church, notably among the folk of Corinth, where *glossolalia*, or 'speaking with tongues', was frequent. Paul dealt with its advisedly, on two counts.

Was it not anomalous, he hinted, that Christians should abandon intelligible language when they served 'the Word' enfleshed, entailing other words of narrative and witness, when disciples themselves were meant to be themselves 'epistles' legible in life as word? How could strange speech convey their meaning or ensure their veracity? The *glossolalia* could only arouse impressions about thus 'gifted ones' and only remotely and bizarrely achieve communication, while drawing attention to the utterance itself and possible admiration for the amazing 'linguist'.

Moreover, Paul insisted, were not 'the gifts of the Spirit' – love, joy, peace, patience, long-suffering, endurance, gentleness and compassion – essentially moral qualities known and shown in the web of social life and the harsh traffic of the world? Should these be confused with, or displaced by, a marvel of strange discourse which, anyway, would need 'interpretation' and so be inevitably circuitous in disconcerting ways? Was faith really commended by an extraneous phenomenon?

Centuries later, if not already in the Greek and Latin context, another consideration throws doubt on *glossolalia*. It has recent exposition in a notable story out of Africa.[28] *Translating the Message* studies how missionary grammarians, in Christian faith communication, pioneered script for oral languages, enlarged their range, furnished them with new vocabulary and thus initiated them into a richer culture. This happened via a painstaking care for local mentalities and a steady commitment to their means of understanding. If there was a 'gift of tongues' it was *to* others, and from the slow tasks of scholarship. It fulfilled the promise of Pentecost by cultural enterprise, not the onset of abnormal utterance.

Charismatic worship is often characterized as more exclamatory than reflective and its preaching highly rhetorical, with congregational patterns responding in mutual kind and with hymns less thoughtful, less charged with awe, than they had better be. Sincerity demands a more exacting form that sobers shapes of public piety and personal demeanour in the praise of God. Does human *charisma*, in these terms, take less than proper stock of divine glory and of the dark and tragic meaning of our Christ-redemption, our full-attained discipleship?

Nevertheless, as with the reach of yearning for, or welcome to, an

< 91 >

omni-sufficing, inerrant Church, or a dogmatically immaculate Bible, does the neutral observer need to concede that there may be types of mind, or moods of will, where a full Pentecostalism fills due human needs and should not, therefore, be decried? Perhaps there is place for such pragmatism in assessments of practical theology. 'Let both grow together until the harvest' was Jesus' counsel to those who thought they knew to read the evidence of 'tares'. In any event, that 'harvest' is the only final verdict. Even so, the obligation remains to be able and ready to discriminate, if only for the better health of what we must query, regret or carefully resist, caring, in all, for what may be 'God's wrong', including – it may be – our own temerity. For the divine is an exceeding patience.

VII

That being so, perhaps the most far-reaching of the pitfalls we are studying is what has drawn many under some 'cloud of unknowing' which belies – it would seem – the clear New Testament confidence in 'the knowledge and love of God' as veritably ours in Christ. To be sure, 'it passes knowledge', but it would be fatal to apostolic Christian faith to hold that 'inexhaustible' meant 'unpossessed'. This 'knowledge of God' in the New Testament is not, subjectively, His of us, but objectively ours of Him, and something in which we are 'kept', even 'garrisoned' and 'assured'.[29]

By contrast, disciples of 'the cloud of unknowing' school have relinquished the Christian sense of reading and receiving human life as a sacrament of the senses in the created realm of nature. Their mental austerity is earnestly meant but it will not be singing with Thomas Traherne:

> We need nothing but our eyes to be ravished like cherubims . . .
> Men do mightily wrong themselves when they refuse to be
> Present in all ages . . . the world the visible porch and gate
> Of eternity . . . There all things receive an infinite esteem . . .
> He (God) doth what He does that He may be who He is.[30]

The unknowing author of *The Cloud* held to a Dionysian concept of divine darkness, wrote of 'the desert of wilderness of the Godhead' where no one could be at home. God was essentially 'unknowable' so that the task of all 'unknowing' was to forego intellect and senses with their reasonings as lost and helpless. The soul had to learn and school itself 'not to see what appears', with all that purports to register it or assume a confidence to 'read' it.

How could this consort with Biblical psalmody or Quranic celebration where 'the heavens declare the glory of God' or life is ever 'returning

< 92 >

unto God'?[31] Was not such 'unknowing' well told as 'a cloud' in which the soul should grope its way beyond all sense-and-mind reliance to where one 'chose for one's love the thing which one could not ever think'. God could somehow be 'loved this way, but not thought on'.[32] 'Unknowing' there had to be, and had, in any doctrinal sense, by a hard renunciation that 'knew itself not knowing'. The mystery of God was only present to the heart in being to the mind unknown.

Did the whole creation, then, become in some near Buddhist way, an illusory foreground and hinterland of this conclusion, thus conceived as never of theological or Christological significance? Can this vision underwrite sacramental living, grace at meals and grateful experience in time and place? Must one 'choose for one's love', in this world of panoramic sense-exposition of phenomena, 'that thing which one could not ever think'? Inside 'the cloud', 'knowing' had to be the hard renunciation itself 'unknown'.

Since it is always well not to reject others' thinking out of hand when so direly held, ardent sacramentalists can readily concede how our knowledge of God transcends all that we can utter, while never silencing our doctrinal praise. Our genuine capacity to 'know' God will not presume to 'grasp' Him. Nevertheless, the 'cloud of unknowing' is surely self-excluded from the entire shape of Biblical trust and the sacramental theme of historic Christianity. It implies a world in which divine Incarnation could never happen.

Furthermore, it is through the lowly senses in attentive register of nature's order that we discern the benediction of creation, our destiny to 'possess possessions', via the arts and sciences, and translate them into wonder, love and praise. 'All that is within me' can then 'glorify God's Name'. So only follows the sacramental principle by which all that we do in the body, as reputedly secular, has its place as the material for a consecrating salutation of joy, reverence, compassion and humility. Unless 'all that is, is holy', nothing could be. Thomas Traherne, Henry Vaughan, George Herbert, these poets did not 'unknow a cloud:' they loved a landscape which brought 'all heaven before their eyes'. 'Past the low lintel of the human heart', comes the temporal as the theatre of the eternal.[33] Nothing Biblical, from Genesis to Eucharist, discounts the realm of sense-experience, where believing to understand and understanding to believe are one.[34] 'God's wrong' in our impoverishment is inherent when we doubt or despise that cognizance which is blessedly ours in the sense-register of nature, life and knowledge.

There is a dark irony in any 'cloud of unknowing' of such order. We mind it two ways. One is the frequent lapse of due confidence in meaning or our sombre forfeitures of hope. The other is the sad futility of a society and its media besotted with unloving sexuality. The former is often characterized as 'a growing up' beyond illusion, the other a willful surrender

< 93 >

to satiety. Since, in both, 'God's wrong is most of all', the only rescue is the authority of an inclusive eucharist.

How else do we renounce some Hardean notion of this earth as 'a blighted star'? Did Hardy know of any stars that had ever proved so happily hospitable as this strange earth? When, in *The Return of the Native*, he depicted 'humanity entering hand in hand with trouble', why not also 'humanity hand in hand with curiosity and privilege?'[35] and thus despite heavy negatives of such plaintiffs against God.

These have their logics but should yield to perplexity without umbrage, courage without curse. They should defer to the sure positives that issue, from wonder and wisdom, into debt and ministry. For, only so, can society in the West be delivered from the harsh materialism, the sight of which too often provokes religious deplorers into the more ardent zealotry.

Intelligent faith instead has on hand an emancipation from this *dêja vu* of current agnosticism and lustful boredom. There is no salvation from these in the de-sacrilization of nature or the virtual atrophy of selfhood. It must be the 'sacrament of being', of being here, of being thus, of being at all, that answers secular notions of futility and the absurd. These deny the premise of selfhood *per se* and face neither its distresses nor its summons. Our 'being has to be received' as from One who has 'set eternity in our hearts'.[36] as the creaturely autonomy of mind and will.

Disowning scepticism this way, do we not quickly find ourselves coming on to Christian ground, shared as the 'receiving' is elsewhere, inasmuch as this 'letting us be' on divine part, entails there a divine 'Self-expenditure', a *Deus expenditus*, proven in our presence in a verifiable world. Might we not, then, anticipate in God the same self-expending quality in history, as manifestly in the realm of nature – alike participatory 'God with us' here in human comedy and tragedy as via the external world? Alike in nature and redemption, we may meet the same 'Emmanuel', in Cross and Passion no less – far more – than in our 'letting be' on His sacramental earth.

If thus we 'know whom we have believed' we shall no longer talk of adult realism, as our 'apostacy' from the illusions of the childish. We may the more share in the re-sanctifying of the world and on every count contribute to 'the righting of God's wrongs' in the glad confession of His rightfulness.

There are for the next chapter urgent questions about the vocabulary by which we say so and the language of their comprehension.

< 94 >

Chapter 8

VERSIONS OF VOCABULARY

I

To have become aware of the circulation of the blood was a famous waymark in the story of human healing by the arts of medicine. Its counterpart in the body of faith and the corpus of theology must surely be a lively attention to the arteries of words. Vocabulary, it might be said, is the life-blood of belief. It is certainly where meaning circulates and where there are multiple recesses to reach. The old academic usage that talks of 'doctors of theology' requires of them an alert attention to their patient's circulation, its major and its lesser arteries. Only words mentally convey what originates in hearts and must return there.[1]

For it is true that faiths exist and belong in the daily converse of their familiar nouns and verbs, the rhythm of their liturgies and the phrasings of their greetings and their creeds. Buddhist instinct finds the theisms rather talkative religions, too trustworthy of pages and enamoured of pens. Yet classics of 'God-breathed' writings variously prove that the Qur'an's theme of 'man taught by the pen' belongs everywhere in the world of the faiths. What can be conceptual for the mind and be vocal for yearning, the 'calling' God that is theology and the 'calling upon' which is worship, alike must concert their inter-acting invocations either way. The *orare* of prayer will be the *laborare* of thought – theologians either way.

A noteworthy 15th century pioneer in the converse of faiths preferred another analogy – that of the lowly sieve in daily kitchen use or the riddle on the farm. He called it in his Latin a *cribrum*. For a wicker basket in which a child might lie (hence the Christmas 'crib' tradition) could also function as a mesh through which grains might be sifted, to garner what mattered and be rid of what did not. This was the imagery about vocabulary devised by Nicholas of Cusa (1401–1464) in his *De Cribratio*

< 95 >

Al-Corani. A Roman Cardinal who had a mind for the Hussites in his ecumenical sympathies, had been stimulated by earlier scholars, like John of Segovia and Peter of Cluny, to concern himself with the Muslim Scripture which he carefully annotated in Peter's Latin version. From earlier still, the thought of John of Damascus had come through to him via the Franciscans he encountered.

He was responding intellectually to the trauma of the Fall of Constantinople in 1454 and the deadly incursions of the Ottomans into the Balkan regions and their devastating victories at Varna and Kosovo. He cannot have foreseen that they would stay in Europe through four long centuries. The Pope (Pius II), who had prompted him to write his *Cribratio*, had also seen him as the publicist of a new crusade.[2] He, alert to memory, was well aware of long hostile 'mindings' about Islam. The *Cribratio* concerned itself with 'holy pages' as Muslims revered them, not 'holy places' as Christians coveted them.

With and beyond his philosophically comparative theology,[3] Nicholas of Cusa realized the prime importance of words and terms and the bearings they imprinted on their habitual usage, to the often inattentive satisfaction of their intimates and the constant confusion of those unaccustomed to their import. Bare translation – if any could be 'bare' – was no automatic help, the less so when the same role was played by them.[4]

Hence something for the mind like the *cribrum* that might avail for the sifting of the sense, as the lexicon that can only partially provide, on the familiar model of Samuel Johnson or Edward W. Lane.[5] For these fine artifacts themselves can often only weave around an elusive definition with yet other words, while all the while meanings shift in the ceaseless flow of language. There are words which, like a *cribrum*, can hold no water and so let no meaning travel, when vocabularies meet in discourse. There is also then the difficult question as to how flexible or fixed terms will be by virtue of their incidence in sacred Scriptures, where again they may be less than definitive, despite their hallowed status. For terms like *fitnah* in the Qur'an or *ecclesia* in the New Testament undergo progressive content. In this situation genuine scholarship with readiness of will can ensure some sifting of the sense.

Doubtless, as all previous chapters have shown, the most question-raising word of all is that 'G O D' – the Benamuckee Man Friday named for Robinson Crusoe in Defoe's desert island story.

> With a perfect look of innocence (he) said: 'All things do say O to him.' He said they all went up to Benamuckee. Then I asked him whether those they eat . . . went up thither too. He said Yes.[6]

'God' could be the recourse of cannibals and cannibalized alike, if with differing, prior savour of Him. Crusoe could only contrive a very apprehensive dialogue but, cannibals apart, theists say an intelligent 'O' to God

< 96 >

that obligates them in ways that Crusoe was hard pressed to explain to Friday, when theology had allowed him to survive. Nor could Friday have appreciated why his Benamuckee managed to hearken alike to consumers and consumed in his cannibalist world. Defoe was merely musing on the human problematics of inter-cultural communication, while reflecting wryly on the skills of theologians.

Some of the issues of theism in the Islamic context were broached in Chapter 3, via the meaning of divine unity as a concept. There is no doubt that the strong emphasis on the negation of the pseudo-deities – that vibrant *la ilaha* in Muhammad's mission and the resultant credal brevity – led to a popular sense among Muslims of a divine 'remoteness', thanks to the imperative stress of 'Exalted be He above . . . ' If we use a pyramid analogy, then Allah is the very apex high above the base, where *al-bashr*, we humankind, belong. More near and intimate were the pseudo-beings, powers, demons, spirits, that 'possessed' the wells, oases, hill-tops, waymarks and other social phenomena, tribes and places. When effectively these were cancelled, abolished and removed, there was indeed a liberation from their psychic tyranny, but there was also a certain nakedness, a 'distance' they had evacuated, now sensed as intervening between *al-bashr* and Allah. In so far as this was so, it was the necessary, if transitory, price of a real emancipation.

Yet the psyche took time to adjust to the new rubric of unity, or perplexity ensued. It is evident, for example, in Surah 2.186 – a late passage – which records how Muhammad's hearers interrogated him concerning Allah. The terms of the answer imply what was in their minds: 'Say: "He is near . . . near to answer the call that prays to Him".' There is an intriguing move away from their query about theology, in his response about 'answering' prayer.[7]

The assurance of 'nearness' and of unfailing 'readiness' for petition (*du'a*) exactly suited the situation left by Islam's urgent anti-idolatry. Any vital mission needs the controlled force of its essential negatives. The problem remained, however, of bringing that divine 'nearness' down into the cares, the anxieties and phobias to which the pseudo-deities had falsely ministered. Was Islam, in some measure, at risk in the psyche, by dint of its valid urgency in the mind concerning Allah's unity? For the theme of divine 'intimacy', the Sufis apart, has long been at risk. There is no need to reiterate the points made in Chapter 3. The point here is set to raise the essential meaning of the root term *Iman* in Islam and its verb *amana* – 'faith' and 'to have faith', or 'belief' and 'to believe'.[8] Both are crucial in any study of the vocabulary of any faith that uses the 'God' word.

For the 'whether' of faith, i.e. the fact of credence, always entails the 'what' or, better, the 'who' in its content. That issue becomes the more urgent as and when the sanction of the political order supervenes on the incidence and the sincerity of 'faith'. The same applies in the very essence

< 97 >

of *confessio* as both a public stance and a personal conviction, with any possible discrepancy between them. The 'politics of faith' are taken up in Chapter 10. Religious vocabulary is never immune from subterfuge.

Meanwhile, the issue within 'faith/believing' has a deeply significant expression in Surah 49.14, when certain 'desert Arabs' came to Muhammad and said: 'We have believed . . . ' (*amanna*) He is directed to reply to them: 'Do not say: "We have believed," Say: *Aslamna*, ("We have submitted", or "we have become *muslim*".)' With the further corroboratory comment: 'Faith has not entered your hearts.' Lip service may lack heartfeltness and so betray words.

Thus the clear distinction is made between 'submitting' and 'believing'. It is one that was renewed later when the second Caliph 'Umar preferred to be termed *Amir al-Mu'minin,* rather than *Amir al-Muslimin,* when the latter were a more dubious and, so, unreliable allegiance. At the time of Surah 49 Muhammad's cause was proving, had proven, physically successful. It is evident that these recruits came thinking it well to join the winning side, while still their pagan selves.[9]

It follows that the quality, even the fact, of faith may still be at issue inside the profession, or notions, of faith. That conveys us to the Qur'an's own care about 'esteeming Allah with a due and right esteem',[10] where the very doctrine of divine unity may confuse theological faith, should the urgent Islamic 'dissociation' of God from the idols be allowed to imply some 'dissociation' on His part from the human world. For the second would deny and defy all we studied in Chapter 3 concerning the signs in nature, our given dominion from them and all else around the summons to grateful worship, cognizance and love, as from wondering creatures to an ever wondrous Lord.

For, on every count, it must be that the 'God with whom we have to do' has to do with us and that what enters into 'defining' Him belongs mutually with what defines us as human, so that full theological faith is also a deep and awed humanism, a faith about who we are, enfolded into 'who He is'. Trusting *that* God is, crucial to faith as it is, has to ripen somehow into *who* God proves to be as, citing Surah 114, 'Lord, King and God of humankind', the harbour of our refuge and the destiny of our mortal years.[11] A theology is likely to be stunted if it neglects or diminishes the clues that rest in the humanity, which in some sense reciprocates or comprehends divine 'association'. For pagan idolatry excluding God is closely akin to current secularization.

II

There are few passages in sundry Scriptures where 'the sense of the word', as a deeply ambiguous usage, is more urgent than the account, in John

< 98 >

18.35–38, of the encounter between Jesus and the Roman Governor, Pilate, in Jerusalem's Judgment Hall. It turns on the second of the three in Surah 114, namely 'king' as applied to Jesus by his accusers in the only – the political – terms on which a capital sentence against him could be secured from the Roman authorities. It is the word due to be cited in the *titulus*, or placard, set over the cross. Every instinct in the context makes Pilate understand the word in the Roman sense of pretension to state power and so a rebel against Rome.

Accordingly, he opens with: 'King of the Jews? I understand.' Jesus cannot answer 'No, I am not', without excluding the sense in which he is. Nor answer 'Yes. I am' without conveying a falsehood. Accordingly, he replies: 'Sir, are you using this word "King" as you would as a Roman, or are you quoting as a charge made in another place?' The point is vital to the whole case. Unaware of any word-distinctions and sensing evasion, Pilate impatiently retorts: 'Am I a Jew? Your own people have brought you here before me. What have you done?' Bent on elucidating the only sense in which the word could be right, Jesus responds with: 'My kingdom is not of the sort you are thinking of. For, had it been, I would not now be standing here before you without a fight. Mine is not that sort of kingdom.'

Still in the Roman sense of the 'king' word, Pilate cries: 'So you are a king then?' to which Jesus answers: 'King is your word. It fits me only in that I came to this world to summon to the truth and there are those who heed my voice.' Pilate remained only confused and, maybe, testily annoyed, when he replied, famously: 'What is truth?' and did 'not stay for answer . . . '[12]

This classic passage illuminates the comparable situations that obtain with all the great defining terms of the New Testament – 'the Son of God', 'Mother of God',[13] 'Lamb of God', 'the blood of Christ', where there is the same need to reckon with the cultural bias implicit in the listener's familiar world. There is the same necessity for pause and a patience that does not override what it sees as prejudice, or worse, but rather lets it have due place in negotiation,[14] as the ever present onus on intelligent communication. Only by giving perplexity and resistance their occasion can truth be entrusted and precious meanings conveyed.

These key terms of Christian faith *and* theology[15] can only be received and understood in the entire context of the Incarnation in which they cohere. Their warrant was in the founding faith of 'the Word made flesh', which resulted from the apostolic experience of the impact of Jesus, via reflection on the parallel emergence of the Church as community in that faith. Outside this context, these pivotal terms of the ' . . . of God' quality have no intelligible meaning.

'God-bearer', for example *Theotokos*, with its Latin *Dei Genetrix*, is impossible, even horrendous, if read in any 'literal sense' concerning Mary –

< 99 >

the sense, that is, in which Margarethe, thanks to Hans, was the mother of Martin Luther, or Mary, thanks to John, was the mother of William Shakespeare. Such a notion would be blasphemous. Why then did the term come, if controversially, into use in the 4th century? For the reason that 'birth' and, therefore 'motherhood', the womb and its mystery, are inseparable from any divine enterprise of purposive presence within human history – a purpose which can hardly be forbidden (on our part) to omnipotence, least of all an omnipotence already enterprising creation and creaturehood and history. Human motherhood affording those womb-necessities may be duly called, with due care for that import, *Theotokos*. Her lowliness, her surrender, her vocation, can then in turn become a sure 'sign' of the 'high estate' of the humanity of all of us, so that this Incarnation is the truth both of God and ourselves in one and the same mystery. The whole context is vital to the inclusive meaning, given a steady attention to consistent liturgical intention in its salutation.

It may help any Pilate/'king' situation here to recall that the entire Semitic tradition understood divine initiation happening via human 'agency'. Otherwise, all prophethoods including Muhammad's would be impossible. Something human is yielded into, because taken up for, divine employ. 'The Word made flesh' is of the same order but with the personhood wholly present as the fullest measure of the divine in the fullest expression of the human.

There seems no doubt that it is in this Semitic, Biblical and Quranic context of divine agency that we have the matrix of the 'Son of God' language in the New Testament, from plural reference, as in Job 38.7 ('All the sons of God shouted for joy', cf. Job 1.6), concerning a retinue of attendants waiting on divine authority, to the Letter of John assuring his readers: 'We know that the Son of God is come . . .' (1 John 5.20).[16] There are those who wait upon, and move on behalf of, the divine sovereignty. For what transcends will surely engage, and where there is rule there is also relation. The four verbs cannot mean otherwise, inasmuch as they inter-define.

To add ' . . . of God', whether to 'word', 'speech', 'messenger', 'Messiah', 'Son' (in languages that have this form of grammar) is to have the eternal be temporal, the divine take human means. It will be the same with grammars that use a nominal sentence without the 'of', as in the Qur'an's formula (and the *Shahadah's*): *Muhammadun* (is) *Rasul Allah*. There is thus in every case a divine employment of the human means and thus, in turn, a human instrumentation of the divine.

Everything, we must realize, will then rest on the intensity, the reach in seriousness, of that engagement, the burden it has in care, whether it be a voice, a cry, an appeal, a prophet, a reminder, an intervener. That issue will turn on two related counts, namely how far eternal sovereignty wills to be engaged that way, and on how much a human expectancy is

< 100 >

bold or timid to construe legitimate hope of such divine concern. For our experience of the created order, and of our liable creaturehood within it as custodians, tells us that resultant history, social and ethnic and political, will have to be the sphere of any such divine dealings with and for the human scene. How not so, unless that divine sovereignty goes, unthinkably, by default – in which case human meaning also would for ever stay unmeant.

Muslim faith seems to have concluded that the measure of any such dealings would be directional, verbal, hortatory, prophetical in the measure of the Book as 'sent down' upon 'the Apostle' and thus entrusted to communal mind as legible and mandatory.

Was it thanks to the weight of its sense of 'specialness' via birth, Exodus and land and then, Temple, that Judaic identity expected some more radical, more intimate, more far-reaching, dimension for them of divine relation to their experience of the human meaning and its claim on YAHWEH?

Be that as it may, the bitter experience of piecemeal, then final, forfeiture of land[17] and the burden of exile engendered that ultimate theme of divine/human occasion which was the Messianic hope. Variously dramatized in imagination and anticipation, it housed for Jewish minds and wills the terms of a divine partaking of their destiny. 'Yet have I set my King upon my holy hill of Zion' would be the dual truth of their corporate hope and His divine fulfilment. Just as 'the place of the divine Name' had initially been read by Moses and his people in that awesome Exodus, so, beyond the failed and forfeit Temple and the 'lamentations' of Jerusalem, YAHWEH would act in their vindication and only so be Himself vindicated as worthily their Lord.

In the defining context of 'Messiah' we trace the formation of the 'Son of God' language, alike in psalmody and prophet. It is heir to the long tradition of 'the Lord for His people'; and of a 'people for their Lord'. It renews and deepens the 'Son of Man' language so evident in the self-description of Jesus in the Gospels. Those Gospels and their presentation of Him enshrine the conviction, from which and through which the Christian faith itself was formed, which held that Jesus, in the terms of His life and death, had enacted that Messianic hope. He did not, could not, have answered the question: 'Are you the Messiah?' with a straight 'Yes! I am' or: 'No! I am not', without distorting and confusing the sense in which the answer could be affirmative. That situation was exactly parallel, indeed involved in, the 'Are you king . . . ?' query of Pilate, as we saw. Jesus only fulfilled Messiahship by first defining, *ex eventu*, who and how Messiah was – in which he was guided by the precedent of the 'suffering servant' in Isaiah.

Into that fulfilment, as nascent Christian faith identified it, and was itself born in the process, several antecedent strands of meaning gath-

< 101 >

ered to warrant and interpret the 'Son of God' language and, with it, the 'only begotten' phrase.

The clue to these strands lies in the unison of wills between the determinant in God and the transacting of it in the 'agent'. It was a unison that could readily be expressed in a 'father' from whom all derives and a 'son' in whom the deriving ensues as the fulfilment. There are sundry examples of this juncture in Israel, with clear traces of the 'satisfaction' the unison tells. Psalm 2.7 says about a 'king in Zion', 'Thou are my Son as if born to me this very day!' There is a clear salute to a personhood in an office, vocation or role-task which takes its very birth from the intending will of God and is set to be personified in the ensuing mandatory carrying these into life-realization.

The 'Father/Son' language fits this originating/implementing mutuality because there is a 'coming to be', or 'coming to pass' of the 'begetting' intent – the more so when in Psalms 80.17 and 144.3, this 'agent' is 'the Son of Man whom Thou madest *so strong for* Thyself', the divine means being so evidently human for ends assuredly divine.

There is a further clue to this sense of 'Father/Son' in the import of the parable in three Gospels of the vineyard and the husbandmen. Their obdurate behaviour is a clear indication of their conspiracy to take over the vineyard – a pattern of events familiar enough in the Galilee of those years. Beyond merely withholding the fruits, they are coveting possession by violating their status as tenants, which is the cardinal sin of God-flouting human wrong. Faced with this situation, there is no further point in simple 'messengers'. What has transpired is 'Messianic' in its clue-response. 'I will send to them my Son', inasmuch as only the son, the heir and no mere 'servant', can assert the Lord's right. Hence the otherwise puzzling logic of risking the son in sequel to the murdering of the servants. The Messianic proportions, in the divine mind, of the 'Son-sending', is the realist measure of the wrongness of human history and thus a further angle on its realization in Messiah Jesus. For the sequel in the parable was the sequel in the story: 'Come let us kill him and seize on his inheritance.'

It follows from all that gathers in the 'Son of God' language in the New Testament that there is an intimacy of will, and also of character, in the 'sending' as discernibly one of identity between the 'Sender' and the 'Sent', as both alike divine. For the divine, in this equation, has no element of 'deity' that shrinks from, or disowns, the human nexus already implicit in the creation of creaturehood as a purposive history (the sort of nexus which other theologies repudiate). Thus the Fourth Gospel can align 'the Word made flesh' in Jesus as the Christ, with 'in the beginning the word: "Let there be . . . " " "begotten . . . before the foundation of the world".'[18] John's Christology counterparts his theology, neither separable from the other.

< 102 >

This unison of divine/human wills, seen as a unison of 'Being' or 'substance', is implicit in the frequent occurrence in the Gospels at significant moments in the story of Jesus: 'This is my Son, my beloved . . . ' with the obscure translation ' . . . in whom I am well-pleased'. This phrase might well suggest some mere admiration as of a disinterested observer, whereas the real sense should read; ' . . . whose will coincides with mine' or ' . . . who finds his pleasure in what is also mine.'[19] The 'beloved' word in this context refers to the benediction of the situation it denotes, the unison of the will that 'volunteers' with the will that presides.[20] 'The 'begotten' language then means that the 'birth-source' of this mutuality is in the nature of God, the God with this divinely human concern.

Hence the shape of the 'God-in-Christ' situation in the Gospel and the First Letter of John. 'To have the Son is to have the Father also', because 'in the Son the Father is always at work'. Thus the rubric of John 14.6, ' . . . no one comes to the Father but by Me'. We misread if we think this contradicts Abraham, or Job, or the psalmist (103.13) or Malachi (1.6) ever 'coming to the Father'. How could it? For they 'came to Him' by the familiar sense of being 'filial' inside the natural order. The 'fatherhood' to which we 'come' through Christ is that, but with the profound further dimension of its meaning that is present only and for ever in the person and the Passion of this God-disclosing Sonship.

John 14.6 is thus not exclusivist but sublimely 'expansionist' from the caring Creatorship the 'Father' word originally meant. It is as if some Beethoven would say: 'To have me for musician is to have my symphonies.' 'Only by these do you reach to me.' Or some dramatist saying: 'Find the mind of the play only on the stage of its *mise-en-scène*. That is where I am.' The truth of theology is made the truth of personality. To know the one is to have the other, where, as John had it, as the 'word' of Jesus: 'I and my Father are one.'

The reaching, on apostolic part, of this conviction is no small part of its veracity. It was of an order of meaning as being first cognized in a history issuing into an experience, not as a proclamation otherwise to be imposed. Thus the double sense of 'he who *has seen* Me has seen the Father . . . ' The substance of the *confessio* was the experience of discipleship from Galilee to Gethsemane and beyond. Thus the Messiahship and thence the 'Sonship' of Jesus were not proclaimed from the housetops of (thus) futile publicity, but only engraven on the mind-set of followers. Thanks, however, to their genesis of Letters and Gospels, it is not withheld from those who were never eye-witnesses, but conveyed to them in documents these would leave concerning 'Him whom, though now we see Him not, we rejoice' with a joy we cannot fully tell.

This leads the course of thought on 'divine Sonship' to its final attestation in the life-story of Jesus. That 'status' was not only set to be the 'ontology' of Christian faith, a dogma concerning, but also a daily actu-

< 103 >

ality about, his ministry. The loved term 'Abba, Father' in his habitual language concerning God, the sense his preaching mediated of 'One who cares . . . ', the perception of 'a cup my Father gives me' around intimations of the Gethsemane ahead – all these were the *de facto* 'Sonship' that came to underwrite, in ways we have reviewed, the *de jure* 'Sonship' of Christology. What the creeds looked back to at Chalcedon was first told in Gethsemane, the 'Father' in the prayers of Jesus.

There is no contradiction in Jesus' 'Sonship' being so deeply human in its being also sublimely divine, so that the measure of the Passion is one with the divine nature, the *Deus expenditus* of an earlier chapter. The paradox – if such we think it – is of the very fabric of the Incarnation.

It may help those with a Pilate-style cultural or other incomprehension of this Christian theme to ponder the language usage by which what has been adjectival can become nounal and so synonymous with what it existed only to describe. This happens notably for Muslims when Allah is denoted as *Rahman*, 'the Merciful'. Then we find the Qur'an ready to have *Al-Rahman* serve as noun in its own right.[21] There is no 'replacement', certainly no 'displacement'. There was always a unison. Either was there already in the presence of the other. 'Duality' is there for thinking, but only incidental to identity, an identity it only elucidates. This is not 'metonymy' where a part does duty for the whole, as if 'ploughing the waves' was all that could be said about 'seafaring'.

These cares for the meaning of 'the only begotten Son' are the more confirmed by the notable way in which the Gospels record its being directly challenged, namely in the wilderness experience of Jesus. 'If thou be the Son of God . . . ' is a threefold encounter with plausible ways in which 'Messiah' might proceed. The decisive rejection of all three made the Cross the only remaining 'Sonship' course. The three were the paths of economic plenty, of sheer spectacular provocation of credulity and of entire political compromise. None of these would have been 'Messianic' in the only terms consistent with the divine mind. None, therefore, would have been 'filial' as 'theology in action'. Faith is distorted, people are confused, but 'God's wrong is most of all', when the 'truth through personality' of divine Incarnation is left crudely open to a miscarriage of language, whether willful or negligent.

III

There is a similar measure of risk in another ' . . . of God' sequence in the New Testament, when John 1.29 has John the Baptist introducing Jesus to his disciples with the words: 'Behold, the Lamb of God . . . ' He did so with words that had a long ancestry they urgently needed to transcend, on behalf of the only sense that could carry his intention – a sense

< 104 >

which, at long remove, owed its adaptation to what it could no longer ever include. Whatever reaction the evangelist would have us anticipate from its first hearers,[22] the expression lands us in the same quandary with the Roman Pilate over Jesus' 'kingship'. Or, as Shakespeare observed:

> A sentence is but a cheveral glove to a good wit, how quickly the wrong side may be turned outward.[23]

And not only to 'a good wit', but to a stupid theologian or a prejudiced ear.

For truly there is nothing less like a lamb than Jesus in Gethsemane. No analogy from crude animal sacrifice, in levitical terms, can feasibly bear with the conscious anguish of heart with which Jesus contemplates 'the cup his Father gives him'. It has been deeply inimical to Christian witness concerning our redemption that 'sin-bearing' in the arbitrary, artificial contrivance of a 'scapegoat' dispatched to 'take away' what was never understood, could bear the Christian meaning of 'God in Christ'.

To be sure, the 'lamb language' of an ancient animal system could and did yield the metaphor of a 'victim' ritually 'bearing' evil and so re-assuringly (?) 'bearing it away'. But that dim and dire 'original' had first to be taken far from Leviticus and its rites of offering and be translated and transformed by – and into – the prophetic experience of a Jeremiah. His sufferings, and those of his kin, captured in the Isaian imagery of 'the suffering servant', took the cost of witness in an apostate society so that, effectively, their conscience 'bore' the wrongs of that society thus, and only thus, retrieving it from 'being overcome of its evils'. Thanks to suffering, socially inflicted but courageously borne, the truth of things was rescued from what would otherwise have been its ruin.

In Hebraic context, it was perhaps instinctive to associate that personal tragic dimension of prophetic ministry with the immolation of witless animals on some 'altar of sacrifice', but only if the analogy was first exempt from all the elements which could in no way 'go across' the utter disparity. Thus, when Jeremiah, in loneliness and anxiety of heart, likened himself to a 'lamb led to the slaughter', there was a wide world of difference between the measures of 'victimization'. We only have the force of his meaning in radical disavowal of the source of his comparison. Unhappily, it has been a dissociation some theologies of the Cross have been unable or unwilling to make, whether from undue literalism or never having watched in Gethsemane. Or their exegesis never met some clueless Pilate, demanding to know why he should 'look at the little sheep of the Lord of the skies', which could be the English version of what John the Baptist first cried.

Caring this way for the feasible meaning of religious language brings the further boon, beyond the urgent liberation from obscurity and falsehood, namely how the 'Lamb language' passes into doxology. 'The lamb

< 105 >

in the midst of the throne . . . ' 'the throne of God and of the Lamb . . . ' – with these verses, the cry of John to the disciples on their threshold has become the faith's climax in the very doctrine of God. The way that 'God was in Christ' in the time and place of the Cross is the way 'the Christ is in God' in the eternity of sovereignty. Mercy and majesty are clues to each other.

Thanks to the 'Lamb language' we come to the realization of the crown of thorns as the insignia of 'the majesty on high'. What 'couples' 'God and the Lamb' in such theology is not the 'and' of addition but of identity. A vocabulary that took the high risk of baffling incomprehension yields the most assured truth. It has been well told by a 19th century Connecticut theologian, Horace Bushnell of Hartford. He writes of 'a cross of patience even from eternity' in 'the great world-containing heart of its redeemer', adding:

> It is as if there were a cross unseen, standing on its own undiscovered hill, far back in the ages, out of which was sounding always, just the same deep voice of suffering love and patience, that was heard by mortal ears from the sacred hill of Calvary.[24]

Having seen this measure, in Christ and the Cross, of the 'Lamb' language in the Gospel, it dawns further upon Bushnell that the same principle of vicarious travail in the heart of God was the before and the after of actual Calvary. 'Christ in vicarious sacrifice,' he wrote, 'represents the feeling of God in all previous ages' . . . 'Nay! There is a cross in God before the wood is seen on Calvary.'[25] Still more so, it is there in the long story of the Holy Spirit in the life of the Church – the 'violated patience', the 'burdened sympathy', in fact 'a Christ continued'. For

> If the sacrifices of the much enduring, agonizing spirit were acted before the senses in the manner of the incarnate life of Jesus, he would seem to make the world itself a kind of Calvary from age to age.[26]

Thus the whole Gospel seemed to Bushnell 'a texture of vicarious conceptions' in 'a suffering sponsorship of our (human) race'. It follows that what we discern this way in Christ and thence in the Holy Spirit historically extends to the Biblical theme also, as being the risk-taking, long-suffering of God in the launching and sustaining of the human story. The love behind all things is essentially a vicarious principle and that principle will be found definitive in the very nature of love in all other realms within creation, since it is explicit in creation itself. It, therefore, determines the entire business of ethics and sets the shape of true believing, as summoned to its pattern and its emulation.

There is no doubt that Horace Bushnell here has set down the inclusive, Trinitarian logic of the explicit 'lamb language', via Isaiah and Jeremiah, of the Fourth Gospel. Explicit in 'Christ-crucified' is the divine

< 106 >

'undergoing' for us and our salvation, which is the implicit hallmark of all else in our human experience and in the theology that knows experience for what it holds, what it learns and heeds. It is thus the more unhappy that 'this Lamb of God' has been so sadly ill-esteemed and disesteemed.

IV

In how to bear your enemy, wrote Bushnell, you have found your Gethsemane.[27] What has made your theology has to make you a redeemer. The word that comes most to mind from the 'Lamb of God' theme is a word central to the mind of Paul, namely the Greek term *kenosis,* as in his Letter to Philippians 2.5–11. It wholly corroborates what we saw in Bishnell who himself uses it. *Kenosis* is no less risk-prone than 'Son of God', 'Mother of God' or 'Lamb of God' in careless hands – and for the same reasons. It needs a Pilate-style, sceptical interrogation. For the sense of 'emptying' (of the self understood) is ambiguous. We might have carelessly in mind a container from which liquid is poured so that its 'contents' are no longer there. Divine 'self-emptying' is of a very different order, so that the ultimate identity is more entirely present when it *seems* to be foregone.

We come at the meaning by noting how, in human society, rank, dignity, status, office are conventionally self-guarding, self-serving themes to which persons instinctively cling and which they expect will be duly acknowledged, never ignored. For if they were socially disregarded, they might lapse into disuse and be forfeit. They can even find register in language usages, in degrees of deference a choice of pronouns will observe. When they are extravagantly flattered we feel we have become obsequious. That excess in no way questions the care for what is due and the vigilance which will monitor its presence or reproach its absence.

It was a revolutionary Christian perception, taught by Jesus, to think this situation of 'dignity at stake' could ever happen in respect of God. For is not the perennial task of theology the worship of the utterly worshippable? The 'greatness', sovereignty, Lordship, kingship and majesty of God – these were mandatory, inalienable, ever to be adored. There could be no compromise of an endless doxology, the perennial 'exalted be He . . . ' Were it thought to be otherwise, 'God's wrong would be most of all' precisely because 'God's right was supreme above all', a glory that could never be renounced – still less humanly neglected, though *de facto* such neglect was happening all the time.

Yet, strange as it must be to all our *de jure* minding, suppose there might be, in divine transcendence, a quality of 'self expenditure', a dimension of sovereignty that (for still utterly sovereign purpose) let itself be laid

< 107 >

aside? This was what Paul realized to be so, in his characterization of Jesus/Messiah as fulfilling that 'office' in history, only by laying aside the 'glory that was his before the world was'. 'The form of a servant' proved the necessary context of the fulfilment of 'the Son'. This was *kenosis*, an 'emptying' by which the reality was more fully *there* in the very foregoing of its majestic secret as more surely achieving it.

We have seen *kenosis* in the 'Lamb-language' as Bushnell told it. It was there clearly in the 'shepherd' analogy in Jesus' parables. Shepherds truly belong with folds, but if they stay in them when sheep are lost, their quality is forfeit. The 'power' the fold, the rod and staff, wield is not eclipsed by the risk of the errand into the wilderness. It is counter-parted by – we must say – the *kenosis* it incurs to be more totally itself. Its resources answer a different situation with complete consistency.

This self-foregoing, self-fulfilling capacity in God most High is the defining faith of Christian theology and belongs with the meaning alike of the Incarnation and the Cross. Reflection quickly perceives that it is 'the beat of the heart' also of human love itself, readily suffering at cost for what it clearly cherishes, as memorably told by Robert Browning in his 'Saul', celebrating the harpist David's love for the broken King.[27] 'I will gladly spend and be spent for you' was Paul's own way with his churches. The vicarious, like the sacramental and for the same reason, is at the heart of society, at the core of history and – on Christian ground – at the crux of theology. It belongs with a faith that has its credentials in creation and our creaturehood, in Christ and his Cross and thence in the criteria of the Church. Yet, in the 'emptying' language, it has always needed a watchful exegesis lest its precious meaning go by default.

We defer to Chapter 12 and 'The Wounded Name', a study of how far human vagaries of agnosticism, indifference and ill-will or guilt, have made things divine seem 'empty' of their due in the darkly hostile sense of these 'God-wronging' attitudes. The very Pauline language in Philippians 2.5–11 has a hint of this in that 'clutching' word, if we let it portray, not the 'self-foregoing' action of Messiah, but the harsh misprision of God and His praise which happens at the hand of human waywardness and moral wrong.[28] Meanwhile, there is the same need for contextual care in yet another 'language venture' that belongs with all those reviewed, namely 'the – cleansing – blood of Christ'. We have it, notably, in 1 John 1.7 and in the Letter to the Hebrews with its solicitude for the blood and altar imagery of the old Levitical system.

V

As with 'king of the Jews', we need here also a puzzled Pilate to disturb the familiarity that assumes it 'knows what it means', that 'the blood of

< 108 >

Christ cleanses us from all sin'. Such a 'novice', mystified, will want to insist that blood does not 'cleanse'. Blood only stains and it is vital that it should, so that crime may be pursued in its traces to requital. The notion that another's 'blood' might cleanse some third party's sins must be altogether damnable.

'Blood language' has long, precious, sinister associations, as the very 'elixir' of life, its shedding the near vicinity of death. 'Blood', in the impulse to sacrifice, whether human or animal, serves as a palliative, on some 'life for a life' principle, which may avail to placate anger and obviate revenge. Only barbarously and fictionally does its 'shed-ness' atone in that context.

The long centuries of Hebrew holocaust as meticulously promulgated in the Pentateuchal writings yielded the ruling dictum – from that matrix – in the Letter to the Hebrews: 'Without the shedding of blood there is no remission' (9.22). That dark and dread rubric, phrasing the harsh rigour of its awesome incidence, is only – and utterly – retrieved when the same Letter, expounding its theme of Jesus' Messianic 'priesthood', notes sublimely: 'the blood of his sacrifice is his own' (9.13, cf. 13.12). The writer transforms and abolishes the old ritual imagery by locating its implicit relevance squarely in the event of the Cross. Forthwith the formula 'Without blood-shedding no remission' has to find some paraphrase now to read: 'Only in the love that suffers can sin find the where and why of its forgiveness.'[29]

The ritual scheme by which some immolated animal symbolically incurs, by arbitrary imposition, the weight of evil done, to 'bear' it at the cost of blood (whether laid on an altar or scape-goated into a desert) becomes – for the writer in Hebrews – the actuality of a history. Crude symbol rises into veritable fact, where the deed done by representative human wrong is so 'taken', undergone and suffered, as to expound for ever the nature of divine forgiveness, its cost and travail. At the Cross there is the epitome, either way, of human sinfulness and divine grace its pardoning answer.

Only so do we begin to see how 'blood cleanses' – this 'blood of Jesus' as the Christ, as the Christ in these historic terms, and the 'words' that speak it from within. It is well that apostolic faith, so careful for right formulation of 'the Word made flesh', has refrained from any single theology about how the Cross saves. It is important, however, to let the event's reality subdue, not be travestied by, the obscurity of antecedent Levites and their holocaust on Temple altars. Those tragic prophets, 'the blood of whose travail was their own', pointed the way to 'how and why' Messiah would be more genuinely redemptive than any anticipations in a Pentateuch. The point has already been sufficiently made in the Lamb language.

'Washings' which were also vital in ancient liturgies readily yield what

< 109 >

can convey the meaning of a sacrificial forgiveness, realized inwardly in the soul. There is no quarrel with 'water cleansing' 'C'est san metier' we might cry. It loosens the mire from the fabric. By its agency a past is undone and a present renewed. To let the Cross mean what it means, in the heart, is to know a moral 'remission of sin', which may perhaps come home to the mind, under the quite different imagery of a 'judicial' verdict of forgiveness. But this dimension – whatever 'peace of heart' it may bring to faith so perceiving it – is doing 'God great wrong'. For it violates the 'God was in Christ' reality of what it formulates and thus distorts Him in terms that alienate divine mercy itself from what happens in the Cross. To this we only do theological justice when we understand the cry there: 'Father forgive . . .' as a soliloquy in the heart of God and not a plea to an external, still less to a vengeful, Father.

The reality of 'separating' the sinner from the actuality of sinfulness is what the analogy of 'washing' purports to capture, however else the experience may be formulated in 'atonement' thinking. It is well that the creeds sufficed themselves with the affirmation of the history 'under Pontius Pilate', and left to hymnology the intimate personal *confessio* of how it avails the soul. The authority of that reticence deserves to solemnize or simplify the sundry terms in which it is enlarged and dramatized.[30]

The 'blood that cleanses' has a counterpart in the 'price that buys'. That we are 'bought with a price' is a cherished theme (1 Corinthians 6.20, 7.23, 1 Peter 1.19) with its kindred meanings of 'slave manumission', 'ransom' and 'redemption'. Though there have been distinguished thinkers who did not heed it, the soundest exegesis here is surely through the simple matter of the preposition, whether 'to' or 'for', and remembering that 'price may be paid for . . .' that is never 'paid to . . .'. The latter may be some kind of 'barter' or 'bargain' situation, whereas the former comes close to the role of things vicarious as earlier noted.

When Herman Melville writes in *Moby Dick* of the 'price of oil' he has in mind the toils and risks of the whaling ship's crew he so vividly depicts, 'occupying their business in great waters'.[31] Even day-to-day vocabulary needs an alertness of imagination, if its meanings are to register as they deserve. This is far more the case with the language of faith. Metaphors and analogies only belong in the sense in which they can be true. Otherwise their ill-judged potential can lead even a theologian astray and, still more, the naïve listener. Then 'God's wrong' is darkly more than theirs.

With New Testament vocabulary, our security is in the knowledge that criteria of significance are for ever with the drama, the biography where meanings have been enacted and lived. 'He (the Christ)', writes John 1.18, 'has exegeted God'.[32] All words have their lectionary in 'the Word'. All the more vital then the intelligence, the discipline, with which we refer to the one and defer to the other.

< 110 >

Chapter 9

THE NECESSARY MINISTRIES OF DOUBT

I

When, in mid 20th century, the Cambridge historian Herbert Butterfield published his notable broadcast Lectures, he ended with 'a principle' which, he said, 'gives us a firm rock and leaves the maximum elasticity for our minds'. 'Elastic' and 'rocklike' seemed a strange unison but 'the principle' ran:

'Hold to Christ, and for the rest be totally uncommitted.'[1] The rock-likeness of 'Christ' had been anticipated by Paul in writing to his Corinthians (1 Cor. 10.4) but the very boldness of this analogy told how diverse and wide the ways in which the 'Christ' word could be read. And 'totally' about all other commitment seems to rule out their being sifted. Perhaps he would have been closer to a precept for faith if he had suggested 'intention' instead of 'principle'. To intend to 'hold to Christ' will give ample exercise to 'elasticity of mind' and the implicit tension in so doing can hope to be faithful with faith.

Whether principle or intention, 'holding to Christ' will learn on many counts how necessary is the ministry of doubt and with it of courage. The previous chapter has exemplified the multiple 'scepticisms' that must happen around the language of metaphor and the ways of analogy. The urgent remit from Chapter 7 was the readiness to 'bethink ourselves mistaken' where we are lulled or lured into premature or complacent confidence in the 'givens' of belief.

There is an immediate example of language and case-making, one that might seem to exclude any authentic role for doubt and so cut short at once the whole logic of this chapter. John 16.8 has 'the Holy Spirit reproving the world of sin because (or 'in that') they do not believe'.

< 111 >

Misconstrued, that might mean that all reservations of mind about belief, any concern about trusting with integrity, had to be condemned. This would plainly be contrary to that same Holy Spirit 'guiding into truth' by gentle persuasion that enabled a growing discernment thanks to a reciprocal patience, that of truth in its loving siege and the self in its questing soul.

The Johannine context, here and in the Letters, is that of Jesus' Passion in retrospect and of its being akin to the subsequent rampant persecution of the Church. This was the 'sin' that was 'exposed' as such by its own deeds. There was no 'doubt' of any seeking sort in the dark verdict they had for Jesus, only the deadly negative of his crucifixion. The Greek verb in 16.8 has the meaning of 'bringing guiltily to light', 'to unmask' so as 'to convict'. Indeed, we might capture the double sense of the persuasive and the condemnatory activity of the Spirit in these Chapters of John by the contrasting senses of 'expose' in English usage, i.e. that of 'expositor' or 'exegete' and that of 'prosecutor'. The former wooes the dubious towards convincing, the latter accuses to condemn. There is nothing to incriminate in the open-endedness of the first, everything to rebuke in the already acted malignity of the second.[2]

This reading of John 16.8, as in no way criminalizing all doubt, is confirmed by other verses that refer to the deeds of evil that already entail their own guilt (3.18, 19 and 36, 15.22–24). It could not be part of the impulse of this Fourth Gospel to give the lie in these verses to the utmost significance of its inclusion in 20.24–29 of the most telling doubt of all in Thomas, the most demanding of disciples and first architect of creeds.[3] The theology/Christology of John 20.28 carries the whole genius of the Gospel, in the perspective of its Jesus, from the cumulative experience of dispersion into 'Gentile' inclusion in Christ and its travail under persecution. Both these illuminate the whole sequence from Galilee and, with it, the gathered meaning of the Cross. Just as Paul's vision on his Damascus road attested a Jesus now 'persecuted' in the persons of his apostles yet belonging with the glory of God, so John in his Gospel narrates the antecedents, as now legible in their eventuation. It is possible to read the whole Johannine text as controversy culminating in the Passion and shaping the self-understanding of the Church.[4]

That enables it to be also the supreme mirror of the 'truth-convincing' ministry of the Holy Spirit, as for ever engaging with the human seeking that can only begin in the will to interrogate. As one reader has it:

> Our Gospel registers an eternal protest against all fixity of dogma. 'The Spirit, as John conceives it, is a principle of inner development by which traditional forms of belief may from time to time be broken up, in order to reveal more perfectly their essential content.'[5]

< 112 >

The Fourth Gospel concludes in 20.31, prior to its 21st Chapter, with a clear note of its deep intention to 'persuade', to serve to have all its readers 'theologians in the knowledge and love of God'.[6] That ambition forms, for the perceptive reader, a lively ministry to the doubts it conspicuously explores in all its *dramatis personae* – those that are reprehensible, but more those that only through doubt put themselves into the answer. The Gospel that has for Prologue the sublime assurance of *Lux mundi* and *Lux Christi* in their unison has place for the Thomas whose desperate doubting first demanded the vital insignia of faith.

II

Is there not an impulse, in all belief systems, to want to absolutize themselves and is not this quality most evident in structures of religious faith? The reasons are not far to seek. For faiths have to do with what must determine all else. One can hardly be tentative or irresolute about that which must resolve the several dependent issues that wait upon its dicta or its dogma. The Jewish tradition must make absolute the call of Abraham, the experience of the Exodus, the Decalogue of Sinai and the 'everlasting covenant' of David and his divinely constituted monarchy. There is something adamant and incontrovertible about this assured scenario, an entire reluctance, within its ethos, to interrogate its feasible sources or to query in its long and tangled story the factors that – for other minds – suggest elements in its unfolding that might qualify the reading – and the readership – of the narrative. Nor are its devotees content – as it were – to 'internalize their conviction as 'truth as they inwardly held it'.[7] On the contrary, no 'truth for' perception can do duty for the 'truth of' necessity. What is claimed others must concede. For 'objective truth' cannot be only privately cherished without betrayal of its given character.

Thus the 'chosen-ness' is for Judaism the *sine qua non* of its world relation, with a persistence that abides and has even proved itself capable of undiminished and unquestioned transit to the ranks of a 'Christian Zionism' unconditionally committed to the entire and innocent validity of the State of Israel.[8]

'The necessary ministry of doubt' is clear enough in the reservations that might arise, once the participant has stepped outside the charmed circle to allow a modesty of self-interrogation – not the abandonment of identity, but its better exploration.

That such a ministry inwardly arose within Jewry itself in the wake of their Exile from the 'land' so pivotal to their self-assurance, becomes clear in two remarkable ways. The experience of 'away-ness' from 'the place of the Name' under foreign rule and tutelage made them more introspective and, by the same token, the more minded of the world beyond. Even

< 113 >

before Exile had transpired and while its menace only threatened below a horizon, the prophet Hosea even called into question the entire theme of Exodus election to intimacy with YAHWEH.[9] Jeremiah deepened that insight by his theme of 'new covenant' of law, written in the personal soul rather than in the corporate destiny.

The 'ministry of doubt' here lay in the refining of an essential reality, the maturing of a meaning, hitherto only too grimly compromised by the proudfulness in its possession which the voice of Amos condemned. They were 'not YAHWEH's people' incorrigibly, in order to be 'His people' the more morally and worthily. What becomes dubious in its ethos, as honest ethics must acknowledge, had to become dubious to its own self, if ever its authentic meaning was to be sustained. 'God's wrong' is the more involved the more this necessity is obscured, deferred or denied. So much earlier chapters have noted.

A further result of this enlarging experience comes in the changed awareness, in the exilic and post-exilic prophets, of the rest of humankind. 'Others' had first been those impeding Philistines, the non-elected people due to be subdued by Abraham's children. Folk had to be assessed by their inimical relation to Israel, whether Goliath or Sennacherib. Cyrus could not have that aura for an Isaiah. A chastened perspective could now discern some positive in 'others' and muse on the reach of Jewry's own meaning, when even those unknown 'islands' might 'wait for YAHWEH's law'.[10] To be sure, a Zechariah in this vein would see the far-off coming to cling to Jewish skirts. Those who came to sense 'where God was' must needs repair to visit a land-tied people, yet one who might now await them through the education of their own Exile. Perhaps it was the very tenacity of their 'land and people' nexus which enabled the bitterness of the 'waters of Babylon' so tellingly to deepen the Hebraic genius in the task of self-possession.

That doubt had this ministry is evident enough. It would be more vital still when, at long range, a Jewish apostolate out of Jesus as the Christ, fulfilled that impulse to mental interest in the wideness of the world. Thanks to the meaning they found in him, they did so, not by awaiting the visiting nations in their own Jerusalem, but venturing themselves, casting off the moorings to the land to make good from it a different 'promise'. There was then no haunting question about 'the Lord's song in a strange land'. Strange lands were meant to sing it.[11]

There was no comparable development in the epic of Islam – the faith which, perhaps more than any other, has precluded the vexations of dubiety. The first Muslims, with Muhammad, had their Hijrah at the onset of the Calendar, but it was into the eventual policy and polity of the haven of Yathrib, soon renamed 'the city of the Prophet'. There were initially elements of doubt about its reception, since it had been offered as a sanctuary only by some of its people. But these were only of the circumstantial sort and quickly to be resolved by the skill and prowess of the arrivals and their leader. What finally ensued only the more firmly entrenched the self-confidence of the faith migrating into a victorious destiny.

Those *muhajirun,* or 'emigrants', had run a risk in setting faith-ties over tribal ones and there were sharp hazards in their evolving story of success. But these did not concern their minds as to faith's content, while faith's warrant was the more ensured to them by their campaign in the field of conflict. Their creed or *Shahadah* might be threatened in battle: it was not tested in mind. On the contrary, a ministry of success dismissed, by its own momentum, any ministry of doubt to the ethos of Islam. At the very heart of its defining narrative lay the prescript of its validity.

Even so, it is possible to discern from the Qur'an itself a setting in which dubiety had played its part in the inauguration of Muhammad's prophethood.[12] It is certainly clear that there was a profound scepticism to overcome in the hostility of the Quraish to his credentials, his notion of 'corpses' brought back to life and his demand for the Oneness of his Allah. Was his decision for the Hijrah then a token that he read them as never liable to be persuaded or, at least, dissuaded from their paganism? If so, did that Hijrah set Islam permanently on a will to impose, rather than a mind to commend, its faith, to by-pass its task with doubt by the very shape of its coming? The defining story of Islam was certainly the expansion of a régime more than patient tuition of the mind. Thus the Qur'an could announce itself as 'a book in which there is no dubiety' (Surah 2.2).

There are, however, two points to be made of hesitation about this verdict, one in the there and then of the 7th century in Arabia, the other in the here and now of a global 21st. Muhammad's Meccan preaching – and indeed some little time after the Hijrah – was full of repeated appeals to intelligent minding. There was everything compelling about this conviction, nothing compulsive about his attitude. He was then himself immensely vulnerable, exposed to obloquy and scorn. That initially he had crippling doubts about his authenticity is evident from the reassurances he received, as for example in Surah 93.6–8, and his sense of sharing the pressures of earlier messengers.

Still more relevant for uncommitted attention to the Qur'an is its steady, recurrent appeal for intelligent consideration. There are many scores of occasion for that *la'alla,* 'perhaps', pleading for *tadabbur, 'aql, tafakkur,* 'reflection', 'minding', and 'thoughtfulness'. It would be false to hold that the Qur'an was mandated to ride roughshod over doubt and misgiving. It would hardly tell the audience that it 'lacked a right mind about Allah' (Surahs 6.91, 22.74 and 39.67) and not be urging them to find a better one. That they 'had locks upon their hearts' was its deep suspicion about their heedlessness (47.24). That Muhammad in Mecca

< 115 >

had a sharply agnostic constituency – agnostic both about him and his meanings – is of vital importance for Islam today, as prior in its original posture to the more combative sanctions of its Medinan sequel. One must draw from Muhammad the persuader for Allah the implicit presence of doubt in the access to faith and, thereby, a factor in the attaining of conviction. That priority abides beyond the different strategy of the Medinan achievement of wide allegiance.

Though Islam, characteristically, has produced few sceptics within itself, the role of the rational and the imaginative has never been lacking in its cultures, even when it has remained a firmly self-sufficient system. Perhaps what has fostered this quality has been its pre-occupation with the will, rather than the being or knowledge, of Allah.[13] Law will more readily dictate than negotiate, while doctrine hardens in the enunciating of rules. Muslims, then, by and large, outside the ethos of the Sufis, were well seasoned to be strangers to serious doubtings until the onset of the bewilderments of more recent secularity.[14]

III

While there are strenuous intellectual duties for the alert Muslim[15] as there are for the scholarly in Judaism by long tradition, it is fair to say that Christianity has been the most doubt-sifted of all the great religious faiths. Exploratory scholarship on the New Testament has been voluminous for two centuries in the wake of the mental labours of the early Fathers, the vitality of the medieval theologians and the ardours of argument released by the Reformation. Chapter 5 studied how burdened with dubiety was the theme of Messiahship during Jesus' ministry and how his fulfilment of it – as the nascent Church perceived it and was born in the perceiving – turned both on whether and how. For only in resolving the second could the answer clinch the first, the reality in the Cross being so far from the sundry norms of expectation.

The disciple Thomas, though deepest in his insight round conviction, was by no means alone in his anxiety about the Resurrection. For there was a crucial sense in which the disciples themselves would become the supreme evidences and, in that story, their own perplexity had to play its vital part. It was for all, belief out of unbelief, dedication after desertion, reborn motive beyond prostrating despair. No one could sanely reckon with the New Testament and find it a journal of fond credulity.

The salutary ministry of doubt can be discerned there in three broad threads of faith found and told in fellowship-creation. They were the perpetuating of Holy Communion; their taking to the road: their attaining of textual identity. Each finds a symbolic capture in the narrative Luke has of the journey to Emmaus, when – at length – around the

< 116 >

table 'He was known of them in the breaking of the bread' (24.35). Then they saw the clue to him which, pointedly, had eluded them in the 'opening of the Scriptures' on the road. It was the more reminiscent of 'the Upper Room' precisely in *not* being a formal liturgy but a home-like meal. All transpired because those two wayfarers had the impulse to travel. 'Three-score furlongs' were scant enough for 'the ends of the earth', but – whatever the immediate factor then – Jerusalem had not retained them. The third dimension of the story, similarly eloquent of the future, was the scriptural horizon of their identity. It would be enlarged by the process of their own corporate dispersion from 'the place of the Name' at Jerusalem.

Each of these three defining features of the early Church belonged with a growing sequence of conviction and impulse, ensuing from decisions born of anxious care.[16] We noted in a previous chapter the strange paradox of doing anything 'in remembrance' of an unforgettable Jesus, when we also found why the memory had its given pattern. It seems clear that clinging to it at the Master's behest was instinctive to the Church's being and that it sacramentalized the deep transition from 'disciples' into 'apostles' through which they passed, as the prelude to all else. That 'he would be for ever known of them in bread and wine' would be the charter of their fellowship, the surest, most constant, antidote to doubt either of him or of themselves.[17]

But it was not confined to where it had inauguration. It could transpire in Emmaus no less than in Jerusalem. For it belonged to a road-taking faithful. This second dimension proved an epic story only because it entailed the liveliest inner question. According to the Lukan narrative in Acts, faith-extension to the 'Gentiles' seems to have been the initiative of nameless pioneers. It could not stay that way. Apostolate had due authority to exercise and the new departure demanded to be found authentic at that level. For it drastically reversed the assumption, even of 'universalist' prophets, that the nations should 'come to enquire at the only place of the Name'. The notion of taking it from native ground was revolutionary.

Divine privilege is never easily shared as the annals of 'special theological relationships' have shown and there was fear for the moral contamination of the 'pure' by the admission of 'outsiders' to hallowed law. There was the contagion of the pagan scene to be excluded. The way to the inclusiveness of the reach of faith in Christ was only taken by way of vexing doubt as to its rightness. In the event, it was more aptly fulfilled by virtue of having been anxiously queried.

The essentials were there in the story that took Peter to Caesarea. We noted its significance in Chapter 6 as having its place in the steady discovery by the Church of divine integrity in Christ reaching for the embrace of 'Gentiles' into grace. It was to prove a signal occasion of how

< 117 >

strong initial doubt was a prime factor in the sequel. Faith learned its full dimensions only in unlearning its first sharp confinement.

Travel is a lively tutor of the mind and a sifter of prejudice. There is no way 'from Judea and Samaria to the uttermost parts of the earth' (the historic formula in Acts 1.8) without crossing rivers, of which there are none in Judea and Samaria, and reaching for the sea. But why is Peter in Joppa on the coast? According to Luke's narrative, there appears to have been a 'lay' movement down to Lydda on the plain where a faith community had taken root. It was they who invited him and from there he proceeded seawards. The transit was not part of apostolic leadership.

It might almost seem from this factor that Peter the leader was learning that there could be spontaneity in the way of Christ arising from lowly sources and putting even apostolic status under tutelage. Perhaps those very human details were all conspiring in the story to reinforce the lesson. It is often precisely where we want to lay the veto that the openness to its withdrawal has to come. As with exilic Jewry what had appertained to the *one* land could belong in *any* land. Covenanted peoplehhood could know itself strong enough beyond a single geography. Initial truths differently abide in what has to revise them radically. Science from the century of Copernicus and Galileo thought it had disdainfully to renounce the geocentric universe of the medievalists. More recently we have come to realize its essential truth. For unfathomable immensity is in fact fathomed by, for example, a Hubble spacescope which only human earth could contrive and launch. We will need the point again in Chapter 11.

In the case of Peter, anathematizing the foreign meats which the cargoes off Joppa suggested to his dozing mind – and the bidding: 'Kill and eat', required him to do – that dietary law was at the core of Jewish separatism and of a Levitical obedience. Only by foregoing – even defying – this, via the hospitality of Cornelius, did he attain to the lesson in its abrogation. It must have been an anxious watch as he wrestled overnight with the treacherous idea. Coincident dreams in the story were no temptation into compromise but the prelude to a doubt's retreat. Peter would experience his case-making for Jerusalem.[19] The wider reaches of travel meant larger reaches of the mind. Apart from that sojourn in Caesarea–Philippi, their travels had been confined to Galilee and the uplands, with a focus toward Jerusalem.[20] Now, thanks to their discipleship become apostolate, they were launched on to far-reaching ventures by land and sea.

This diaspora, given its evangelical intent, meant a further education into meaning – an education in which scruple around issues its outreach engendered excited its mind and entered into the very telling of the story. If there had been doubt over 'Gentile' circumcision in the early thrust of

< 118 >

mission, there were other doubts to be resolved in its ongoing course, as local communities multiplied and the distance from the Jesus-origins lengthened.

We had reason earlier to note that the New Testament as 'document' derived entirely from 'New Testament' as an event on the ground. When the 'document' became a definitive 'Canon', a 'Scripture' in its own novel right, that development became the more conclusive. The Scripture came with and via the geography. Had there been no purposive travels there would have been no definitive text. Gospels became mandatory because lapsing decades pass and because memories belong with the living. That time factor operated with the place factor, so that Galilee needed narration in Corinth and the parables their currency in Ephesus. Thus, time and place, given insistent reach into both, occasioned the textuality which would enshrine its story. Hence the onus on self-interrogation.

The same convergence of mission and 'document' accounts no less for the ministry of 'epistles', of apostolic correspondence teaching and nurturing the churches – letters which, in large part, preceded the maturing, if not the genesis, of the Gospels. There was much that was precarious and now beyond certain tracing in the whole documentary process, but of its crucible in missionary expansion there can be no doubt. The scattered communities needed apostolic bonding, alike in faith and ethics, and they were often rawly born out of pagan culture. They were not exempt from circumcision to be exempt from 'righteousness'.

Thus, because Christology was pastoral as well as historical ('Let this mind be in you which was also in Christ Jesus') the faithful needed its discipline in both private and corporate terms. Those at Corinth who had no scruples about 'idol meats' must curb their liberty and defer to those, 'weaker brothers' in their view, who still held to them.[21] There could be no absolute attitudes that did not yield to the constraint of love, no imperatives without that 'if' implicit in the fellowship. 'Giving no cause for another's stumbling in anything' was an over-riding factor. The restraining patience involved would be the salvation of both parties, the one from arrogance, the other from compromise, and both from absolutist banishment of doubt.

Likewise, in the same often disquieted Corinth, the precedence of humility with spoken wisdom over the pride of luxury in the gift of 'tongues'. Spiritual exuberance could readily degenerate into exclusifying self-esteem. It was well to appreciate the diversity of spiritual gifts and to serve generously with those one had, in a self-acceptance that was ready to reciprocate. Elsewhere in Galatia, the 'care' of this Church was occupied with a local trend to vacillation, alternating with excess of wild ardour in a people too volatile for steady nerve and sane discipline of will. Or those Colossians, so readily prone to esoteric cult and Gnostic wander-

< 119 >

ings from the criteria of the faith-consensus still proceeding in those decades.

Evidence shows that only at Philippi did the Pauline correspondence have unanimous occasion for congratulation to a Church – it would seem – immune from necessary cautions, except apparently for feuding ladies (4.2). All the letters show a remarkable familiarity on Paul's part with the comings and goings in each community. What is also noteworthy, not least in Romans and Ephesians, is the depth of mind and reach of theme of which recipients were capable. But throughout, it was matters that gave pause, issues lurking in doubts, that elicited this epistolary tuition both of mind and spirit. 'I stand in doubt of you', Paul tells the Galatians (4.20) so that his 'perplexity' relates to their vagaries, so that these, in turn, serve to set forward a knowledge that could only emerge from a correcting truth of apostolic response – a knowledge alert to its own critique.

It is in this way that the New Testament Letters function still, as resourcing the ensuing Church down the centuries with precedents from which right minding could deduce a present guidance in a different age and world. Only so can we accept that the Scripture has 'sufficiency' now, given its lamentable brevity and the perhaps premature closing of the Canon.[22] How the Letters handled doubts and misgivings can afford us clues now about how like issues may be resolved, both as to the temper in addressing them and the criteria by which they may be judged.[23] Doubtfulness, in this sense, plays its salutary part at every juncture.

At the core of all was that *haplotes* which Paul, in 2 Corinthians 11.3, yearned to find in his readers. He used the word elsewhere in Romans 12.8 and 2 Corinthians 1.12. Often translated 'simplicity', it is not the 'easy to understand' sort but, instead, a 'single-mindedness', the absence of 'duplicity' alike in thought and in intention. It is the quality which belongs to them 'in Christ', and its benison was the whole intent of the scripted education of the churches.

In that process, it is noteworthy how epistolary tuition harks back to 'remembering the words of Lord Jesus'. Thus, for example, Paul on 'idol meats' borrows from Jesus on 'unclean/clean vessels' and who can doubt that the praise of love in 1 Corinthians 13 derives from the Beatitudes?[24]

If the saying holds that 'truth will be found at the bottom of the well' (whatever the coiner meant) it was certainly down in the minds and wills of dubious attitudes and learning loyalties that the faith and sacred text of Christian formation moved and cared. It exemplified 'the necessary ministries of doubt' to corporate faith and exercised the sort of authority that left room for them. For only the doctrine that is patient with confusions is honest and forthright with conclusions.

< 120 >

IV

But, crucial as these aspects were and are, there are more radical measures of the place of doubt in the growth and sanity of faith. It will be false for theology to think

> There is no justification for doubt itself. No one should flirt with his unbelief or with his doubt. The theologian should only be sincerely ashamed of it.[25]

'Flirt' – a loaded word – is never what genuine doubt will do. For it can be pain and anguish, and 'shame' will be absent from 'sincerity'. The religious mind, as argued in Chapter 7, must be reconciled to accepting how many things stay relative and so forego the anxious craving for the absolute. For only so does faith stay within the obedience of love, which contains what it may not totally explain. And what fully contains the 'open questions' that remain for such obedience is the divine meaning in the Passion of Christ. In that measure, we can borrow what Shakespeare has in another context:

> I hold it cowardice
> To rest mistrustful when a noble heart
> Hath pawned an open hand in sign of love.[26]

For 'trust' is always the other hand in the mutual grasp of faith. The best 'certainties' are thus the self-critical ones that do not withhold the will from the going, even as a ship will answer no rudder until it is afloat. By the same token there is about much 'atheism' a mood that does not venture.

Yet human capacity for 'trust' in the sense of these lines of Shakespeare, as they might tell of 'God in Christ', is all too often limited, then crippled and deadened by the cruelty of time and tragedy. That could only be a false and facile faith that took no cognizance of the grim toll of human weariness and woe, 'the slings and arrows of outrageous fortune'. Honest faith means an imaginative awareness of the Empedocles and Thomas Hardys of this world and of the steady toll of suiciding farmers in third worlds through the poverty that western patterns of trade inflict on struggling national economies.

No religion can be honest which immunizes itself from facts as they are, below the horizons of its dogmatic assurance or its ritual practice. If there is truth beyond the forms of truth, there must be conscience beyond the consolations of belief. The ministry of doubt will the better care for the integrity of faith.

His 'orb' word had a suitably religious aura, but Tennyson made the point in his earliest poem 'The Two Voices':

< 121 >

As far as might be to carve out
Free space for every human doubt,
That the whole mind might orb about
To search through all I felt or saw.
The springs of life, the depths of awe
And reach the law within the law.[28]

He would write better poems later in the wider suspicion that no such discernible 'law within the law' existed, but 'space for every human doubt' remained a watchword. For it belongs with believing theologians, no less than with agnostic poets, to marry their vocabulary to the whole reach of human experience.

This is the more urgent in that deep sources of agnosticism lie in the follies and excesses of religions themselves. They can readily seem to external assessors bastions of prejudice or havens of willful illusion. Aspects of their dogmatism suggest long measures of self-delusion. The cult of certainty repels those who are learning to love questions they will not prematurely answer to their own ease of mind. And, of late, there has been a spate of the will to suicide which can only mean – to an incomprehending world – a faith bent on dying for what it refuses more patiently to live for. How cheaply it holds its own private mortality can be no intelligible commendation of its sanity or its moral relevance.

These more dark aberrations apart, the mind of the doubtfulness that shuns commitment and stays critically outside the appeal of a faith has to be the touchstone of that faith's liability for its image and its duty in witness. The challenge to its authority tests the quality of the authority it claims. For he would be an odd witness to the integrity of his creed who left the impression that he had no will to appreciate the reach of another's perplexity.

Yet that re-assuring openness needs to retain a lively grasp on the right of his faith to offer it. Anxieties are not relieved by those who indecisively share them. The deeply Christian poet R. S. Thomas might be cited as a case in point. One poem every fortnight for fifty ministering years, twelve hundred in all, in the pastoral ministry with unpretentious fidelity, was a prodigious witness to a Christianity utterly self-aware, yet moved to ask:

Will nobody explain what it is like to be born lost?[29]

The question could only be asked in a state of self-despair, never as the query ever arising from Christian faith. For grace means a sure inherent inheritance of meaning, which is only forfeited in the conspiracies we mount against it in the concreteness of active living. To write of 'dreams . . . of happiness unfounded', as 'a child's memories out of the womb', flouts the Christian hallowing of the womb, the hope creation holds and the mystery of open grace.[30] Had the priest-poet somehow slackened the

< 122 >

thrust of his Christianity by the very intensity in which he registered the ache of humanity? If so, must we conclude that he had yielded to a captivity to doubt instead of accepting its ministry?

It would seem to follow that, for those so minded, the relations between faith and doubt must truly be reciprocal. If faith has a steady duty to the dubious, as is clear in its *confessio*, so radical interrogation serves to alert believing to the full measure of its task. Examples of language confusion or miscarriage were noted to Chapter 8, in meanings only conveyed when critically challenged.

Such critical correctives, so urgently needed in the art of words, are the more vital in the realm of conscience. The clarifications which illuminate the one must be the correctives which purify the other. Religious faith may be beset by misconception: it is more prey to moral exploitation. It can too easily be engrossed in satisfying consolation. John Henry Newman's 'nor prayed that Thou should'st lead me on' lay wide open to ambiguity. Was he musing on his Oxford career, or was he seeking verily to resolve the vexed issue – as he laboured with it – of veracious authority in doctrine?[31] Purity of heart can be an elusive quality inside the tensions of faith and commitment. 'And with the morn those angel-faces smile' could be rightly, or only wrongly, rewarding. Likewise also the merit in the humility meant in 'I was not ever thus'.

Admittedly, the famous hymn, like its kindred 'Abide with me', may be utterly sincere in its self-pre-occupation. But it might not. It is from this complexity around faith-honesty that some, like the novelist Iris Murdoch, have urged the religious need to be 'good for nothing', that is 'good' or – by obvious sequence – 'faith-holding' for no other reason than a pure heart.[32] The 'interest' that claims commitment must be somehow 'disinterested' – paradoxical as the demand must be.

Here is the deeply moral ministry of doubt that can interrogate the unworthy reasons that may have motivated allegiance, some reach for consolation, a cult of self-esteem, or coveting some final escape from doom or pledge of eternal security. Faith needs to know itself, not as a gesture of cowardice but as an act of courage – courage, that virtue so often claimed and flaunted by the brave old agnostics who see themselves grandly aloof from the naïve rescue-seekers of faith.

Such ethical self-scepticism is at the heart of all Christian *confessio*[33] – hence, perhaps, the strange enlargement of that word into 'confession', seeing that self-examination in the mood and mind of Psalm 139 belongs in the outset of Christian liturgy and with the integrity of the private heart. Yet such can be our deviousness that even self-scrutiny may yield a subtle self-congratulation which then requires another confession. If that sequence is not to be perpetual, we can only end it in the reality of grace.

That there is here the ever open question of moral integrity in the art, the act, of faith means there must be the ever present ministry of doubt

< 123 >

towards the readily closed question of doctrinal statement. It is a relevance calculated to clip the wings of pretension, to acknowledge the elusiveness of meanings in formulae and to guide commitment into maturity. Only so are we preserved from the arrogance of indicatives that do not live with interrogatives, and of those of whom Charles Williams wrote:

> Lord God, the mystics gather
>   To Thy familiar tones,
> The sons who know their Father
>   Assume their judgment thrones.
> With terrible assessors
>   Thy seat is thronged about.
> We too are Thy confessors,
>   Lord, hear us too who doubt.[34]

In the grammar of verbs, indicatives can always pass into interrogatives. Must it not also be so in the grammars of faith, and be so both in intellectual and ethical terms? The issue we have examined about 'being good for nothing' is perhaps most acute for those whose faith has committed them to 'holy orders', or whatever other shape of priestly and teaching ministry serves the faith they espouse. Since these 'ordinations' engage them in a task they will not relinquish until death 'makes the sacrifice complete', have such 'clergy' also relinquished a still open mind about its theme and content? Moreover, since they have attached a livelihood to their office, will there not be a vested interest in sustaining the beliefs that under-write it? In that event how open can they afford to be to ministries of doubt?

The question is not about 'stipendiary' ministry *per se*, but about sustained integrity in the continuity of conviction, lest unworthy sanctions maintain it in being. Though acute for such stipendiaries, it is in fact a situation common to all religious conviction understood as commitment immersed in, yet immune from, the ravages of time.

How religions answer this predicament is for them to say. On Christian ground the dilemma of continued integrity through transitory years lies in the real distinction between the *what* of the faith as held, and the *who* in the faith as trusted. Paul the apostle, who emerged from 'deep searchings of heart', was at pains to insist: 'I know *whom* I have believed . . . '[35] Unlike a fixed dogma, a personal relationship is free to ripen, mature, deepen and enlarge. Moreover, the commitment is mutual. The Master-Keeper to whom we are committed has his 'trust' committed to us. The relationship is mutual. *Servare est regnare.* To trust is to be entrusted and the two capacities enclose and ensure each other. Thus *teneo et teneor* is the language of Christian discipleship and together takes care of authenticity and thereby also of integrity. Such discipleship is a self-examined

< 124 >

life only in being also a self-unpreoccupied one. Its scrutinies are inside its mastering by Christ.

V

All the foregoing about faith honest with itself on every count duly impressed upon it by ministries of doubt is darkly jeopardized, as and when it is entangled with the compromises or attentions of political power. While duly ordered power is indispensable to the welfare of society, any weddedness of power to faith, especially in unilateral terms, is highly inimical both to power political and to faith religious. This angle on how 'God's wrong may be most of all' is remitted to the chapter following. Only then shall the course of thought arrive at a perception, implicit throughout this chapter, that authentic faith turns finally on an act of will. The will to believe and belong and behave – that triad of the right disciple – has to be the study of Chapter 11. 'He that willeth to know let him do.'

< 125 >

Chapter 10

EXPEDIENCES OF POLITICS

I

'If you let this man go you are not Caesar's friend.' There was a veiled threat in the words of the Jewish leaders to the Roman procurator, Pontius Pilate, in John's narrative of the trial of Jesus. Cunningly they used the official term, *amicus Caesaris* only applied to the Emperor's inner circle to which only improbably Pilate belonged. Their flattery apart, its import was sinister enough and captures here the dark territory between two vested interests – the political kingdom and the religious order. Jesus' accusers, for their part, represented a hegemony, a structure of credal and cultural authority held and exercised, as they believed, on behalf of God and by His warrant.

Thus the classic confrontation in Christian faith-history brought dramatically together the appeal of religious belief-system to political power, the answer of politics to the claims of religion. The dilemma with which the scene confronted Pilate made the trial of Jesus the trial of Pilate also and, no less, the trial of the accusers. Conscience for both active parties was at stake in their encounter with each other around the role of Jesus as their catalyst.

The otherwise obscure Roman Governor of Judea for a mere decade in the 1st century stays perennially named in the Christian Creeds. 'Suffered under Pontius Pilate, crucified, dead and buried.'[1] What does 'under' gather to itself of 'regime', 'verdict', 'watch and charge' as the role of power's exercise in a single fated episode? Symbolically the Gospel narrative characterizes it as 'the sin of the world'.[2] Present co-actively with the political compromise of Pilate were the religious moods of malice, the clamour of a volatile crowd and the dark calculus of a disciple's mind.[3]

< 126 >

A faith pivoting credally on this haunting Pilate figure in his telling context can never be careless about the machinations of human politics, the tangled obligation of power to truth, of rule to right and of faith to politics. To see 'God's wrong most of all' in why and how Jesus was cruci-fied immerses Christian faith, as a theology of history, in the most radical relation to the realm of power, the political business of the state. If, as we must ponder closely in Chapter 12, as arguably its most incongruous measure of itself, it must hold to a crucified Lord and set a crucifix at the centre of its sacramental life, conscience in politics will always be its burden.

For there is no refuge *in absentia.* The great Muslim sage, Imam al-Din al-Razi, Qur'an exegete and legist, records of Emperor Kaykhusro, tired of his throne and task, how

> His soul inclined earnestly to the divine world and realized that it was not possible to have both the worldly kingdom and the nearness of the divine world. He, therefore, abandoned his kingdom and journeyed to a place in which nobody knew him and he engaged himself with Allah.[4]

The motive may have been admirable, though uncharacteristic of norma-tive Islam, but it could only prove a personal escape. The business of the political order is inexorable, in that 'the sin of the world' admits no resig-nation from its taskmaster role. The Emperor's resignation merely bequeathed its incidence.

II

'Taskmaster' is apt imagery in a double sense. For the power dimension which must rule and regulate society as its due and proper task, is – and must be – itself 'entasked' to do so with justice and compassion.[5] Al-Razi's story is pointed, as indicating what might be a Muslim option (in Sufi terms), in only being also against the grain of every other Islamic instinct. For Islam is the most uninhibitedly committed of all faiths to the political order, yet most insistent that *al-mulk li-Llah*, 'the sovereignty is God's'. The two belong in one. Precisely because 'Allah rules all', His agency via the Islamic state and legacy of 'His messenger' is seen as the more manda-tory. If we speak of a 'theocracy', it is in tandem with a human-set commission to discharge it.[6] 'Obey God and obey the Apostle' is the dictum in Surahs 3.32 and 47.52, while 4.59 and elsewhere link this 'obedience' to God with 'those foremost' (or 'in authority') among you – an ambiguity which occasioned the Sunni/Shi'ah divide in the first half-century of Islam. The essential point is clear. Faith pre-supposes rule and rule serves faith. Believer and subject are to be one and the same.

It was not always so in Islamic origins. For thirteen defining years in

< 127 >

Mecca, Islam was no more than a preached faith in a hostile world, one which neither sought nor enjoyed the sanction of power. It was a situation closely analogous to the first three centuries of the Christian faith, prior to the arrival of an Emperor resolving to take over the Church, as the religion of his Empire. In effect, by the Hijrah from Mecca to Medina in 622 AD, Muhammad became the Constantine of Islam, setting a pattern of religio-political hegemony to this day with duly appropriate benefit of the power factor.[7]

This Islamic situation is relevant here only as a superlative example of the ultimate faith–power nexus and its propriety to either, so that religion is unashamedly political and politics congenially religious.

It is a salient, yet fallible, expression of a principle long held right and urgently imperative – even with the fact of expediency lurking on all sides. Despite that perpetual likelihood, there is a pragmatic place for the *imperium,* the domain and exercise of political power. There is a moral obligation to truth and justice in and over the control the political thing enjoys and employs. Pretension to absolutism in the first means violation, even repudiation, of the second. The sub-sovereignty which the sovereignty of God entrusts to the first is evermore beholden to the obligations of the second.

The political order has legitimacy conditional on its non-primacy. Religion only rightly receives its ministries of order and social control, when it retains and fulfils its own moral and spiritual judgment on their incidence and worth. 'Seek ye first the Kingdom of God and His righteous dealing' is the divine summons to both in their inter-relation. It may not be allowed to read, as fit for either: 'Seek ye first the political Kingdom,' since faith doing so would be no longer religious, and a power-structure totally unaccountable betrays its trust by usurping prerogatives that go only with its service.[8]

Those defining experiences of Islam's thirteen years and Christianity's three centuries need to be kept firmly in view. For they witnessed and indeed nurtured and launched their essential identity and did so in a manifest absence of the power dimension which, in either case, came to be so strongly – if differently – characteristic of their world establishments.[9] In the Christian case, Emperor Constantine, with his dubious 'baptism' and his imperial pragmatism, was an incubus on the original genius of New Testament faith, its gallant survival under the mingled tyranny and indifference of the many featured sequence of his predecessors.

Yet the innovation of his adoption and recruitment of the faith proved immensely durable and coveted over long centuries, in the successive forms of 'Rome East and West', 'the Holy Roman Empire' of Charlemagne and the Papacy, medieval rulers and the nation state Catholic and Reformed. The marriage of Church and State seemed fasci-

< 128 >

nating and imperative to both parties. How could it be that faith should not covet, demand and retain unilateral control of political auspices? How could it be 'faithful' and ever be content to let these pass into custody elsewhere? The sole duty of religion was its utter immersion in the business of power, however the *modus vivendi* with its organs was devised and assured. *Cuius regio ejus religio* was the ever reversible principle. *Christos Pantocrator.* In the West there could be no 'reformation' of or from the faith of the Papacy not obliged, by the logic of the Papacy itself, to nest itself within the political patronage and protection of some crown or rulership. Thus struggles over issues *within* faith became, by the same token, conflict between their political guardians who drew succour, in turn, from rivaling truth claims.

Yet, entrenched and seemingly axiomatic as this pattern was and persisting durably so long, it did violence to the very nature of religion. It obscured the originality by which Christianity had once been a minority conviction, ready for jeopardy and finding its mettle in that very circumstance. It forfeited all that might be salutary faith-wise in that vulnerable condition, or it only renewed the experience when – as with William Tyndale and his kind harassed by their Thomas More – minorities found themselves on the dangerous side of political permutations and auspices.

Furthermore, that Christendom pattern, imperial, papal or national, left no – or only minimal – occasion for genuine, moral and personal impulse to claim exemption from conformity. Or it allowed these only through long and costly partial surrenders of its hegemony, in tardy recognition of a painfully emerging 'secular' mind, to which – in the event – it would learn heavy debts of its own.

Was there not, in this protracted privilege with power, a willful negligence of the deep and necessary quality in faith, that of liberty in the confession of belief, freedom of conscience in its profession – and these as integral to its very health and authenticity? Was not a Christian truer to his origins in being vulnerable to outsiders at liberty to stay such? Should he not be willing to be a citizen in patient faith-fulfilment, rather than a sanctioned conformist inside a political safe-haven? Were there not, for any Christian, profoundly theological reasons for a 'secular' statehood?

They were surely there in the doctrine of creation, the mandate to human dominion in creaturely trust with the sciences, and the fidelities of a natural order, apparently indifferent to faith-allegiance as part of the very integrity of religion? Were not the elements of wind and rain, of season and soil, the chemistry of laboratories and the processes of the good earth, all impartial *vis-à-vis* belief and unbelief? If there was no elemental sanction on being Christian, with 'the Lord sending rain alike on the just and the unjust', should not the political order be likewise ready for 'the un-restricted greeting' that Jesus commended?[10] Need the

< 129 >

slow retreat of establishment religion have been so tedious, the claim of some 'open arena' so arduous?

III

Yet there was meaning in that slowness. The reasons for the long obduracy ran very deep. Could power ever be safely 'secularized' if 'sovereignty belonged to the Lord'? If His created order had 'dominion-holders' over it, should not the political order be likewise in proper custody? If human vagaries were left at risk in the one, why not also in the other?

The statesman, however, is in a different category from the farmer, the politician from the engineer, the ruler from the forester. Here we come upon the supreme irony of all. Because power inherently 'corrupts' and because the 'governance of man' is territory quite contrasted with fields and orchards and constructions in science, politics lays unique claim on moral integrity and politics is the realm where it will be most at risk. The paradox works both ways. Religious faith alone must be the security of the political order: the political order will always imperil its religious guardian.

Or, if it is not to do so, the price for faith, as for human liberty, will be 'eternal vigilance'. For the liability of the power quest or the power-possession to corrupt the power-wielder is in no way diminished in the case of religion but rather intensified. Thus, added to the foregoing about the circumstance of power in relation to faith, is the menace of the temptation it presents. Concern for its doctrine may provoke it to panic, or draw it into false alarms and the loss of a sound perspective that puts its moral vision awry.

There was a striking example of this near panic at the outset of the Oxford Movement within Anglican Christianity in John Keble's famous sermon in 1833. Identified in retrospective as its starting point, the preacher's charge of 'national apostasy' on the part of the English State had to do with the recent 'secularization' of the Irish bishoprics.[11] By more wisely Christian lights there was every moral reason why they should be 'secularized', as serving a minority community at the harsh expense of an impoverished majority. Yet minds that coveted the continuance of state privilege and protection could only read the measure – with certain others at the same time – as 'apostasy' against which they would 'never cease to pray'. Their language was as alarmist as their emotion.

A random example has kinship with the Pilate/Caiaphas situation, except that in 1833 the State was not amenable to what a priesthood would seek of it by way of what was 'expedient', as gauged by its perceived 'interest'. Keble deplored a disappointment only because he pleaded a satisfaction. His faith was the less resolute in being the more petitionary.

< 130 >

It would have been better if he had applauded what his perceptions could only accuse. Self-interest had induced a blunting of moral discernment and the political order itself had been ill-served by false expectations of which religious faith was guilty. There have been many such examples in the story of Orthodox Judaism in the politics of Israel and of some U.S. Christianity in its manoeuvres with the White House, whereby both State and religion have been suborned.

Yet an irony persists in that tangled Keble sermon-story. For the Oxford Movement's apprehension around the de-privileging of the Church had impulse from the long decades of latitudinarian complacence in its recent story, when it had forfeited its authentic mission and the due awe of its liturgy and worship. In measure that complacence had proved the more damaging by rejection of the Methodist incentive it had disdained to heed. But a Keble-style renewal of the true priestliness of the English Church could not be well achieved by appeal to state protection of that status in erstwhile medieval terms.

There was also the corollary here of the emergence of new 'secular' factors of which a Church-mind needed to have more cognizance but from which it held aloof because the auspices were uncongenial or threatening to its familiar status.

If, in this example, the body politic has better relation to justice and right than the religious community, and thus the service of the latter to the former is muted, the price is paid in the integrity of religion. What when the situations are reversed? Or, if not reversed, where both faith and state are mutually culpable, as was manifestly the case between Pilate and Caiaphas?

Between them, and their like, expedience dominates the scene. Having an unpredictable Jesus out of the way was expedient for the preservation of the uneasy compromise between Jewry and Rome, by which a mutual aversion between them could be contained without the sort of wild catastrophic disruption which supervened four decades later. It was expedient for Pilate, concurring, to let it be so. He was an office-holder with a religion of his own, the inviolate service of imperial Rome personalized in his Tiberius. Office, like all power, is vigilant to perpetuate its tenure. Victim of the system as he was gave him no mind to victimize himself for some duty to transcend it. Pilate had already learned, in the episode of the banners he had brought into Jerusalem by night,[12] how stubborn these Jews could be. This enigmatic prisoner, this 'king' Jesus, might be expendable, a trifling incident readily forgotten, once the creditable details had been duly reported to his Caesar. Pilate could be 'Caesar's friend' in a 'Caesar's' way.

Even so, as the narratives disclose, there were moral reservations. There could be something also Roman in resisting vulgar pressure. These Jews might 'have a law', a curious figment about 'blasphemy' by which

< 131 >

this Jesus 'ought to die'. But was it one a bold Roman should implement, despicable as its enforcers were, forcing his hand as the only legal warrant-holder. What humiliation for an *amicus Caesaris*! Yet that sinister reminder of theirs about that very role – and in this dire scenario – tormented his mind.[13] There was no escape in exploring the alternative, via Nazareth, of 'Herod's jurisdiction', nor did the popular clamour allow of more equivocation, while the prisoner unmistakably ruled out 'king-ship' in any Roman sense, most king-likely communicating its reality in his own bewildering terms.[14]

The rationale of Pilate's final surrender to the intimidation of the expedient enshrines for all time the moral crisis of the political order, the power-dimension, in their betrayal of the ethical by connivance with their own subversion. In that New Testament situation both Caiaphas and Pilate were power and religion, coalitioned in either by the nature of their confrontation.

The faith-element at stake is evident enough. Caiaphas was annexing it to power in the vicarious terms of grim enlistment of Pilate to his Jewish ends. Judea under Rome's yoke would be Rome under Judea's will, as creed and power in one would successfully demand.

In so far as Pilate's Roman loyalty was religious, he served his gods in holding the Emperor's commission. Power was faith and faith was power. If conscience could be forfeit to the one it would conveniently be also victim to the other. Pilate must be applauded for whatever reservations he had about the sentencing of Jesus. They did honour to his Rome. That he let them be over-ridden was his and Rome's guilt and shame, no less, no more, than the guilt and shame of Jewry's Caiaphas in cajoling the verdict from Pilate's reluctance.

How strange a circumstance it is that the central faith-event of Christianity should have so direly coincided with a time and place where 'God's wrong was most all', amid all that 'crouched' at the door of human will and deed. Yet, perhaps, how fitly so.

IV

Two questions emerge. Must *all* be political? Can all ever not be? What then, it follows, must power mean to religion and what role has faith towards power? The dilemma of Pilate, read as representative every-where, lay between integrity and expedience. Faith with the first militates against power's innate bent for the other. Faith and power painfully share the same territory of society and structure, of action and conscience, of culture and the sciences.

It would seem to follow that religious faith must be dispossessed of power in its immediate exercise, only in order to be more dynamically

< 132 >

energizing it critically and morally. Faith unilaterally wielding political power coarsens its own soul, obscures its own moral vision and withdraws from society at large the proper right of political dignity. It must be a confession of cowardice for a religion to say that, unless we exercise exclusive political control, we cannot authentically be ourselves.

Such relinquishment, however, is far from meaning that it opts out of the business of politics, as if its relevance were now confined to rites and ceremonies and consisted entirely in devotions. On the contrary, it will be more truly engaged with it in the more appropriate terms of living faith, counsel, criticism and a sifting, probing moral ministry. Like the great Hebrew prophets, it will address the corridors of power the more tellingly by not occupying them. Like those Micahs and Hoseas, that Jeremiah, of their Hebraic generation, they may well seem to their politicos as in 'treason' to the state interest by the very honesty of their accusation of its deeds. Such reputation will be their vindication.

It will be so because they have not bartered with the corruption and the lures of self-serving office, which regularly plague and beguile those corridors of power. Their business will mean ensuring, as far as in them lies, an order and régime of politics, of statehood and suffrage, of discipline and debate, most consistent with personal dignity and the ready exercise of conscience, in bearing on the decisions and policies of the power realm. This will be believing citizenship in terms more pointedly Christian than any hankering after an earlier 'subject *qua* communicant' equation.

Faith as 'political' this way involves two other factors acknowledged. The one is its recognition of a now global situation; the other its current negotiation with a long tradition of history. On both counts this 'discrete'[15] relation of Christian faith to political power belongs with contemporary needs. Has there not been a certain obsolescence of the national state in the increasing globalization of economic factors, the information revolution and the technological changes making for an incessant co-mixturing of humankind? Such is no world in which religions should continue to endorse hostilities or connive with stark confrontation, as if humanity could only be right under their singular auspices and their religious rule. When nations, in their ever diverse emotions, are nevertheless constrained ineluctably towards some common 'good' survival, ought religions to continue to sanction their enmities and not, rather, sustain their peaceful mutuality by whatever resources of wisdom or 'maze-exegesis' they command?

But the corollary must be that they have long histories of abiding cultural identity with nation and location. Histories are not for emotional undoing, nor memories eroded from identity awareness. It follows that faiths 'discretely' political, in the sense argued, do not abdicate their traditional nexus with place and story. It must be assumed that some

< 133 >

primacy of historical faith can properly persist within a political expression or a nation state and enjoy a kind of 'seniority' among minority or
once 'alien' elements, provided that these enjoy equal political occasion.
In Anglican terms, this may well embrace some continuing measure of
'establishment', if only as a symbol that no political order is a law unto
itself, subject and accountable to none, ever and only the creature of its
own expedience.[16]

There is a third consideration worthy to bring home the other two. It
is that religious faiths may be too readily complacent or aggressively reac-
tive, in face of such co-existence in shared political responsibility. The
current urge to dialogue, the displacement of 'Divinity' (of whatever allegiance) by 'Religious Studies' too quickly superficializes both the inner
and the outer tasks of *confessio fidei*. It therefore ill-serves the political
ministry we have argued as now their vocation. For this means a livelier
possession of their possessions as to truth and conscience – hardly a time
for a quiescence in their content or their temper, such as some 'dialogue'
is liable to induce. The issue is a tangled one and reaches beyond the
present context but – by the same token – it is not one to be ignored.
'Dialogue' assumes – problematically – that things are somehow 'negotiable' between parties, given the necessary goodwill. That may be so, in
some measure, in the realm of 'meanings' as these are 'told' or 'held' in
doctrine, where many factors, like those of language and symbol examined in earlier chapters, afford 'space' for a more open mutuality. But
what of the sterner realms of revealed law, of 'commandment' rather
than the 'commendation', which must be a theologian's anxiety and a
lawyer's duty?

V

The onus of divinely promulgated law incumbent on the community
around some 'Sinai in Arabia'[17] must surely require a regime, a 'governance' committed to its rigorous enforcement. The Jewish law and
Roman arm to enforce it, we have already seen in play in the expedience
of Pilate. Only the Roman occupancy and his tenure stood between the
law and their own duty from it. It was its being mandatory which *in situ*
made them so deviously political.

Significantly, it was a law about 'blasphemy' as a capital crime. And
what is 'blasphemy' if not alleged violation of the divine law and so the
Divine Name? Jesus, as they saw him, had somehow pitted his personal
'conscience' against both law and Name.[18]

Any encounter, actual or implied, between 'conscience' and 'blasphemy' must imply that revealed law from God constitutes 'the theocracy
of heaven' and, therefore, implies a custodian 'theocracy' on earth to

< 134 >

ensure its sovereignty. To be sure, no such 'theocracy' is possible, since the custodian on earth will always be human and fallible. Thus Pilate's quandary over Jesus was none other, in essence, than the entire liability of human conscience – and so in turn of human institutions to the obedience of revealed law from God. Can any 'conscience' survive?

The issue has been most acute for Jewry and Judaism with their Torah and its Talmud, for Muslims and their *Shari'ah,* as alike in their legal and ritual provisions the mandatory obligations of their faithful. How should conscience, personal or corporate, handle that onus and how might political structures accommodate it? The questions belong where they arise and where alone they can be resolved. It is easy to see how 'God's wrong most of all' turns upon their answers – indeed on how or where 'wrong' is committed, whether in the rigour that obeys or in the obedience to conscience that rebels.

It would be honest, yet also naïve, to claim that – thanks to Jesus – the issue does not exist in Christianity, honest by virtue of the Messiahship in which he lived and moved, naïve because long generations of Christendom have lived and moved with a version of theocratic legalism, often grimly allied with the political order, its engines and sanctions.

There has always been a deep paradox about the relation of law to love. One might borrow an analogy from human physique. The body needs a skeleton frame and structure to function at all, but what these afford it will never be supple without the impulse derived alone from mind and will through nerve and sinew. For the New Testament, from Jesus to Paul and John, 'Love is the fulfilling of the law', thus neither its abolition nor its tyranny. Rather law is interiorized in the authority of love. Genuine love of neighbour in these terms – stemming from the love of God[19] – makes the *command* of law unnecessary yet critically retains its import in obedience. Thus it finds reconciliation between the necessity of law and the menace, otherwise, in its compulsiveness. For unless thus reined in by love, that compulsiveness leads into futility.

The futility of law in this sense has long been the burden of religious thinking. For law is 'futile' in its own ends, when it becomes only punitive, where its precepts and rulings have been defied. Requital may uphold its warrant. It only frustrates its intention in that its 'righteousness' is thwarted and its failure is manifest. Yet without courts that apply and penalties that enforce it, law falls down on itself in desertion of its task and renunciation of its trust.

In this situation of the force-prerogative[20] of law and the force-futility to which it is prone and liable, it would seem evident that law, in this territory of its meaning, belongs with the political order and never with religious faith. For the nation-state, or 'imperial' rule, is where the dilemma alone arises, inasmuch as common order and the public peace and moral justice require this legal pattern of things. But that pattern can

< 135 >

have no authentic place in the appeal of religious faith, despite the long centuries when Christendom and Islam saw it otherwise. To what dark perversions did they resort to enlist political force to the imposition of their 'lawful' ends and means, whether juridical, ritual or doctrinal.[21] This instinct to 'co-tyrannize' with political power recruited to its will was the negation of the very essence of 'love to God' and the religious role of conscience in His Name about how that 'Name' should be read.

The due role of such reverence for truth was to have religion bear upon the politics of the rule enforcing state in the critical quality of a citizenship which conceded the necessity of the state's role but schooled the discharge of it with lively criticism and constructive vigilance for compassion, justice and integrity. Only the utmost perversion of faith and love alike could think to recruit such power auspices for the enforcement of *Shari'ah* or Torah or *religio* for purposes other than those that duly fall within the purview of the political order in its liability for common good honestly pursued. All else, liturgical, conformist, traditional and spiritual, in these several 'shari'ahs' of the faiths, has no place in the power-wielding of the state. They belong only with the witness and the moral resilience of the faith itself, monitoring the political but not usurping it.

It is grimly evident that long centuries of Christendom and Islam have violated this understanding of faith and politics. Not content to care religiously, they have domineered politically, 'If you let this man go, you are not Caesar's friend' has a strange ring down those centuries. 'Friendship with Caesar' is requisite for the partisans of God according to the light by which they see the hand they play. Expedience avails for both parties. Constantine can serve the Church because the Church can serve Constantine. The Caliphates flourish with Islam: Islam fulfils the Caliphates – or however a like succession might be now.[22]

If, by contrast, the political order is relieved of such onus to enforce religion, it may the more genuinely fulfil its proper task. The faith-order, likewise liberated from the pretensions that belong with the exercise of political power, can the more honestly attain its true vocation as 'salt seasoning the earth'.

All returns us to the primacy of love to God and neighbour, where truly the writ of law runs but only in the interiority of a true discernment of its intent and the impulse to obedience which love alone supplies.

The Book of Leviticus – as its name implies – represents for all time a supreme model of an omni-present ethico-religious code to be imposed by due constraint. At its heart in 19.18 it has the central injunction of 'love of neighbour', while seeming to associate it with avoiding to hold a 'grudge against the children of thy people'. On the basis of Exodus 23.9 and Leviticus 25.6, that 'neighbour' might well include 'the stranger also', though all the 'woes' upon Moab, Edom and the ever-listed 'seven tribes', fit to be expelled from 'promised land, persisted. It fell at length

< 136 >

to Jesus of Nazareth to embrace Jew, Samaritan and 'Gentile' alike in an inclusive humanity fitted for a mutually human inter-active love. In political terms, this will be the most exacting and conclusive pattern of all, precisely in having only a ministry of conscience and vigilance towards the order of necessary, yet always only approximate, regime of justice with force and force for justice.

This will be the end of laws of apostasy, of papal decrees with civic intent, of recusancy fines and state sanctions on purely religious allegiance. 'Treason' can be only a political charge against a political crime – a principle under which neither William Tyndale nor his persecutor, the blessed Thomas More, would have paid with his life. Since 'perfect love casts out fear', then fear-mongering and its agencies have no place in the kingdom of heaven.[23] If it be asked whether states and corridors of power can ever have a 'conscience' – as consistent with their legitimacy they surely must – the answer will lie in the moral capacity of their citizenry's faith.

This primacy of love inside the legitimacy of law is not reached by the logic of reason nor achieved by appeal to goodwill. It obtains inside that other primacy of divine love to humankind. As John wrote, in the mind of the whole New Testament: 'We love because He first loved us' (1 John 4.20) in that 'love is of God'. The two commandments that sum up all others are inseparable. The ethic of the Gospel belongs squarely with its faith and both were rooted in the Christian reading of Messiah Jesus in the teaching and the Passion of that reality of 'God as love, manifest in the flesh'. In so far as there would be anger, it would be 'the wrath of the Lamb'.[24]

If weighing thus expedience, and Pilate conveys us to this conclusion in negotiation between law and love, between politics with power and faith with love, the conclusion in turn urges on the course of thought the honesty of a will to faith – the faith that takes and knows itself this way.

< 137 >

Chapter 11

AN HONEST WILL TO FAITH

I

In the heyday of a popular 20th century empiricism it was a matter of insistence that statements could only be proved and upheld by their verifiability. Since legitimate verification was assumed to be experimental and scientific, it seemed impossible to say, still less to mean, that 'God is love' or 'sin is original'. No longer the venerable 'queen of sciences', theology became the unhappy pauper outside an inaccessible market where no business could be transacted.[1]

At the close of the previous century, however, a certain William James had published a cluster of essays which he entitled: 'The Will to Believe'.[2] His academic and personal interests were deeply in the human psyche and in, memorably, what he later called 'The Varieties of Religious Experience'.

Here the idea of what might be encountered lay outside experimentation under a microscope or via the skills of the chemist and the physicist. Perhaps verity itself could defy the bounds of verification if these were arbitrarily contrived to exclude elements of experience to which they ought to be alert. He argued for 'the lawfulness of voluntarily adopted faith', castigating those so

> . . . well imbued with the logical spirit that they have as a rule refused to admit my contention to be lawful philosophically.[3]

His case was for a more 'radical empiricism' than the merely experimental type, one that claimed the right to think of issues in metaphysics that was not deterred by any limited verification principle. Hypotheses, if we stayed with them philosophically, so that they were barren of action and exempt from decision, left genuine living behind, however far they

< 138 >

might indulge and gratify mere intelligence. Indeed only 'a willingness to act irrevocably' gave the maximum 'verity' to a proposition or truth-conviction.[4]

There were dangers, as we must note, in William James' zeal for action, but real life was with him and, surely, the very nature of time. For time's flux means that, at length, abeyance of decision or suspension of judgment will be a verdict all the worse for having been only drift and delay. Procrastination arrives willy-nilly at a feeble choice. Time is inexorable and only admits of neutrality, if some uncommitted stance is deliberate and purposive. The rank empiricism which forbids theologians to think and theology to speak has wantonly circumscribed the whole business of living, has failed to appreciate that risks ventured before they are ever 'verified' are perpetually present in the fabric of life. They are also discovered to be in the very nature of love and truth.

Hence the study of a will to faith in any context of 'the wrong we do to God' – a wrong akin to 'the primal suspicion explored in Chapter 4. If faith is a response in the will, as well as being a responsibility of the mind to meaning, and if only each legitimates the other, then withholding of the will is a sort of rejection of God more harsh than intellectual demur. Atheism, if it has bothered to be intellectual at all, begins to be a manner of divine spurning. Since the volitional is inescapable, an unreadiness for faith becomes, more sharply, an unreadiness to love, and almost a self-exemption from life.

It would seem that, in point of fact, much scepticism or agnosticism is more an act of will than a conclusion of mind. If there is 'a will to believe', 'a will to disbelief' must be no less actual, if what is intellectual in the disbelief connives against what is crucial in the will. The situation is not, then, so much about 'halting between two opinions', as of 'halting over the other dimension', the answer of the will. Human life is like verbs in grammar which propose in the indicative but present themselves in the imperative. William James' 'maximum of liveliness' meant 'willingness to act'. When he added 'irrevocably' he was urgent to arouse his hearers, overlooking how a discerning prudence would be part of doing so, the risk-taking not taking leave of wit. The will to engage should not be blind to its own fallibility. We are not using the language of the gaming table. Rightly to deliberate is congruently to decide. Life's being is to be received.

Every 'will to faith' is thus an act of response. We can usefully take the argument further here by reference to an earlier philosopher of 'the World as Will and Idea'. There are two reasons why. The one is that he saw how a centrality of will on the human side had to mean a responsiveness to 'will' in some cosmic sense reciprocal to ours. The other relevance lies in his intense sense of the gloom and doom when he pondered any 'willed' relation to our earthly predicament. For if, by

< 139 >

contrast, we read the 'will' behind our whole scenario here in the Biblical Christian terms of benediction,[5] we are close to the sacramental reading of the world, as the clue alike to our willed context and our willing selves.

The philosopher is Arthur Schopenhauer (1788–1860). The heavy accents of his pessimism became highly influential for successors like Friedrich Nietzsche and poets of the malignant scene like Thomas Hardy and essayists like Winwood Reade. Thus reference to Schopenhauer suggests that belief in God and being positive about the world are one and the same. For, to his mind, a 'world by divine idea' is hardly a 'world accordant with human minds'. Has it not long been the main theme of atheism that our significance, if hard to identify, is no desideratum if and when we do?

Must it not further follow that honest faith in God is, in fact, 'an ode to joy'? No, the Schopenhauers will say, 'a threnody to pain'. The burning question, then, either way, becomes that of honesty. Either way too, 'God's wrong will be most of all' – that of a guilty futility or worse, if the pessimists are right, that of false accusation if they are wrong.[6]

That issue about honesty on our part in any 'will to believe or disbelieve' has aspects to which we must return. But has 'good faith on God's part' not been present all the time, in chapters on 'divine integrity'? If how we humans conclude, as between some Schopenhauer and the author of the Johannine writings, has to stay among our options, then at least the crucial role of the will in faith or unfaith is the more evident.

II

Seeing how far intellectual agnosticism, on its own showing, opines or insists that so many open questions remain and that to be honestly persuaded about faith is impossible, and seeing, further, that living necessitates decision, does not the will come, either way, into a decisive role? It is manifestly so in the narratives of the Gospel. 'Wilt thou . . . ?' was the issue, with believing ensuing as the experience of acting. 'Follow thou me' in Jesus' invitation could hardly be construed as a case in logic, though answering it in its inviting terms might soon become such, but thanks only to the volitional response.

How often does the word 'must' in the New Testament have to do, not with capitulation to argument, but with devotion to a purpose. Jesus 'must needs to through Samaria' (John 4.4) not from conning a route map, since other routes to Jerusalem were feasible, but from a set of the will anticipating Samaritan encounters. 'I must work the works of Him that sent me while it is day' (John 9.4) was about vocation reading a destiny. The primacy of the will lies behind so many attainments of discipleship, as it underwrites the mountaineer scaling his peaks or the pioneer strug-

< 140 >

gling against the odds. It is often that ventures languish, marriages collapse, trust erodes and compassion falters, not for any logic that has undone them, but for lack of will to see them through. 'One here *will* constant be' in John Bunyan's prison song is not about mere futurity. It has to do with present resolve, 'come wind, come weather'.

It is as if such set of soul, as it were, believes to see the divine will behind all else, acting to give being to a mastery of the cosmos and presiding in terms that duly warrant the trust on which we proceed and, so doing, truly have it so. Then 'volunteers' can indeed be a verb in the sense that a posture of human will, firmly held and translated into active courage, confirms the goodness of the world in corollary with the goodness of God. Such 'have believed to see the goodness of the Lord in the land of the living' (Psalm 27.13), and, so believing, evidence its being so. This, then, would be the Biblical, Christian antithesis to Schopenhauer's view of a cosmic enmity to humankind reciprocal to the (his) set of human will that took it so.

In entire reversal of this dark stance was Robert Browning, asking – of divine love in the goodness of the world: 'Has it your vote to be so if it can?' He was too diffident in phrasing things that way. It had been better had he asked: 'Is it your will to make it so in finding that it is?' For how much of 'will' enters into the very word 'mind', as in the New Testament call: 'Let this mind be in you which was also in Christ Jesus'? (Philippians 2.5).

Such 'letting' is a willed attitude that reproduces in living what it registers in mental conviction. This is no 'Believing makes it so' in Hamlet's laconic sense. It is that minding wills its content into life.

All this, however, in an integrity matching what it finds. It is readily clear how this criterion of truth could hold attraction – and temptation – for apologists about religion and the rationale of a 'will to believe' that might be less than fully honest. Might the will to faith be commended as having desirable consequences for personal living? James was deeply interested in those 'varieties of religious experience' and so conversant with their effects in individual lives, whether benign or adverse.

A will to believe might then be advisable on grounds of psychic composure, peace of mind, a focused set of the soul freed from intruding anxiety. Might not 'the peace of God' surpass all misunderstanding and thus be desirable on that account? Should it not matter, however, how much of real understanding of the faith was present in the psychic benefit? Was faith well perceived as a crutch for cripples? Were churchgoers justified in so doing because the 'good feeling' involved was salutary elsewhere? 'What works is right' – always the Achilles' heel of pragmatism – needed to stay to ask: 'Works at what cost to integrity?'

The art and practice of prayer might well enable people to offload their troubles, singing: 'What a friend we have in Jesus', but not to shed

< 141 >

their own tasks thereby, nor de-value their theology by missing other lengths of that 'friendship'. Honest belief is more than soul-comfort. It is well to remember that the root meaning of 'the Holy Spirit the Comforter' is 'the Holy Spirit the Fortifier'.[7] The pragmatic case for Christianity does 'God in Christ' much wrong by its strange reductionism.

These benedictions in the will to faith are less suspect, more legitimate, when answerable also to the perplexities of the mind in faith. With the honesty of their own scrutiny, they need the other honesty of faith's intellectual integrity. If Christian faith in God is *ipso facto* faith in the goodness of the world as parties to one divine intention, then – on both counts – it is duty bound to take real stock of the near despair of an Arthur Schopenhauer in the seeming enmity to humankind of the 'cosmic will' with which our mortal will has to relate.

Adjusting his ideas from his heritage in Kant, Schopenhauer read beyond phenomena to 'the thing in itself' which phenomena concealed, and on which sense-experience is based and, with it, the desires, avoidances and impulses of will by which we decide. These were no sufficient clue to the 'cosmic will' itself, as something scarcely conscious of us or the world in its own self-sufficiency. All here is a far cry from the Biblical concept of a 'wanted creation'. The cosmic will with this 'idea of the world' takes no cognizance of the necessity in our wills to cope with what we find and know.

On other grounds also – those of despair about human nature and history and the horrors of recorded time – Schopenhauer was possessed by a deep human pessimism. The necessity to will held out little promise of success. Suffering was almost the norm. Empiricism might make for pragmatism but action could never solve the riddle of existence *per se*. If we could bring ourselves to take actual delight in the world and cultivate it by our *will* to such faith, it could only be in spite of what decried it, and mean some odd capacity to think even misery a boon. One might, he thought, find solace in the appeal of beauty, in aesthetic experience that entailed no active burden. Otherwise, one should reconcile to the implicit dissatisfactoriness of life and perhaps surmount it by the ascetic discipline of sainthood.

Schopenhauer serves eloquently enough in present context. He represents a deep stream in western, indeed in Buddhist, literature. Thus he points graphically to the sharp contrast it presents to a Christian sacramentalism. It requires all 'will to faith' to search its own honesty in believing in such urgent contrast to any Schopenhauerian perception of what is at stake between the will behind the world and the wills of mortal humans, its conscious indigenes.

For the Christian mind, alike theologically and liturgically, holds a blessedly sacramental view of that human scene. It reads there the intimations of invitation, of hospitality, of a purposiveness evidently

< 142 >

reciprocal to our mortal needs, our mental and physical capacity for wonder and utility. It presents a 'dominion' for which these capacities are meant. Their fruitions prove how dependable the partnership remains. For it has a normalcy on which we can rely – a normalcy by which we can sustain and repair the strange vagaries from which it is not exempt.

These, the re-assuring experience of our sciences, have continually excited and equipped the celebrations of poetry, music and the arts. These have been its salutation by a sort of answering gratitude, as of a reality not taken callously for granted, but reverently for given, given so generously into our pioneering hands. For pioneers have been requisite in what has ever been a cumulative story. Thus history as well as nature proves a second sacrament, posing to us the question: 'What hast thou thou didst not receive?' Our creaturehood within this created order is a long theme of generational indebtedness.

Hence 'things grateful calling the grateful' could be a formula descriptive of human experience, panoramic and intimate, when duly greeted in these sacramental terms. Hence again the propriety of letting worship of God the Giver focus around some Holy Table where human community might gather and, in 'bread and wine' – those elemental products of a natural order under human hands – signify a human guesthood inside the hospitality of God.[8]

Hardly anywhere in Christian devotion has this dimension of worship in its grateful meaning been more steadily expressed than in the 17th century writings, poetic and reflective, of Thomas Traherne, priest at Credenhill in the diocese of Hereford.

Thy Soul, O God, doth prize
The seas, the earth, our souls, thy skies;
As we return the same to Thee
They more delight thine eyes,
And sweeter be
As unto Thee we offer up the same,
That as to us from Thee at first they came.

'You never enjoy the earth aright,' he wrote, 'till the sea itself floweth in your veins, till you are clothed with the heavens and crowned with the stars, and perceive yourself to be the sole heir of the whole world, and more than so, because men are in it who are every one sole heirs as well as you.'[9]

Such minds 'give all things an infinite esteem', regarding the world as 'the visible porch and gate of eternity', where every day is an event and a sacramental possession. They have willed to turn the tables completely on the stern and sombre distrust of such significance in that temper of mind in Schopenhauer's 'will and idea', where 'will and idea' consorted so darkly.

< 143 >

III

But is this Traherne style of sacramentalism duly honest? How well does it cope with human perversity and the disorder in nature? Could it be more than a wishful aberration, blithely eliding all that must belie it? Was not a Schopenhauer simply renewing and deepening that primal suspicion breathed in Paradise itself? The privilege of creaturehood had its reservations which longer time would bitterly accentuate. If there was a beneficence at the heart of things, it was sadly ambiguous or tragically inefficient. Sacramental gratitude ought to fold its wings, heed the discord in its music and give place to lamentation. Its happy credentials were dubious, its greeting of experience dishonest. If there was 'cosmic will' at all we must read malevolence in its 'idea'. Arguing from amenability to man opened more problems than it recognized. For all the burdens and miseries of history lay also 'in its wake'. Thomas Traherne should concede to Thomas Hardy.

That the goodness of the world can only be a comforting illusion must always remain a poet's human option. Yet, in defence of a sacramental hospitality given and received, it is right to note that only on something like its premise can a divine reproach be argued. Either way 'some will to let exist' is present, unless all is pointless, vacuous, illusory – a 'vanity of vanities'. Given 'will' and 'idea' undergirding all that is, these can only be reproachable, in some Hardean sense, because we take them as malign, they violate what ought to be. We need the moral good in order to identify and incriminate the immoral wrong. The God we must accuse has failed to be the God we could approve. Total enigmata apart, and allowing *any* human standpoint, the charge of evil against God assumes His intention ought to have been good. Thus, indictment rests on an assumption it promptly disowns and the *problem* of evil cancels out.

To be sure, the pain and distress, the anxiety and burden, of its incidence abide all too tragically, putting experience at a loss how to endure, but not the mind with a case to arraign. For the latter could only arise in the essential goodness of the world, a goodness which our tragedies interrogate only because effectively they call it into question.

It is this which makes a situation in which the necessary goodness of the world has to be an act of faith, but not of blind, unthinking faith. For just as the 'cons' are not to be ignored, so the 'pros' stay vulnerable as innumerable despairers witness. Mere logic will never resolve us. The will to believe must decide but without evading the burden of its mental role.[10]

Clearly, in this situation, the motivation of the will must locate away from the hither and thither of assessments of the natural order, the physical sciences, the space-probers and cosmologists. For it is among these

< 144 >

that the doubtings and misgivings arise about any final good or even about any discernible significance at all. But where, otherwise, could it locate? If nature and physical history are cripplingly ambiguous for the theologian, will human history, political and social, prove less so? Will not any attempt to locate the proof of goodness there be even more adversely taken? For it is in the long and loaded human story that the evidences of good and gentle meaning are most ruthlessly obscured and wanting.

Might not that be the very reason for seeking there the index to an honest faith, one that precisely in centering there acknowledges where the crux must be? It is assumed throughout these chapters that issues lie, not in external nature alone or in a scientific empiricism, but in what some have termed 'the anthropic principle', or the entrustment of that natural order of creation into human creaturehood whose annals thus become its story too – and not its story only but also its crisis and where its anguish belongs.

It is in this way that historic Christian faith identifies a quality in history where the ultimate case for the 'goodness of God' and so, in turn, for the goodness of the world, is verified for wills that fully read and learn it.

It has that quality as also an event – some might even say an episode – though one against a long protracted vintage. Its sharp particularity may deter many from its recognition. While its character strongly addresses and resolves the human will, its honesty does not disguise how far from merely logical proving it necessarily remains.

Perhaps the quality it has, as event from character, might best be told in question form, since compulsion is never its language. Might it be that the goodness of God in the world we will, sound-mindedly, to learn and greet is there for our recognition where the New Testament arrives at 'God in Christ' (to use the Pauline summary) in whom we encounter 'the Christ in God'? For we only have the first as the insignia of the second. The one derives from the other much as Shakespeare the play derives from Shakespeare the mind, or Beethoven the music from Beethoven the musician, or – in credal speech – the 'Son begotten of the Father'.[11]

This 'Christology', narrating or expressing 'theology', houses – we might say – in the time and place of history the credentials of God. Chapter 6 has already explored its Biblical hinterland and heritage. The concern now is with its invitation to the will, how it might resolve for us the inconclusiveness of all prior or subsequent terms of honest theology.

At least this Christhood in the Jesus' shape of New Testament history, in the measure of the Cross, the dimensions of Gethsemane, is close to the realities of the human scene, the travail of its contradictions. That cannot be an ultimate divine goodness that obtains only in the realm of law, with its punitive measures in face of its violations, subverting or frustrating the good it has in view. Can the power which law must invoke – as noted in the previous chapter – amend or retrieve the evils it addresses,

< 145 >

and only can address, in powered terms? Can there avail for this wrong-doing world a forgiveness so trite or sanguine that it confronts no guilt and stays majestically effortless[12] and so measures no wrong? Must there *not* be a forgiveness deep and wide enough to reach where our guilts and griefs must take us, if the will to faith in a divine goodness in creation and its history has any kindling ground at all? Might such ground be comprehensively realized in fact and faith in a single but representative event?

It is just such a one that New Testament discipleship believed itself to have found. The Passion of Jesus as the Christ, against the background of long Messianic hope, had enacted the meaning of the goodness of God.

The sharp particularity in such a faith will offend many, the 'here and now and thus' of one Good Friday telling of a 'Father, forgive them' *vis-à-vis* 'the sin of the world'. Yet drama cannot avoid to be dramatic. Or perhaps, as two Shakespearean figures had it: 'Our tears are not yet brew'd' about 'so foul and fair a day',[13] as that dark Friday was. Only when there we recognize our world do we there recognize our God – 'the God who was in Christ reconciling it'.

We noted in Chapter 8 some of the issues for language and its words in expressing this faith and how continguous it is to the meaning of a good creation and to the re-making there of this our human nature. The metaphors that occupy its theological telling wait to be taken over in the commitment of a willing yet not willful faith. This means – as noted earlier of ministry – that they may enrich and ripen in the using.

IV

There are three elements in such a will of the self to faith. All will to believe – we might say – is the very *argumentum* of selfhood: it stands in the nature of courage; and it conforms to the nature of love. Or, put negatively, it does not indulge in evasion of life: it will not be forfeit to cowardice; and it makes full proof of love as the due facing of risk. These three belong together and can here describe what an honest faith in a sacramental world and a divine redemption learns to live by.

Thus understood, the will to believe, while alert to the limits and constraints of an intellectual theology, is no party to the wildly irrational. Its concern for decision takes thought into the very sanctuary of the self as 'doer' and 'deed'. Some of the factors that make decision imperative in the narrative of life have been noted at the outset. The old Latin sense of *argumentum* can help us take them further. The English 'argument' has come to mean only what is 'debated', 'refuted' or 'contested' in order to reach what is conclusive in these terms of logic and reason. But what of the 'argument' of the self *per se*, its 'theme' or 'plot'? Is there not an *argumentum* in a sculpture or any work of art, a statement it is making by its

< 146 >

very being how and what it is? The play *Hamlet* is an *argumentum* about indecision, that 'one particular fault', just as *Macbeth* is an *argumentum* on the theme of compelling, unbridled ambition that 'o'erleaps itself'. In both cases they are themes of selfhoods. They are what these characters are 'meaning with their being'.

This kind of will-based wisdom is a far more crucial argument than debate about abstracts of metaphysics or the pros and cons of a practical pragmatism. It is more urgent even than the 'unexamined life' of which Socrates mused as 'not worth living', if he meant a bare inquisition rather than life without a theme. The fluctuations of circumstance will be more testing than the ebb and flow of philosophical debate. The difference between them will be 'one here will constant be' and some concluding Q.E.D. 'What do you make of it?' will be a question which might ask about a riddle or an enigma. It will be far more crucial when posed by a life.

There is something here that answers to the concern in Chapter 7 for the centre of gravity of faith as doctrine, given that the self is the centre of gravity of faith as conviction and commitment, so that believing informs belonging and both decide behaviour. The soul is no longer rudderless but resolves to be its own helmsman with a read and readable compass. Thought becomes intention and intention action. In any event, we 'live and move', but in Christ 'we have our being'. 'Lord, in Thee have I trusted, let me never be confounded' is not praying never to think inconclusively about this or that. It prays ever to think conclusively according to 'the mind of Christ', as one so possessing his part as to be possessed by it. Analogy from the theatre is not inept, since 'all the world's a stage', and faith is belonging with the 'plot' as Christ-allegiance writes it. There is neither drift nor thrift in such devotion, only a settled argument about the self.

Yet argument it has been, duly circumspect and logical. It is not rightly told in any terms like those of Blaise Pascal's gamble with a wager or even Søren Kierkegaard's 'leap of faith'. There is no bravado in its sanity. For, like the courage and love we must come to, it is wise enough to reckon with the odds and navigate the waters. It senses and has read elsewhere the folly of 'unchartered freedom' which 'tires' both mind and heart.[14] It knows that heart-commitment is the saving prerogative of faith, letting the unbanished attentions of doubt be present from the margin to its set of soul.

Doing so, it pays honest tribute to mysteries that must abide around it. Its discipleship is not shielded, when to be undismayed would be a kind of treason. Rather it lets perplexities be contained inside its larger confidence in what they leave secure. There is thus a willingness to trust what persuades the soul in Christ to undertake what, elsewhere, continues to oppress the mind. This quality of faith would only be evasive if those persisting problems were ever susceptible of intellectual resolution. Their

< 147 >

being not so – and life being requisite of policy – we take life in the affirmative that holds a sacramental trust in 'God in Christ'. The life that sought an answer has become the answer that it sought. It reads its New Testament credentials and owns them subject to long scholarly scrutiny but finds them divine insignia on which it can rely.

Doing so is one aspect of its open courage. For it is aware of whether anything mortal and temporal can have the eternal indwelling its transitoriness, or whether the historical can ever under-write the theological. There is something, however, in the very nature of life itself to suggest such intercourse. Or why else would wonder appertain or mystery arise?

Just as there is much cowardice in brash unbelief, so there is much courage of another sort in faith-conviction. 'Will you hold that faith against the world?' was Robert Browning's question when he took Christology so energetically into his poetic lines.[15] It was more than rhetoric and banter, however wary we need to be about baptizing him. If often he stayed thus in the interrogative, it was because indicatives were real and actual. Christianity did indeed exist and he would reckon with its secret.

But in this 21st century we are not Victorians. The many are distant from confessional believing. They see the Church as distant also from their mind-set, the assumptions by which they live. Press and media express a cognizance of life too often vulgar, crude and listless, one obsessed with gain or sex or glitter or the trivial. There is something sordid in the air. We seem to have lost the wholesomeness where a playwright sang:

> The west yet glimmers with some streaks of day.
> Now spurs the lated traveler apace
> To gain the timely inn.[16]

Nor, for the most part, do we see and treat old age this way.

It therefore takes a certain courage to believe in a life-enlisting Christ. Or folk are confused – as noted in Chapters 7 and 8 – by the sundry terms and symbols in which the enlistment would recruit them. 'How hard it is to be a Christian', Browning cried with less reason then than happens now. Popular indifference fosters a different kind of reluctance to believe than does perplexing confusion. It suggests that 'things worthy to be looked into' need merit no such care. A sort of *consensus non fidelium* or *Adeste, non fideles* mark the commercial recognition of 'the Saviour's birth' and Good Friday is fused, with Easter, into a bank holiday weekend.

All this needs no down-heartedness, only the 'valour' John Bunyan came by during twelve years' captivity in Bedford prison. It also needs a clear perception of the nature of the secular and its urgent separation from an outright secularity. There is much that is elusive and deceptive about the notion, so fluid these days, that 'there is only us'. 'We are on

< 148 >

our own' with no divine referent, no 'great Redeemer, holding with his powerful hand', or 'feeding us (incongruously) till we want no more'. Devour hyperbole apart, we are 'on our own'. As we have seen in Chapter 5, the theme of creation makes it so. What we puzzlingly call the 'secular' is our creaturely *imperium*, our privilege in the trust of a comprehensible creation. 'Let us make . . . ', 'have thou dominion . . . ' – these are its watchwords. There is a divine 'over to you, you humans' about all things economic, societal, political and privately personal. These are not spheres of divine meddling or disruption. A certain normalcy prevails and admits of our arts and sciences, our structures and our scenarios.

To think, in this sense, of the 'secular' is also to know it for the potentially sacred – a character which will turn altogether upon our human attitude. Because it is 'ours', it is not withdrawn from 'God's'. It is only more critically there. Biblical faith in final Christian form does not evade this task of sanctity. It summons to it. It is when this calling is refused, denied, repudiated, that a total 'secularity' is reached. The distinction from the (other) 'secular' is vital. Christian faith means to make it real in deed and fact as witness to a sacramental goodness at generous risk in human minds and wills. Faith, then, should not deplore and fail this world of the secular as merely 'worldliness', but embrace the common task of an inherently sacred meaning. Hence the central role of the Christian sacramental, alike in worship and in life, in sexuality and society, no less than in the sanctuary. The Lord who 'looks for us in the sanctuary' (Psalm 63.3) would have us know that sanctuaries are everywhere.[17] It needs courage to 'hold this faith against the world' of outright secularity, where it is so far the ignored truth of the secular itself.

But the needed courage here has another test as well. Scholarship around faith sources and faith's story may deter it, popular negligence dismay it and cultural attitudes oppress. But, beyond all these, is the inward doubt of private sinews waiting for the race. Resources in the self may falter like an empty well. Some aspects here will belong in Chapter 12 with the fear that somehow Christian faith is in danger from morbidity. How shall we be, or stay, adequate to this 'high calling', how surmount sustainedly these counter pressures? The answer again can only lie in 'Him we have believed' as 'able to keep' our living in Him. For, both ways, such believing is always 'trusting' and the sufficient answer to all apprehensions must be: 'I believe in the Holy Spirit, Lord and Giver of Life.'

It is here that what we are calling a strategy of courage yields to the authority of love. For the ways of faith are so far akin to the ways of love.[18] Love yearns for that by which it is endeared. It rejoices in the society where it is exchanged. It senses how the sacrament of the body prompts the desires of the heart. It delights to belong where it responds. It is spontaneous in commitment when sure of its adventure and both features abide in its authenticity.[19]

< 149 >

What ripe analogies of 'the will to believe' are here! Faith is an answer only because it hears a question: 'Lovest Thou Me?' If it lives for the question, it lives by the answer and all else in Christianity concerning the goodness of the world is had as well.

< 150 >

Chapter 12

THE WOUNDED NAME AND ITS KINDRED SERVANTS

I

'The wounds of Jesus' have very central place in Christian devotion but in those terms find no mention in the New Testament, where – apart from John of Patmos – the only 'wounds' are those of the Jericho road (Luke 10.34). Can we ever move, as Christian theology has long been bold to do, from 'the wounds of Jesus' to the wounds of God?

If so, that parable of the stricken traveler from Jerusalem, who may well have passed by, or through, Gethsemane, will be where to begin such venture of faith. For the story of how he 'fell among thieves' and came into desperate need of a rescuer with his 'oil and wine' is a classic tale of the two dimensions at the heart of all human experience. 'Bound in the bundle of life' in the human condition means that the vulnerable has somehow to be countered by the vicarious. The mutuality of these two – if the second responds – is the very essence of human society and, if the second is lacking, its deepened pathos. Experience from day to day is filled with jeopardies taking their toll on the well-being of body or mind, potential inimities on every hand, and society ever prone to mutual damage or distress in the traffic of the world.

This ever vulnerable life harbours the past and stores for the future by the power of memory and so cries, on every present count, for the amends a future might afford. But some cleared name in time to come is no reversal of a present wrong. The urgency of acts vicarious answering the griefs of the vulnerable is the more intense. The grim end of *Hamlet* leaves him crying for a vindication for which only a fellow-suffering can avail.

< 151 >

O God, Horatio, what a wounded name,
Things standing thus unknown, shall live behind me![1]

Can this friend Horatio be proxy beyond the royal death for the burden of the tragedy, be vicarious in the telling and so the sharing of the story? 'A wounded name' must find a wounded voice.

Our theme throughout of 'God's wrong most of all' has held a double sense. Chapters 1 and 4 are occupied with divine reproach, with God as 'ever blameworthy', loaded by human enmity with alleged guilt about the world, about the savage vagaries of nature, about the pattern and policy on heaven's part of the entrustment of the cosmos to human management with so dark a sequel of miscarriage at our hands. So runs the negative, the agnostic accusation of the divine in creation and history.

By its very nature this verdict against God as humanly 'wrongful' implies that all *should* have been otherwise. As we have argued, there can be no negative indictment that does not imply a positive liability. But can the tables be turned? If God is thus vulnerable to evil charge, may He also be vicarious in sustaining it? If so, the animus in the accusation must become the substance of the suffering it inflicts. In any event, what we popularly charge against God recoils upon ourselves. For it has to do with human wrong and wronging. His 'wrong is most of all' only because of what is maximal in ours. Given that, divinely, there can be no 'holding guilty' without occasion for the vicarious, can the divine nature undertake positively what our wrongs assert negatively? If we, in our humanity, have so insistently made God vulnerable, both by word and deed, by blame and by act, may He have made Himself vicarious in the ultimate expression of His Name?

Such long-suffering, via an original Hebrew, came squarely into Christian theology. That 'He bear them and carried them all the days of old' (Isaiah 63.9) was the story of their being His 'burden' (cf. Isaiah 43.24: 'you made Me to serve with your sins'). This Name, or 'character' of YAHWEH had disclosed itself to them in the experience of exodus which had told it (Exodus 3.10f). That divine Name was understood to have emblazoned itself in the dual 'place' of land and people in perpetual unison.[2]

As *makrothumia* this divine 'long-suffering' passed into the New Testament conviction as the ultimate measure of 'God in Christ'. It signified a mind capable of far-distant reach. Intriguingly, the *makros* word tells in Luke 15.13 'the far country' into which the wayward son wandered and where the wistful mind (*thumos*) of the father reached for him in the sort of yearning that allowed him to visualize an unchanged, unresentful home to which, at length, he might 'arise and go'.[3]

Can such quality of heart belong truly with transcendent power? Did

< 152 >

not Proverbs (18.10) describe 'the name of the Lord' as 'a strong tower', not a gentle heart? Yet it is at the heart of Christian conviction that the only honestly divine Name is a wounded one. The 'God in Christ', that is God in this Christ-told way, is defined so in 'a man of sorrows and acquainted with grief'. The place where Christians worship is where Christ's feet trod and they took him to Gethsemane and beyond.

It is there we read and possess 'the knowledge and love of God'. Ours, then, is a theology prizing the principle Samuel Taylor Coleridge was often commending to his friend Wordsworth, namely that 'all truth is human truth'. It proceeds from a perception of the world as purposive, that purpose enshrined in the natural order and that order answering to our intelligent human cognizance, thus yielding (in human truth) the moral realm of values spiritual.

These obtain among us as both ethical trust and spiritual liability, but their authenticity for us lies beyond their manifestation in our human realm. They address us humanly because they dwell beyond us divinely. They are 'human truth' in our experience, yet their capacity to be secure from us belongs with their divine ground. What we may not deny and do not ordain is our experience of their divine affirmation.[4]

Since in this sense 'human truth is divine truth', we can see already a situation where 'sovereignty divine' is invested in human cares and realms. What is 'of God' is 'with us' and vulnerable to our wills and doings and, in that capacity, therefore, vicariously at stake in our wrongs.

This reading is confirmed if we state the argument the other way round and move from the ever present notion of 'agnostic' theology (or its secular corollaries) which hold any divinity there be utterly immune from connection with the human world, whether as to a language that might describe or a relevance that might relate. The Infinite must be unknowable and indescribable, aloof alike from word and deed. But such 'absentee divinity' makes a contradiction in terms. To distinguish the divine from the human so utterly that no inter-analogy is allowable is not only a negation of all worship. It perverts the truth that, if the word 'God' is to mean at all, it must mean relationship. The truth of God has to be 'human truth' but in divine measure, so that the limitations of the finite are clues to an infinite awareness of them. Having them so points to the condescending quality of divine transcendence. Via the values inherent in the human sphere we are alert to their incidence in God. Our involvement in them in time and place witnesses to how they are divinely His.

This conveys us to measures of divine magnanimity in no way incongruous or incompatible with Omnipotence but fully present to it. We can perceive a divine/human relationality where the vulnerable and the vicarious, so deeply present among us mortally, belong also there eternally. All the glad springs of love and forgiveness, self-giving and

< 153 >

compassion that flow so dearly among us have their rise in the divine nature they fulfil.

The defining New Testament term is *kenosis* as Paul has it in Philippians 2.7–8 in his exposition of the Christhood he reads in Jesus and the Cross. This is no 'emptying' as if the content is no longer there. Rather, it only seems to demean itself in the more truly being itself, more truly present because of the situation it has faced. There is a partial analogy in the long English love-affair with what is 'royal'.[5] But what is 'royalty'? Only the kingship will define. Crowns will be known by the manner of their wearing.[6] Could the divine show its referent in a crown of thorns? What, there and then, was so much part of our humanity was, in that very capacity, insignia of the divine. 'God's truth is then human truth' in the double sense of 'a wounded name'. It is double because it belongs where we are, in guilt and grief, and with God engaging these in the love that they necessitate. As Robert Browning came to say: 'The creature' does not 'outdo the Creator', instead the Creator outloves the creature.[7] His truth is our truth, costly because apposite, eventful because eternal. It is where we fully know ourselves in wrong that we learn God in His sovereignty, with Jesus crucified as the place of both.

Just as – given any Biblical doctrine of creation – divine indifference is a contradiction in terms, so also is any notion of divine immunity.

II

Per necessitatem Christianus is thus the logic of our discipleship and discipleship celebrates it as also being a 'necessity' about God.[8] Yet an incredulity persists from many sides. Such theology has altogether betrayed transcendence. A suffering omnipotence takes paradox too far. Also what seems to many intellectually impossible is to others emotionally bizarre. Moods like those that afflicted Thomas Hardy resist and resent the strange alleged pre-occupation of Christian worship and imagination with wounds and nails and blood and tears, and all these as ever notionally associate with God. No 'human truth' framing a theology could be of that order. How many in the throngs that greeted the late Pope John Paul II on his frequent travels paused to wonder about that crucifix he carried with its tortured figure on a ghastly rood? Was this the utmost emblem of the pastoral meaning he brought?

It is clear that the New Testament itself has a deep reserve around the physical anguish of Jesus' Passion. The Christian piety that later gathered round its vivid detail found no warrant in the antecedent Scripture. Plainly the Gospels and the Letters would have us see the Cross rather than the crucifix in the gaze we bring to 'survey its wonder'. Christian architecture has loved cruciform churches, its art enshrined the unadorned Cross for its fuller adoration. The unburdened symbol is in better line with the text and its deep reticence about the physical horror of death by crucifixion.

There is no doubt there about 'God's wounded Name' but yet a telling silence around the literal agony of the wounds. The garden of Gethsemane is more explicitly narrated than the sequel. There is a wide disparity between the terse 'there they crucified Him' with 'soldiers sitting down to watch',[9] and Isaac Watts' language of 'dying crimson like a robe' that 'hangs o'er his body on the tree'. 'Him there' suffices.

It was – we may assume – faith in Jesus' Resurrection with explains this reverent silence, drawing a veil across the narrative as the lurid might have told it. But not only so. 'Being numbered with the transgressors' was no light obstacle to any heralding of Jesus as Messiah – and in that Judeo-Roman context. How could a common felon be so hailed in a constituency loaded with Jewish sense of scandal and Roman measures of the ignominious? In a 'crucified' there lay offence to the pride of Greek culture and harsh affront to Roman dignity.

The faith about Christ crucified had to be 'placarded' (the term they used) in its essentially redemptive terms of 'God's wrong for our righting' not in its incidental harrowing physical detail. What sacred memory held of 'words from the Cross' sufficed to comprehend the anguish in the larger relevance.

That deep reserve and its emphatic focus on the central meaning of 'God in Christ', of 'Christ' this way, could not preclude the preciousness with which centuries of devotion would clothe it. Nor could it conceal the great theological meaning of the vulnerable – and so the vicarious – in the Christian experience of God. On the contrary, its very focus made it the more provocative of confrontation with the wisdoms of this world, with the protests of human self-sufficiency and the zealots for divine immunity as the due safeguard of omnipotence.

Yet the consensus of the New Testament remained undeterred by the weight of the resistance to its 'folly'. And so essentially it has remained through all the vicissitudes of faith story. For how can bringing together omnipotence and immunity ever make theological sense? By the latter the former would have no role for its power. All-inclusive power would be meaningless in complete excuse from its exercise. God's competence, in relation to the 'human truth' of things, could only be proven by engagement with it. If, as R. S. Thomas has it, writing of the *Furies*: 'All nature acknowledges the crucifixion', so – far more – does human nature and so, in turn, divine nature.[10] That the Cross confirms, because it pre-defines and fulfills 'the power and the wisdom of God' abides as the anchorage of Christian theology.

Nevertheless, because of the 'man of sorrows' image it for ever carries, to which piety gives full rein in hymn and art and icon, the critics too

< 155 >

abide, the accusers stay entrenched. Can this measure of things human and divine be more than wishful and perverse? What lunacy was it that could set pity and piety, forbearance and compassion, at the heart of human society? How did the meek in fact 'inherit' the earth? Must not the 'hunger and thirst after righteousness' be fated to stay that way in any realism about the hope of it in this power busied world? Did this whole 'beatitudinal' *mise-en-scène* belong any further than an idyllic hillside in Galilee, surrounded even there by zealots against landlords and miscreants of the Barabbas sort against an occupying power? Could Jewry be so emasculated as to forego its priestly cunning and political expediency, or Rome tell its imperial self in Jesus' terms?

To think 'God's wrongs' dramatized in a gross human occasion of them and yet read that occasion as redemptive grace 'bearing them' 'for us and our salvation', was surely to violate any 'majesty on high' and betray all sane Messianic hope. That the heart of the New Testament Gospel was so far scandalous only makes the more remarkable the confident education into it which the first disciples underwent in the aftermath of such unnerving events.

The aphorism 'All truth is human truth' certainly belonged to them. For everything around that Cross and Passion turned on real encounter between divine wronging on our part and human righting on God's part, and both in the one story of the Christ.

III

Yet the incredulity which greeted those first perceivers of divine/human truth has variously persisted down long centuries despite what are dubiously called 'ages of faith'. It found unusually vehement exposition in the mind and pen of Friedrich Nietzsche (1844–1900) to whom it is well to turn as a classic representative of hostility to Christianity. He had earlier rebelled against the Lutheran piety of his childhood nurture and developed a disdain for what seemed to him the enervating, crippling, de-virilizing impact of the Church and its Gospel on human society, creating the submissive 'herd-instinct' and shaping a race of 'camels' 'cameleered', made submissively to accept a 'load' of destiny they should refuse.

He had been deeply affected by Schopenhauer's 'will to power' but yearned to defy the pessimism, the conflictual doom to strife and ultimate futility to which it led his mentor. Nietzsche would both accept and reject the 'nihilism' – accept it as a logic rightly drawn from theology and devout tradition (since these had now become relics) but repudiate it in the quest for – if only in an able few – some positive 'will to power' to escape the negativism and achieve some ultimate liberty of 'the joyful science'.

< 156 >

This theme, as Nietzsche shaped it, was not susceptible of rational argument as in a Socratic converse of minds. He could only romanticize it in passionate aphorisms which made fervour itself their plea and case. The strange irony around the vehemence was that the ardour of his self-projection in the mastery of his meaning precipitated the final collapse into a madness lasting eleven tragic years, in which he came into desperate need of the tender compassion he had reviled.[11]

Another irony of his philosophy lay in how it would be distorted into a racist Germanism he would have utterly disowned. Christianity has not capitulated to his denunciation. Indeed, it would be fair to read beyond his hate for it a sifting of its abiding authenticity. For Nietzsche's fascination with it was no small part of his animosity towards it, as the titles show of *Ecce Homo* and *The Anti-Christ*. If, as he claimed, 'the answer was to discover a religion in which it was possible to love',[12] it would be compassionate to think that this was the goal of his mind and its anguish and see him as a soul in positive intent. One might forgive the extravagancies of his style and self-conceit, and allow them a benign intent.

For, if firmly rejecting his 'over-man' ideal,[13] the Christian mind can readily concede that dogma can make for 'camels' meekly loaded and church authority be like some 'cameleer' riding a submissive beast. The closed mind needs to open to its private tasks and seek the grace to do so, while a caring church must know that spiritual 'nursing' is also an honourable calling, since not all are capable, whether *in media res* or in tragic grief, of the price of greatness. Nietzsche meant to alert and prepare human society for a final 'God-forsaken-ness' ensuing on His demise. This was the 'nihilism' that demanded the new resilience of an undaunted 'will to power'. Faith would have to say, inside any such 'nihilism', there would remain the un-forsaking divine presence 'going after all such that were lost until they were found'. In such divine venture (how could it fail to be incarnational and Cross-like?) God would be known as the provenly present and the 'nihilism' be the forsaken thing.

Yet Christian faith may only thus refute Nietzsche, while first reckoning well with how God may be made a crutch for cripples and how these must then be the loving liability of an honestly strenuous faith. We might all lapse into madness by failing to realize that only one 'meek and lowly of heart' could ever invite to 'rest' 'the weary and the heavy-laden'. The fervid passion in Nietzsche's thought conveys back to the redeeming Passion of the Christ of God where that invitation lives. Nietzsche read 'God's wrong most of all' as requiring His abolition, which had happened anyway. Christianity had made 'the wronging' supremely the costly evidence of His unfailing reality. The paradox in Nietzsche advantages that faith.[14]

His youthful brilliance in philology had given him a rare insight into

< 157 >

words. His genius deserves longer study for which there is here no context. Might there, by his lights, be a play on meanings in the English word 'excruciating'? Such verbal subtleties were much to his mind. The word has to do with what causes pain and anguish, but these derived that sense from their 'crux' as a cross. It was this, with the other, that he wanted to 'take out' of life, to expel from all thought whether of God or tradition, no less totally than he expelled all metaphysics from his mind-set and all familiar ethics from his 'beyond good and evil'.

For, as with some warrant he saw it, the Cross in Christianity had inspired much pseudo martyrology by a false idealization of suffering and the cult of self-immolation.[15] Early and medieval Christianity had glorified the hermit, the anchorite, the lunacy of a Simeon the Stylite perched on a pillar. All such was escapism and a denial of the genuine will to be as essentially, a 'will to power'. 'We would be where no storms come' told the false lure of the monastery, where minds were overtly concerned with self-offering, when 'self-realizing' should have been their ruling passion. If Jesus was not 'the pale Galilean', as the poet thought, he had 'conquered . . .

> . . . the world has grown grey from Thy breath:
> We have drunken on things Lethean, and fed on the fullness of death.[16]

From plight traced to the cult of 'the Saviour', Nietzsche meant to rescue those who could see how deceived they had been. In the process he would abolish the 'God' who had done them this wrong. It was a strange gloss on what 'God's wrong' meant in Shakespeare.

A sane Christianity could well heed Nietzsche's strictures without accepting the negative venom on which he was bent. It was well to take the point of less than robust personhood and register the fallacies into which excessive devotional self-depreciation could lead. Yet here the tables had to be turned so that 'the hiding place' became 'the come wind, come weather' of an only physically imprisoned John Bunyan. Have some Christians been heavily pre-occupied with guilt, only the more to invoke and magnify divine grace, as answer to a helplessness within? Has the promise and prospect of heavenly rest diverted the will from immersion in the earthly tasks, postponing all solace? Ought Christianity, in fact, to disqualify us from realism about the actual world and from courage in taking it as it truly is without comforting illusion?

The final answer to these and other aspects of an indictment of this Nietzschean order is to rebuff them with the courage of faith, with the courage that faith perennially demands and enables. The role of suffering – on the part of Christ – at the core of that faith must be rightly known in its authentic significance as divinely redemptive. All has to do with that ancient prescript about not 'taking the Name in vain', distorting the very nature of things believed in the very shape of believing them. Taking it 'not in vain' means its imitation.

The point was before us in Chapter 8 with its 'Versions of Vocabulary'. If we externalize to God the events of salvation, by the same token we absolve believing souls from the lesson in their very nature. To have the Passion of Christ a mere artifice, a transaction of legal formality, is not only to falsify history but to forfeit its due summons to discipleship. Examples of both abound on every hand. Not to understand *how* 'God was *in* Christ' is to misconstrue how the meaning must be in us. Otherwise, we open the door to many kinds of selfish interest in its 'benefits', whether of comfort, or complacence, or refuge, or satisfaction, in their self-serving incidence.

Thus, for example, Irish figures in the sundry IRA struggles and martyrdoms drew analogies of 'greater love' to sustain their spirits. Patrick Pearse wrote for his mother a poem about Mary having also 'offered her first-born son as a sacrifice to the Father'. Echoing such mis-reading, Wolfe Tone also had a Christmas poem which ran:

> O King that was born to set bondsmen free
> In the coming battle help the Gael.[17]

Such vested interests, apart from distorting the story, miss how the claim of the crucified Christ to discipleship is to no cause but His own. The theology that makes from Christ's Cross an arbitrary borrowing makes of His 'benefits' a mere strategy in another cause, a cause utterly different from His own.

The point here at issue, as we saw, is made by the place of Holy Communion at the heart of Christian worship, of 'bread and wine' as its focal sacrament. It starts by asking – since for his disciples and indeed for all history this Jesus was unforgettable – why anything 'in memory' was remotely necessary. Was not the Cross etched in them indelibly? Words and sermons might well pass but in that case different means to recollection, like some formal recital, would be fitting rather than a table spread. Then on reflection, it emerges that the 'bread and wine' to be partaken had not to do at all with *whether* their ever memorable Jesus would be 'remembered'. They had only to do with *how*. There would need to be identity in the meaning, inside the recalling. Such has always been the point in *anamnesis*, 'Take this and divide it among yourselves'. Participation there had to be. Credence, recollection, retrospect or only devotion in those terms – these could not suffice. The Cross, so internal to 'the sin of the world', was truly interior to the being of God and must come to be so likewise in the nature of Christian discipleship. All self-serving from it, in the shape Nietzsche so grimly arraigned, must be subdued to self-enabling allegiance.

< 159 >

IV

Hence 'Its Kindred Servants' in this chapter's title. It had always been assumed that there could be a collective meaning to the calling of Messiah. To be sure, in the very nature of the event, 'he trod the wine-press alone'. Discipleship could not then follow but, alike before and after, 'ye are they that have continued with me in my trials' was the counterpart of the Jesus story (Luke 22.28).[18] In the very nature of redemption in its Christian eventuation, those who know themselves redeemed must become in turn redeemers. The meaning of divine grace is not truly known as pardon unless it is understood as education. Forgiveness has not become an experience if it is not also adopted as a policy. A collective emulation of the once for all redeemer belongs to its once for all and singular expression in the Cross.

Is not the meaning here explicit in 'the Lord's Prayer', every clause of which is rightly understood as Messianic. There are its insistent plurals – 'Our' 'we' and 'us' – with its repeated 'Thy', and every plea relating to a Christ anticipated. How, then, still apposite as prayer in retrospect to the Christ event? Surely as concerning its appropriate perpetuation in the being and the doing of discipleship. We saw this point already as the active *anamnesis* of the Eucharist.

'Hallowed be Thy Name' is the timeless cry, the present continuous tense of faith: likewise 'Thy kingdom come'. 'Thy will be done' – so wrongly often prayed resignedly, as if 'Thy will be suffered' – calls to active partnership with what that once for all achieved on its abiding 'Good Friday', 'as in heaven' being there defined with onus 'so on earth' as then 'on earth' it was.

Is the Messianic less far to seek in 'Give us this day our daily bread'? Hardly, if we see through the problem there has always been around *epiousios*, so often translated 'daily', though we have already said 'this day', where the words are plain enough. That rarest of Greek words *epi* and *ousios* has 'futurity' about it but is it 'tomorrow' about bread? Why then this day? Is it about some 'coming bread' at all in any 'eating' sense? What of 'bread' as 'destiny', as in 'My meat (bread or food) is doing the will of Him that sent me' (John 4.34)? Could that *epiousios* be 'the coming *one*', the Messiah once awaited? The disciples might have read the words as the immediacy of the Messianic banquet but for steady warnings about long times ahead. Realistically, it meant 'let us be partakers in Messiah's task'. For all sequential time and faith must it not now mean: 'Let us daily live on Messiah's diet, and make His service our daily bread'?

Then 'forgive us . . . as we forgive' only states the abiding principle of Christ's redemption – the divine vulnerability in its ever vicarious virtue reproduced in the day to day Christian. All is confirmed in 'Do not bring

< 160 >

us to the time of trial but deliver us from the evil.'[19] Even when wrong is at its seeming maximum let us not be overwhelmed therein. The ascription about 'kingdom, power and glory', whatever its source if appended, congruently follows.

The theme of Messianic emulation stands in its own truth, whether or not this reading of the Lord's Prayer be allowed, powerfully as it does, to reinforce it. Christian faith reads in 'God in Christ' – in 'His Christ this way' – the sure sign of divine vulnerability to us humans, 'God's wrong most of all', and that 'wrong', thus both ours and His, manifestly 'endured' and 'undertaken' in vicarious suffering whence grace and mercy flow. These cannot honestly be our theology if they are not also our ethical pattern, our 'likeness of mind' in life and conduct.

'Vulnerable omnipotence' is no contradiction in terms, however dimly to many it must seem so. There was always the vulnerable in the will to create and be involved with a creaturehood on which, so evidently, an autonomy had been bestowed. There was a vulnerability on the height of Sinai, as proven by the obscenity of 'the golden calf' at its foot. Divine law was always fraught with human obduracy, beset by human perversity, caught between the dilemma of retributive assertion and a punitive futility. History showed only too grimly how righteousness must concede defeat, if its only resources were the law's own majesty, its armoury of requital. 'Throw away Thy rod', George Herbert's poem advised.

> Let wrath remove. Love will do the deed:
> For with love stony hearts will bleed.

But what if they do not? Should we perceive only a worthier divine failure, since man 'frailties hath'? May grace succeed where law so plainly fails? Perplexity persists, if not for the poet in context, certainly for an honest faith. He pleads:

> O my God, take the gentle path . . .
> Thou art God, throw away Thy wrath.[20]

Either way, 'the wounded Name' of God is there in history. We cannot believe in love and deny its suffering. If the 'wounds' abide either way, and He is God by dint of them because of us, which will be the more God-like – their avenging or their being experienced as love's burden? Is not 'the gentle path' the logic of 'Thou art God'?

V

It would be true to say that the *lex talionis*, the 'law of retaliation', has been the bane and blight of all human story. 'Leave room for the judgment of

< 161 >

God: Avenge not' have not been precepts of power, nor policies of society. We studied in an earlier chapter the inevitability of power structures in the traffic of the world and both the currency and the menace of the expediencies by which they operate. Jesus' 'Resist not evil' could not be read as a 'pacifism' that supposed these never present in the scene. Rather, by reason of their ever present reality, the human world needs the non-pursuit of anger, the open absorbers of hurt, the saving practitioners of forgiveness. The fact of being vulnerable will always be our lot in the ever battling, ever fluctuating world: the will to be then vicarious will always be our crisis of decision. The vindictive or the generous will be the vital option and on it turn malignity or benediction for 'our neighbour' and society. The right option will be no cowardice or door-matting of our self-hood. It will rather be the courage of a divine obedience, an occasion of the ongoing Messiah of God, the corporate peoplehood of God translating 'as in heaven' to 'so on earth'.

Such quality in our humanity can only be inside the like economy of God. For the seer of Patmos, no stranger he to a cosmic *lex talionis* of dire visions, trumpets and swords, it was 'the Lamb' he saw 'in the midst of the thorne'.[21] Where 'God's wrong had been most of all' in the vulnerable/vicarious Christ, all surmise, misgiving or perplexity as to some ever blameworthy, ever oath-worthy deity had decisive answer. The love-worthiness of God, of 'God in Christ', had borne the blame. In the worship of that 'wounded Name' the necessity of love pledged us to be and stay its kindred servants in the utmost meaning of ourselves.

< 162 >

NOTES

Introduction

1 William Shakespeare: *Hamlet*, Act 1, Scene 5, the cellar where actors, prompters, musicians gathered and the nether regions of the Elizabethan universe.

2 'Ultimacy' being the Christian corollary of Biblical 'unity', seeing that Gospels and Epistles are committed to the radical enlargement of divine/human peoplehood by the ready admission of those hitherto excluded as 'the Gentiles'. This faith can readily co-exist with how Judaism now reads its unbroken private continuity with God.

3 More than invoking it trivially in jest, the term – at the heart of all these chapters – must cover all false usages in word or deed that denigrate or flout the integrity of God.

4 'Mental and manual' in that all human 'empire' must move from the first to the second, pursue the second by warrant from the first. All our technology – by a cosmos enabled – is the fruition of the mind and an extension of the hand.

5 The issue here pre-occupies Chapter 3. Unity is not counting out all idols, so that only God is left, who was never among them. It is not about counting at all. Idols matter, not because they are plural and many, but because they challenge, contest, refuse the divine sovereignty. Unity consists in the capacity to be undefeated in the end.

6 Where the intensity of the singer's awareness of God breathes in the depth of his cognizance of the self, his wombing, his shaping, the sheer mystery of his coming to be – all within the divine foreknowing but turning on the human parenthood.

7 Inasmuch as the will and the way to 'make poverty history' across the globe seems fated to fail by reason of the ever demanding claims of growing population where poverty is most acute. Is this not 'making poverty history' all the time?

8 The Asian tsunami in December 2004 alerted an urge to develop early warning technology and apply it to the Indian Ocean area and make still more effective study of the earthquake potential of the sea-bed.

< 163 >

9   The 'covenantal' character had its exclusive, ethnic expression in the self-awareness of Jewry as 'a chosen people' in a land meant expressly only for them. That Sinaitic 'covenant', however, transpired within an earlier Noabid 'covenant' which assured a like tenancy of mutual people and place across the earth.

10 This unison of creation and incarnation is evident in the Prologue of the Fourth Gospel and in Paul, e.g. in 2 Corinthians 4.

11 Echoing the theme of e.g. Psalm 35.27 and Isaiah 53.10 concerning 'Messiah which translates into New Testament celebration of divine 'good pleasure' realized in Christ, and 'associates' of 'good-will'.

12 Yet something oddly like it is present in notions of 'infallibility', or 'immaculacy', or literal 'transubstansiation' or Biblical 'inerrancy' added to the heart of the Gospel for 'better ensuring' of its validity, seeing there is something like the risk of perjury if it be otherwise.

13 *Panourgia* is most used in an evil sense as both artful and unscrupulous. It was alleged against Paul by his detractors. He may have felt that he was its victim at their hands.

14 The Hebraic yielded the 'price', 'blood', 'ransom' and redemptive language: the Greek that of Christology and 'incarnation', while something of Roman hierarchy, law and structure passed into the shaping of 'ministry' and 'authority'. It is noteworthy, however, how far these also penetrated each other. The long tradition in the Hebraic scheme of 'divine agency' in prophethood augurs the Messianic and thence Christian ministry, without which classic Christology, for all its different verbal vintage, would have no theme. Dressed in 'letters of Hebrew, Greek and Latin', Christian faith had a far sharper task when it told itself in far distant worlds of culture.

15 Nietzsche's entire philosophy, so liable to misconstruction, needs to be read in the whole context of his biography and his long, last decline into a desperate need for compassion. How far was he responding to paradox with paradox? How was it that he could write in *The Antichrist*: 'The answer was to discover a religion in which it was possible to love'? (Section 24). Was he then yearning for Christianity in the very act of rounding on it so furiously? See further Chapter 12.

1 *God – Ever-Blameworthy: Ever Oath-Worthy*

1   Oliver C. Quick: *The Christian Sacraments*, London, 1932, p. 81. He adds: '*Mere power is mere potentiality and potentiality by itself is just a long word for nothing.*' Power in no context is itself vacuous. This matter of 'omnipotence' is central to Christology. See Chapter 3.

2   Seeing that 'monotheism' is never rightly about 'number', as in arithmetic, but always of sovereignty. The whole thrust of Islam against false worships is not about 'counting them' as plural but about 'discounting' them as real or operative. That Allah is God alone matters because Allah alone is God. In *Tawhid* ('Oneness') we neither add nor subtract. Hence 'that God is One' has to pass into 'Let God be One' – 'Thee alone we worship: on Thee alone we rely' in the *Fatihah*.

3   William Ernest Henley (1849–1903) published a *Book of Verses* in 1888

included the well-known 'Invictus' – The 'undefeated' – 'captain of his soul', and 'master of his own fate'. He had his share of adversity, to be sure, but a mood prone to be at odds with life. If all was so bitterly menacing why should 'the shade' be so unwelcome a Buddhist might enquire?

4 F. R. Higgins' 'Cradle Song', in *Poems of Our Time, 1900–1960*, ed. Richard Church *et al.*, London, 1959.

5 Fiddlers and the gallery might be frivolous or noisy otherwise than from their instruments, while one single organist at the keyboard could be more controlled. But for Hardy's love of his choirs, see 'The Choirmaster's Burial' in his *Collected Poems*, London, 3rd ed. 1932, p. 502.

6 The key verses are in Surahs 21.16 and 44.38. Divine 'purpose' in creation is rooted in the privilege of delegacy with it as entrusted to humankind in their status as *khulafa'* or custodians of earth's amenability to their wits and skills. Whereas D. H. Lawrence averred that 'man was the mistake of creation', the Qur'an sees us as the clue to it. See Surah 2.30 and its relevance through all these chapters here.

7 Cited in Tom Paulin: *Thomas Hardy: the Poetry of Perception*, London, 1986, p. 109. There is plain bias in the 'grocer' gibe and, for all his leisurely sojourn in Florence, Browning was far from being an 'optimist'. His 'Christianity' was scrupulously interrogated against self-deceit.

8 *Collected Poems, op. cit.*, pp. 112–13, 261 and 307.

9 *Ibid.*, 'The Death of Regret, p. 371.

10 At the heart of *The Dynasts* is the sheer 'loneliness' of Napoleon's egoism.

11 Thomas Hardy: *Collected Poems*, London, 1932, p. 60. 'The Impercipient', 'this bright believing band' of worshippers in their Cathedral, with whom he 'had no cause to be'.

12 A. E. Housman: *Collected Poems, and Selected Prose*, ed. C. Ricks, London, 1988, 'A Shropshire Lad', Stanza xlviii.

13 Chinua Achebe: *Arrow of God*, London & Ibadan, 1964, pp. 284–5. Two earlier novels *Things Fall Apart*, 1958 and *No Longer At Ease*, 1960, had borrowed from W. B. Yeats and T. S. Eliot notable phrases carrying tones of western disquiet about any religious integrity and human meaning. Achebe was a pioneer of the African novel in English, interpreting Nigerian dimensions of the same near Hardean travail of social existence in its private quality as local culture made it. Ezeulu is the priest of Uhu and, as such, no more than 'an arrow in the bow of his god'. Yet he is against 'ways of the new age' (1.17) and feels like 'the priest of a dead god' (p. 197) among the encroachments of the missionaries' 'other God'. There is also a subtle issue as to 'authority' between the 'god' and 'his priest'. Cf. the comment (p. 266): 'A priest like Ezeulu leads a god to ruin himself' – what of theism's 'custodians' likewise, Muslim, Jewish, Christian?

14 *Ibid.*, p. 285.

15 For a study of Abu-l-'Ala al-Ma'arri and of his 20th century admirer in letters and blindness, Taha Husain, see my: *The Tragic in Islam*, London, 2004, pp. 178–92.

16 Louis MacNeice: *The Strings are False: Unfinished Biography*, London, 1965, pp. 115 and 172.

< 165 >

17 Winwood Reade: *The Martyrdom of Man*, London, 1872. It was remarked of him that, in respect of Tennyson, 'Tennyson saw more clearly because he saw more largely.' Reade would hardly have written 'In Memoriam'.

18 Did he mean 'fated' (divinely made to be so by dint of a crooked body?) or 'resolved so' by his own response to that condition, like Edmund 'standing up for bastards'?

19 William Shakespeare: *Richard III*, Act 4, Scene 4, lines 303–4.

20 The point raised by historians about the 'repute' of this Richard, and the complex views of scholars over variants in Shakespeare's text, do not affect the argument in ethics. The drama moves within the ethical tradition, either way.

21 Such language has become frequent in the late 20th century with users like A. N. Wilson and Richard Dawkins, in slighter sequence to the more serious musings of Friedrich Nietzsche on 'the death of God'.

22 'Suffering' in the older sense of 'letting' or 'allowing', while still retaining the sense of something 'undergone'. The point is a vital one due to recur later.

2   *Shakespeare's Dramatic Mind and Art*

1 Una Ellis-Fermor: *Shakespeare's Drama*, ed. Kenneth Muir, London, 1980, p. 29.

2 It is in Shakespeare the expertly dramatic/poetic unison of action and imagery, and that imagery natural as well as verbal, which engage the viewer as if moving with the character in the thrust of the plot. See below.

3 John Milton's closing conclusion to his *Samson Agonistes* where he used drama as if also a sermon. In *Hamlet* or *Macbeth* we are drawn to 'care' with no remission in 'dismissal'.

4 Una Ellis-Fermor, *op. cit.*, p. 26. The lines from *Macbeth*, Act 1, Scene 3, lines 138. What tries to be briefer about God, as in the Islamic *Shahadah*, is liable to be thereby in default – a danger to which Shakespeare puts us on our guard, if ever, for example, we ask: 'Where is God in *Hamlet*?'

5 'Taciturnity' may seem an odd term for a mind and pen so fertile in expressive imagery and poetic fervour, one so gifted, as the Sonnets tell, in intellectual debate and the capture of a passion. Yet, in his leaving the lessons of his drama to the comer to them, it applies. The town-crier shall not speak his lines.

6 Among the liveliest studies of Shakespeare's imagery is that of Caroline Spurgeon, with that title, Cambridge, 1965, if with the rather lame sub-title: *And what it tells us*. See chapters viii, ix, x and xv.

7 Here, doubtless, is the whole moral problem of eschatology, and the nature of *post mortem* retribution. As for 'revenge' among the living (Hamlet's 'cross') all turns on how truly 'vicarious' – and so 'redemptive' – humans can be. See further, Chapter 12.

8 William Shakespeare: *Henry V*, Act 4, Scene 1, lines 291–3, 298–9.

9 The two final Surahs, 113 and 114, known as 'The Refuge-Seekers'. 'Whisper' and *waswasa* are onomatopoeic words in each language – what stealthily insinuates sinister ideas and impulses in the 'cellars of the soul'.

< 166 >

10 It is noteworthy that the four major tragic plays bear the name alone of the central focus of all else. No 'all's well that ends well' or 'as you like it' for these dark, heavy-laden places of the human self.

11 Being Gertrude, no mother with a daughter to yield or deny and already herself in a demeaning marriage. We are no longer in the History Plays with dynastic interests so pre-occupying in Tudor times. Shakespeare is in wholly tragic muse beneath all surface politics and inside the human self.

12 See the penetrating study of *Shakespeare's Doctrine of Nature*, by John F. Danby, sub-titled: *A Study of King Lear*, London, 1948.

13 It is well to realize how long, in and after the 18th century, the play was given a happy ending, by popular demand, with the reprieve of Lear and Cordelia.

14 And the one as only index and 'progress' to the other. It is likely that exonerations will plead: 'I *did* nothing wrong', rather than admit to 'what I am becoming'. Cf. Paul in Romans (7.24) crying: 'O wretched man that I am . . . ' Or Oscar Wilde in *The Picture of Dorian Gray*. The point is relevant in that, in his time, Wilde was never described as *being* 'homosexual' but as *doing* homosexual things. There has been a strange shift late in the 20th century between the two usages.

15 How frequently have theatre-goers, watching *Othello*, almost risen in their seats to shout warning and protest at the tragic speed of his gullibility, his credulous surrender to Iago's wiles.

16 It is significant to note the many references to 'offence' and offending in the corpus of the plays.

17 We cannot 'unstring' this bow, without abandoning all else.

18 This double sense of 'to carry and to carry away' is exactly that of the Greek *airon* in John's Gospel 1.29. See below.

3 *Comprehending Divine Unity*

1 All turns here on the basic Islamic concept of *Shirk* and of the *mushrikun* who commit it. The root idea is of Allah seemingly being made to 'share' His divine status with pseudo deities who then 'participate' in the worship, veneration, credence or invocation due only to Him. The frequent translation 'association' is unhappy in that, while telling these meanings and emphasizing 'remoteness', it implies doubt of divine 'association' with the world. While other aspects of the Qur'an take due care of nearness, mercy and presence, Muhammad's preaching situation demanded this rigorous 'dissociation' of Allah from daily phenomena, with sad consequences for the 'feel' of faith. The inclusive relevance of Allah must surely survive the ousting of the daimons. The issue only matters here for its bearing on divine unity as only real in sovereignty and involvement.

2 Murad Wilfried Hofmann: *Journey to Islam: Diary of a German Diplomat, 1951–2000*, Leicester, 2001. Born in 1931, Hofmann became Muslim in 1980 and married a Turkish wife. His strictures on Christianity are those of one who has not duly reckoned with what it holds. His entire neglect of the theme of divine unity having any relation to our human perversity is perhaps its largest feature.

3 *Ibid.* Delumeau is cited on pp. 156–7. Perhaps one might recall the 'tradi-

< 167 >

tion' of the great traditionalist Muslim, *Sahih*, Book 1: 'When a man calls his brother an unbeliever the criticism recoils upon himself.'

4   See note 1. There is discussion of what might well be called the divine humanism of the Qur'an in my: *A Certain Sympathy of Scriptures*, Brighton & Portland, 2004, and also in *Am I not Your Lord?*, London, 2002. That title is the Qur'an's own question to all humankind, of great significance as being divinely put at all. Concern here, independently of inter-faith discourse, is simply how divine unity and human perversity relate. The inter-faith aspect can illuminate but should not impede.

5   It is, of course, rooted in the Judaic 'God and His people' formula. If this had its source in a historical tribalism, it issued into a fascinating divine/human nexus in which, however, sadly no other 'tribe' might share, even as an aspiration. 'God and' is plain enough in the Islamic Creed or *Shahadah*, if only as something like a colon between 'God and His Messenger'. Christianity would be disqualified in lack of 'God and His Christ'. How the subtle 'and' works in all three contexts it differs profoundly between 'people election', 'messenger employ' and 'the Word made flesh'.

6   It seems important to note that the three dimensions which belong to this Judaic conviction about YAHWEH and His Jewry are the three identical constituents of all self-aware peoplehoods, namely birth or breed, territory in tenure and memory with story. These are the universal Who? Where? And Whence? of all human ethnology, geography and history. What made Jewry unique was the intensity with which they read their experience.

7   'Heirs to the Sinaitic' in terms of its threefold incidence already theirs but without those insignia, like circumcision and the ritual (as distinct from the moral) Torah/Decalogue which Judaism cherished in its necessary self-esteem and self-presentation to the world.

8   Thomas Traherne: *Centuries, Poems and Thanksgivings*, 2 vols. Ed. H. M. Margoliouth, Oxford, 1958, verse and prose celebrating divine blessings in the natural order. Or, as Wordsworth has it: 'The human form to me became, An index of delight,' and only so because of how the senses related into nature's realm of wonder and surprise, when – as for Charles Lamb – every day was an event. George Herbert wrote and sang much in the same glad vein.

9   Echoing an observation in Colin Turnbull: *The Lonely African*, New York, 1963, p. 157 on the problems of translation. How an African language rendering of John 1.1 ('In the beginning was the Word, etc.') ran 'At first a Word came and the Word came together with God and the Word became the God' as it would read if translated back into English. What it would have inwardly meant to the African hearer would have been: 'In the beginning there was a great argument and the argument came with God and the argument entered into God.' There is deep significance here. For truly human perversity – at odds fiercely with God's will and law – is an argument that enters into God, His being and His response.

10 The name and 'existence' of Allah were known already to the Quraish of Mecca. The Prophet's own father had been named 'Abd Allah some four decades before Muhammad's birth. It was not about some primacy among

< 168 >

many gods that Muhammad cared. It was Allah's sole, utterly exclusive sovereignty. Hence the sharp negation in the Creed, that *la ilaha*, the 'la' which grammarians call the 'la' of absolute negation. 'There does not exist any deity but . . . '

11   See Note 1. The analysis there needed to be made because the root idea of Allah's non-association with the daimons, to whose power (or malice) phenomena were attributed in that pagan world, often suggested Allah's non-association also. Situations in nature – and notions about them – have a durable persistence in the human imagination. Animism was a very powerful illusion which then needed great emphasis to overcome, often at the cost of God's presence also. Driving out the demons needs the immediate entrance of the rightful Lord.

12   This raises the intriguing question as to how – and how far – the content of a revealed Scripture is conditioned by the time and place it addresses. Much turns for intelligent exegesis on this factor. For discussion in the case of the Qur'an see: *A Certain Sympathy of Scriptures*, Brighton & Portland, 2004, Chapter 7.

13   The point is well made in A. N. Whitehead: *Science and the Modern World*, Cambridge, 1926, pp. 15–16, where he writes of the confidence in reason which took theologians into complexities of metaphysics and which he sees as having stimulated an emulation of their probing rationality in the realms of investigative science in sharply empirical ways. Contrariwise, it must be acknowledged that established religious authority did much to harass and deter the sciences (as Copernicus and Galileo knew to their cost). But this hostility stemmed from the vested interest of ecclesiastical prestige and fear for the collapse of authority, as if honest faith had anything to fear from pursuit of human truth. But therein lay a hard lesson only reluctantly learned.

14   Since 'divine unity' must mean that nothing is exempt from the range of intention of a creation entrusted to, and shaped to the skill of, a human 'subaltern'. But see the caveat in Note 13.

15   William Shakespeare: *Julius Caesar*, Act 2, Scene 1, lines 69–70, used in a somewhat different sense from that meant by Brutus.

16   See Surahs 21.16 and 44.38. The 'intentionality' and so 'meaningfulness' in creation is a vital, precious truth of Semitic theism as, at the same time and for the same reason, of a serious humanism. Because all was not 'meant in vain' makes 'taking God's Name in vain' a veritable blasphemy. For 'all that is is holy', always so yet, paradoxically, only so in our reciprocating handling.

4   *That Primal Suspicion*

1   Oscar Wilde: *De Profundis and Other Writings*, 1996 ed., pp. 98, 130, 155. He wrote (p. 172) 'every human being should be the realization of some ideal'. The will to art demands to be 'achieved', translated into act. This can lead to the insistence – about everything – 'what we think we must pursue', no will should be left un-acted. It was also this way with his homosexuality. What is 'made real', i.e. actual, 'done', acted on, is 'right'. To suppress is to deny. If this be a text for the artist, it is close to disastrous for life in general. We are close here to the point of 'thou shalt not eat . . . '

< 169 >

2 There was no need for 'hypocrisy' under duress in Mecca. Feigned allegiance was a menace in the very success Medina attained. *Zann*, then, is not about 'suspicion' of Allah but only of pseudo-allegiance.

3 The passages are reinforcing the overall affirmation of a genuine human vocation in the habitable, negotiable human scene. The passages are in Surahs 21.16 and 44.38.

4 'Knowledge' here has to be understood – as is often the case elsewhere and notably in theology – in the sense of 'mastering' and so 'controlling' and so, in turn, 'conferring the right of'. To know is to own. In this way the transcendent might cease to transcend. The reach of human authority has to stay inside a creaturely status, while – by its very warrant – prone or ambitious to exceed it in disavowal of God over all.

5 John Milton: *Paradise Lost*, Book viii, lines 505–11.

6 *Ibid.*, Book v, lines 521–34.

7 Friedrich Nietzsche: *The Antichrist*, Section 24, and here Chapter 12. Can we rightly live 'regretting nothing' as Nietzschean 'man' proposes to do, having forsaken inter-human compassion in the repudiation of all Christology as ever undergirding it? We need care to understand Nietzsche's subtlety rightly. For there was a yearning wistfulness beneath its high rhetoric. See further Chapter 12.

8 Echoing the theme of W. H. Vanstone's *Love's Endeavour, Love's Expense*, London, 1974, a notable study of Christian personhood drawn into the meaning of Christ's redemption.

9 *Paradise Lost*, Book viii, lines 8, 9, 640, 641.

10 See his autobiography: *The Strings are False: An Unfinished Autobiography*, London, 1965. pp. 108–15 and 133. Cf. also the titles of some poetic collections – 'Epitaph for Liberal Poets', 'Homage to Cliches', 'Holes in the Sky' and (his first) 'Blind Fireworks'. Cf. above p.14.

11 *Ibid.*, p. 172.

12 Michael Schmidt: *Modern British Poets*, London, 1979, p. 226.

13 Louis MacNeice: *Selected Poems*, ed. W. H. Auden, London, 1964, p. 110. 'Jigsaws, V'. He ends: 'We need the Unknown: the Unknown is there . . . a God to phrase it fair.'

14 *Ibid.*, p. 74. 'Prayer before Birth'.

15 Thomas Traherne: *Centuries, Poems and Thanksgivings*. Ed. H. M. Margoliouth, Oxford, 1936, Vol. ii, p. 6, Stanza 7. 'If only I were born' is his prospective greeting for the privilege of coming to be.

16 A. E. Housman: *Collected Poems and Selected Prose*, ed. Christopher Ricks, London, 1988, 'Last Poems', ix, p. 106.

17 Housman had his own heavy share of personal reasons for the plaintive notes his lyrical quality could so tellingly capture even when they were most privately hidden – the curse of devastating World War, the perplexities of sexuality, and an acute sense of the pain of transience, given deep registers of pathos and mystery. We return to the role of will in Chapter 11.

18 Thus John Bayley rejects Rick's verdict, as editor of Housman's verse, on Housman's 'blasphemy' in *Housman Poems*, Oxford, 1992. 'Ricks is surely misleading in continuing to rub in his point about Housman's habitual and straight-faced blasphemy' (p. 131, re also pp. 27, 138–9). Bayley pleads that

< 170 >

'joking' may be involved and notes the 'dignity in Housman's natural use of Biblical language' (p. 138). When, however, he adopts the rhyme and pattern of a hymn, as in 'For my Funeral', his 'handling' of God is mordaunt and ironical.

19 *Loc. cit.* note 16, or in his 'Easter Hymn! Where only some grant of oblivion eases the ache in being mortal as the victim of time, where – as in 'A Shropshire Lad' (stanza xliii) 'Every mother's son travels with a skeleton.'

20 In the familiar carol about 'oxen kneeling on Christmas Eve'. Thomas Hardy: *Collected Poems*, London, 1932, p. 439, written in 1915. Hardy was a powerful influence alike for Housman and MacNeice.

21 In the case of MacNeice there was his Ulster nurture and the complex relation he had with his episcopal father, Bishop John MacNeice of Down, Connor and Dromore. A. E. Housman betrays a strong familiarity with Biblical imagery.

22 *The Poems of Housman*, ed. A. Burnett, Oxford, 1997, p. 71, 'The West', where he 'thinks eternal thoughts and sighs . . . 'twill think your thoughts and sink them far, Leagues beyond the sunset bar.'

23 MacNeice in *The Poetry of W. B. Yeats*, London, 1941, p. 16, cited by Esna Longley in *Louis MacNeice: A Critical Study*, London, 1988, p. 137.

24 The point here about 'proxy' sub-authority under-warranting prior truth authority are the concern, in part, of Chapter 6.

25 'Content' being either the 'satisfying significance' or what 'duration' held anyhow, experience *per se*, of which he wrote in 'A Shropshire Lad'.

26 Cited by Anthony Heilbert: *Thomas Mann: Eros and Literature*, London, 1995, p. 542.

27 Adapting John Keats' celebrated theme of 'negative capability', the ability to be 'in uncertainties, mysteries, doubts, without any irritable reaching after fact and reason'. *Letters of John Keats*. Ed. Frederick Page, London, ed. 1954, No. 32, p. 53, December, 1817.

28 Louis MacNeice, *loc. cit.*, London, 1941, p. 196.

5 *Divine Integrity in Human Covenant*

1 Endless writers have made the point, though some have resembled a plaintiff in a court action who opened his case by denying the existence of the defendant. Nicholas Berdaev is not among them when he observes: 'The rationalistic mind of modern man considers the existence of evil and suffering . . . the most important argument in favour of atheism . . . This argument (and it is the only one) has become classic. Men lose faith in God and in the divine meaning of the word because they find evil victorious.' *Freedom and the Spirit*, trans. O. F. Clarke, London, 1935, p. 158.

2 Seeing that the 'human relatedness' concerned 'submission', and *jihad* in the ending of all *shirk*, yet with a deep – almost sacramental – sense of the natural order, via its *ayat*, or 'signs', as a realm in grateful trust inside the meaning of a creation for a human creaturehood, to which guiding 'messengers' came by divine sending.

3 'Surreptitious' in the strict sense of 'fraudulent' and 'devious', in the meaning of the *Shaitan* term.

< 171 >

4   We shall need elsewhere the force of 'passionate' in the ultimate credentials of divine 'good faith' with us, in the Jesus of a Gethsemane.

5   What Biblical faith knows as the 'Noahid' covenant found in the fertility of land under human husbandry, a universal agronomy known as the human privilege and trust, has been sufficiently expounded in Chapter 3's study of its telling in dominion, nature's answering signs addressing human cognizance and gratitude. For this is the crowning theme of Biblical 'divine humanism' and need not be further elaborated here. Biblically, however, the Noahid is narrowed or focused into the Mosaic and the inclusive tenure/tenancy of all centred on a uniquely 'chosen' people. It is relevant also, here, to note that the Qur'an has no mention of Eve, the 'mother of all living', by name. She is 'Adam's wife', but both are beguiled by Satan to violate the interdiction. Thus Satan is the deep culprit and the human vagary of 'Adam and his wife' more 'forgetfulness' than express rebellion. See Surahs 2.35–36, 7.19–20 and 20.117–122. Thus the theme studied here in Chapter 4 is somehow less 'onerous' in its Quranic than in its Biblical form.

6   Not that our global scene now lacks insistent tribalisms but that who and where and whence 'we' – people, place and memory, things ancestral, territorial and historical – were then so much more locally intense and psychically urgent. Co-existence pleads and posits modern factors.

7   There is something of the same people/place nexus with Allah in the Qur'an's emphasis on Islam as 'religion with Allah'. Hence the perpetual centrality of the Meccan pilgrimage.

8   In the context of the Book of Joshua, 'the hosts of Sabaoth' would seem to be the 'armies' of Israel that he led. Elsewhere in the majestic imagery of Isaiah 40, they must be the very stars of heaven. Then the prophet has in mind a military parade where the stars, named like soldiers at attention, respond to their summons and cry: 'Here we are, present, Lord!'

9   *Ecclesiasticus*, or *The Wisdom of Ben Sirach*, Chapter 24, verses 7–12. New English Bible translation.

10   'Complete', that is, in any terms of a Biblical unity as truly comprising the 'two' testaments.

11   It has to be 'careful', i.e. 'circumspect', in that the analogy is, like all analogies, dangerously partial. Brutus and Portia are in the 'oath-laden' situation of marriage. (The passage is one of the clearest expressions anywhere of the sanctity of marriage vows.) Thanks to books like Hosea that 'bridal' quality belongs to the YAHWEH/Israel bond and has often been cherished since, e.g. by the redoubtable Solomon Schechter in his *Aspects of Rabbinic Judaism*, New York, 1909. That apart, we need caution in thinking of what is between synagogue and church as 'in the suburbs of good pleasure', either way. Portia suggests that what is dubious is absent from 'good health' and occasions the 'stumble' of misunderstanding. Her solicitude is totally compassionate, not accusatory.

12   William Shakespeare: *Julius Caesar*, Act 2, Scene 1, lines 266–7 and 281–2 and 284–5.

13   Though there are occasions where, in the Hebrew, 'neighbour' means a fellow Jew and not a 'Gentile'. It is the very nobility of Shylock that he pleads sheer humanity and the reproach of his baitors is that they spurn it.

< 172 >

14 See the memorable description of her wares and the reach of her merchandise in Chapter 27.

15 This is a central point to which we must return especially in what will be involved in Chapters 6, 9 and 11. There is this deep 'risk element' in the theme of divine pledging which takes divine stakes on into human wills and stories, whereby His purpose is vulnerable to the hazards, latent or active, of the realm with which it has willed to engage.

16 As just argued, i.e. Jewry-directed and transacted but for reasons belonging with all human yearning, all mortal frailty.

17 Knowing 'the Name' means, in some sense, having a power – or a claim – over its possessor. In asking what it is, Moses is explicitly wanting to be assured of the divine competence. In this anxiety he is relaying what he knows will be his people's scepticism (' . . . They will say to me . . . ').

18 For the future sense of the Hebrew – and its significance for the whole nature of Biblical faith as to history, see Martin Buber: *Moses*, London, 1946. Chapter 7 to follow here will need the same principle, with the Christian faith saying – of the whole event of the Gospel as the Christ-story – 'God has been there – and for ever will there be – as He whom He there has been.'

19 Borrowing Paul's analogy in Galatians 3.24 of the Greek slave whose task was to convey the boy to school – a duty which ended when he reached there. All education exists to make itself dispensable.

20 Some effort to study this dark vein in anti-Semitism and the tragic suffering on Jewry which it occasioned was made in: *Semitism: The Whence and Whither*, Brighton & Portland, 2004.

21 One might use the adjective here in something of the sense Charles Wesley brought to his theme in 'Amazing Grace' with its deep feel from an intense surprise. Retrospect to the Exodus was of similar order in Hebrew awareness.

6 *God's Integrity in Christ*

1 Science, of course identifies and exploits them but all our techniques would be stilled and nullified if the natural order, the chemistries of things, were not dependable. Science assumes their constancy: they do not subvert that trust.

2 Echoing the frequent theme in later prophethood, but occurring in Psalm 35.27 (cf. Psalm 122.7). It brings together the twin claims of righteousness and peace, and is closely linked with 'the pleasure of the Lord' in Messiah's hand (Isaiah 53.10, cf. 48.15). In Christology it belongs with the mutuality of 'the Father and the Son and ' . . . with whom I am well-pleased.'

3 The meaning of the pledge to Abraham is not only that the nations would be 'blessed' because of him but that they would 'bless themselves' because of him.

4 The 'seed time and harvest' covenant was one in which Jewry shared along with 'all peoples'. It was, therefore, 'even-handed' in contrast to that of Sinai and its Decalogue in which only Jewry contracted. 'Election' is in contrast to how 'nature makes us all kin'. It is not, however, 'even-handed' in its physical incidence or its climatic diversity.

< 173 >

5 Plainly Moses had a different perspective on the Pharaoh of the Exodus than Isaiah had on Cyrus of Persia.

6 'Bias' here in its sound, good sense of something latent actually conducing to the process that attains it, as in the game of bowls.

7 This summary statement of the New Testament situation is, of course, subject to intense scrutiny by New Testament scholarship – a situation that can only be saluted and never shunned, for reasons that will concern Chapter 9 anon. This, however, is vital at the outset and much of the scholarly task is alive in what follows. Everything, anyway, is party to the twin situation of drama and *confessio*, of event and testimony.

8 How this blending of 'zealot' and the likes of Matthew in the story and how a 'zealot' impulse behind his discipleship may have motivated Judas before and up to Gethsemane, were studied in my: *Faith at Suicide*, Brighton & Portland, 2005, as also throwing the right light we need on his suicide in the wake of tragic mis-calculation.

9 Namely the familiar, recurring debate about some 'Messianic secret'. Since the Messiah factor became so prominent after the Passion, why had it not been articulate publicly during the ministry? Therefore, the disciples retro-actively ascribed it to Jesus falsely. The obvious, simple explanation surely is that Messianic claim could only have been dangerously ambiguous until its very nature had been defined – as it could only be in the event – and that event so disconcertingly uncongenial.

10 Depending on how we relate the visits to Jerusalem. John mentions several with the apparently final one above narrated in the Synoptic Gospels and that 'triumphal' entry.

11 Is there a pointed echo of Hosea 1.9 where Hosea has YAHWEH disavowing the 'I am' of Exodus 3.14: 'I am not the "I am" you think I am'? For the disci-ples had similarly wrong impressions which had to be re-educated.

12 As defined in John 1.36 where the Greek word *airon* has the double sense of 'bearing' and (only so) 'bearing away'. Only the love that suffers affords the forgiveness that reconciles. All this is is thus very far cry from a mere sacrificial system, a ritual of propitiation, an arbitrary scheme of ritual par-don.

13 'Liturgically' is the right word, meaning, as *leitourgia* does in origin, that which serves to, and offers itself for, the public good.

14 It meant only in Isaiah's case the names he gave to his children, whereby his family symbolized in their growing and their attendant presence the meaning he would thus convey – all a fair analogy of the Church.

15 To clarify the difficulty between 'new Testament' as written text, a literary document *and* the term as denoting what we have in 'God in Christ' as event and faith. See below.

16 This, of course, is to hold a Christian perception of that 'election', one which at length majority Jewry disallowed although the initiative had been signally Jewish. There were understandable reasons in holding back, since foregoing of privilege is always puzzling. Yet there was no 'supersession', but only a 'real-ization' that would for ever retain its historical memory in tribute of debt. That 'glory of Israel' would ever endure.

17 This feature is often forgotten in a neglect lulled by the familiar title. How

< 174 >

18   much we are deprived of by Luke's limits and his brevity. There were 'acts of apostles' to India, Egypt, Armenia and Persia.

18   Namely the 'gospel' about a Jesus crucified which Paul as Saul so aggressively denied, maligned and escoriated. See further.

19   As 'imports' seeking entry. Ezekiel in his fulminations knew well enough how cosmopolitan was the trade of Tyre. One might recall John Masefield's poem, 'Cargoes' heading 'down to sunny Palestine'.

20   This form, alike of *confessio* and worship, was basic to the slow formulation of the Creeds. The three terms and the possessive pronoun could be in any order.

21   The term *kurios* was very elastic and could belong fully with the divine as well as with the human serving in a discerning 'mastery'. Its breadth admirably fitted the 'incarnational'.

22   Any 'Peter to Rome' story is lacking in the New Testament, thanks to Luke's pre-occupation with Paul – one of the sundry vacua in the Scripture – if not the better to inform our faith the larger to have its claim on our discernment.

23   The saying in John 12.32 cannot mean a universally successful salvation, if this should override the principle in 'whosoever *will* . . . ' in the personal response of faith. It means a universally accessible salvation, one that is not conditioned by prior ethnic, or other, requisite.

24   The sequence is significant. One would expect it to be the other way round. There is a similar point when in Acts 15.11, Peter, reporting on the Cornelius event, says: 'We believe that we (i.e. we Jews) will be saved even as them ('the Gentiles'). The Gospel was not a prior Jewish thing being allowed to admit 'Gentiles'. It is a universal reality which had its matrix in Jewish vocation.

25   Galatians 4.22–31. Hagar, the slave-woman, mother of Ishmael, who has to be 'cast out' as representing the works of the flesh, is said also to be 'Mount Sinai', the very place of covenantal destiny in the Abrahamic line. She, Hagar, is figuratively 'the bondage' in which Sinai's lawkeepers are said to be, in contrast to 'Jerusalem, the mother of us all'. It is not clear where Sarah comes in here (so important in Romans). Yet only her Isaac is 'the child of promise'.

26   The 'grafting' analogy strains to do any justice to Paul's own insistent doctrine of justification by faith – a faith needing no 'sap' or 'niche', no life to 'tap', no 'stock' in which to be, only such faith alone. All analogies are liable to fall short, but some more than others. How is 'Christ the true vine' according to John, if Jewry must also be?

27   We have noted earlier the problem of this double meaning to the one phrase. It is important both to distinguish either from the other and to know why the words fit both.

28   Echoing Luke's phrase in address to Theophilus in the preface to his Gospel (1.1).

7   *Cares and 'Bewares' in the Trust of Doctrine*

1   This 'centre of gravity' phrasing acknowledges that faiths carry ample ancillary dimensions and that where they cohere and are distinctively defined is

< 175 >

often a question within them. Yet the need to be identifiable and definitive cannot, by any sane reckoning, be neglected.

2   The passage in 2 Corinthians 4.5–7 is surely a 'centre of gravity' passage for the whole New Testament, with its echo of the Aaronic blessing of Numbers 6.24–26 and its language of 'the face' as bearing the entire meaning of the Incarnation, the face being the most physical amalgam of sinew, nerve, muscle and blood, and yet also the steady residence of a whole panorama of emotions – joy, anger, puzzlement, scorn and soul-inquisition by its glance or stare.

3   What was and is the meaning of that negative precept of the third Commandment in the Hebrew Decalogue? It is certainly more profound than verbal swearing or vocal blasphemy. It must intend every false or willful invocation of divine favour, warrant or sanction as cover for sin, wrong, pride and every human violation of nature and grace.

4   This in Ephesians 4.30 is surely an epitome of the whole theme of these chapters about the strange vulnerability of the divine. Or of how we humans – in a phrase of William Temple – could arouse 'the dreadful astonishment of God'. See his: *The Church looks Forward*, London, 1944, p. 71. Is it akin to where the Qur'an finds Allah enquiring: 'Am I not Your Lord?' (Surah 7.172)

5   Thus one may 'believe' that the Norman Conquest of England happened in 1066 but the fact neither invites nor engages me now, whereas I 'trust' the aircraft, its mechanism, its pilots and its navigation and would not board it if I did not 'believe' in these.

6   The significant repetition of the formula ought to alert us to how malice, not to say tradition and propriety, can 'use Scripture for their purpose'. How sinister loaded recourse to Biblical quotation can become. 'Establishments may be less vigilant than personal conscience in 'rightly dividing' holy writ.

7   If, as seems warranted, we see the violent opposition of Saul to the Christian conviction about a Christ crucified, a prolongation of the enmity which occasioned the Cross, then it becomes clear how the event on the road exactly captured that situation. Saul, in persecuting the Church, persecuted the 'me' of the vision. That 'me' identified 'Jesus', the crucified, speaking from where 'the Christ' should be as 'the one from heaven'. Thus Saul became Paul in and by the 'gravity centre' of a faith thus 'glorified', i.e. 'accredited' in him.

8   These, of course, like all else about 'the mind of the Spirit', are prey to human frailty and vagary, since they avail or happen only by divine/human partnership, the Spirit being uncompelling when most mandatory. Even so these organs of that partnership remain His *modus operandi.*

9   Explored later. Some minds handle the Virgin Birth and the empty tomb as if susceptible of investigative proof. Even if ever feasible, such investigative 'evidence' could only be extraneous to the meaning – and vindication – inside the faith concerning divine Incarnation.

10 In its abiding fondness for the troublesome word 'is' and seeing a nominal sentence as in 'apposition'.

11 A Queen reported formula at the time of the Elizabethan Settlement in the Church of England, eluding the sharp controversy between Catholic and Puritan reckonings with the Mass and 'the Lord's Supper'.

12 For these, in bread and wine, are never mere objects to visualize, contemplate or savour in imagination, but only personally to receive – and be aware of fellowship in so doing, as at any table.

13 See the large, long tribute in Gregory Dix: *The Shape of the Liturgy*, London, 1945, and how 'every local church . . . received the rite of the eucharist – the way of performing it – as its first evangelization . . . ', p. 6.

14 *Op. cit.*, London, 1927, pp. 225f. The same writer has memorably stated what must belong to all partaking intention: 'We desire to understand that the crucified Saviour is in space and time the one perfect sacrament of the power by which in the end, and in the whole, all evil is redeemed,' p. 84.

15 John MacQuarrie: *Paths in Spirituality*, London, 1972, p. 86. If 'Presence' is – in liturgical action – ever sacramental can it be only 'visual'? He clearly holds to 'the personal presence of Christ among His people', but is there ever a 'discerning of the body' in visual terms that remains a sacramental reality?

16 Their centuries' history is diligently presented in Dix, *op. cit.*, note 13.

17 See the study of Henry Barbussi (1873–1935) in John Thurrock: *The Word from Paris: Essays on Modern French Thinkers and Writers*, London, 1998, note on p. 120.

18 Miguel de Cervantes: *Don Quixote*, Part 2, Chap. 3, trans. John Rutherford, London, 2000, p. vii.

19 The whole theme of 'priesthood' being altogether 'ministerial' is argued in the old but masterly text of R. C. Moberly: *Ministerial Priesthood*, London, ed. 1927, to be read together with his *Atonement and Personality*, London, 1901.

20 There have been many conjectures around the Infancy narratives unique to Luke's Gospel. Has *Magnificat*, with its deep paradox of 'the mighty unthroned', links with the Maccabees and their celebratory mothers, or – rather – with the song of Hannah? Perhaps how it 'fits' is all we need to know.

21 It is thus with Paul in 2 Corinthians and with John in his Prologue. There is an inaugurating 'word' alike to creation, humanity and their Gospel in the Christ.

22 There is dark confusion here, if the word 'original' is taken as some inherent 'sin' in the act of intercourse, the cycle of pregnancy or the incidence of birth. Such a notion would disavow the goodness of creation and the dignity of the human mandate and the procreation that fulfils them. 'Original' means that *ab initio* none are making a clean, unconditioned start on some *tabula rasa*. We enter a world where 'wrong' and 'wrongs', collective and societal, are already in place and which none may elude or escape. Birth as such does not have these inhere in us pre-natally: it ushers into them as our 'original' context as creatures of time. 'In sin has my mother conceived me' could only – intelligently – have this meaning. 'Original' is 'natal' only in this sense of our way into what we find and discover with us and our bias by it.

23 As rumoured in Matthew 27.63–65, the 'sealing' and the 'setting of a watch'.

24 Sheer longing might arouse a credulity which could then find a longed for theme of imagination credible, as 'compensation' for the utmost despair through which the disciples passed.

25 And that answer will be right. But, if Incarnation is historic, at a time and in a place, it has in those terms, *ex hypothesi*, an 'end'. Thus its 'for-everness' must

be in the truth – as the Scriptures plainly say – of 'the post-existent Christ', the eternally divine. Likewise the concept of 'the pre-existent Christ' means that God eternally was whom, incarnationally, He came to be known to be. 'The Word' came 'into flesh' and 'parted from flesh'. The bodily sight of the Ascension could only have been on the 'sight-side' of the 'cloud', since the event was not a space journey. The point is inseparable from any 'time-incidence' of, from and in eternity. See below.

26 Both in the Gospels, the Letters and the Creeds, if only for the danger from the Docetic heresy of which there is clear trace in the Qur'an's Surah 4.151f. There were Christians who believed that Jesus, being divine, could never suffer. If, therefore, it was said that he did so, it could only have been 'in the realm of seeming', only 'apparent'. There were sundry ideas as to how this 'semblance' of dying might have transpired. Only the fact of bodily burial could disown them.

27 Echoing the Greek verb in John 1.18. 'The only begotten . . . He has expounded (exegeted) Him.'

28 See Lsmin Sanneh: *Translating the Message: The Missionary Impact on Culture*, New York, 1989. Establishing alphabets and stimulating literacy, as the effect of mission, are studied in Nigerian and Gambian context. Vernaculars prove to be both the agent and the beneficiaries of trans-cultural encounter and, thence, of religious dialogue.

29 The verb *phrouresei* in Philippians 4.7 has the sense of 'the fortress warden' of your hearts. 'Keep' here has the sense of 'secure' by adequate resource against subversion or threat.

30 Thomas Traherne: *Centuries*, ed. H. M. Margoliouth, Oxford, ed. 1960, pp. 18, 43, 57, 59, 79.

31 A recurrent phrase in the Qur'an: 'Unto Allah is our returning', mostly as a reference to death and dying but Traherne uses it in his sense of being always 'brought back to God' by lively awareness of the earth.

32 *The Cloud of Unknowing*, ed. Justin McCann, London, 1924, Cap. Vi.

33 'Theatre' to capture something reciprocal between a presentation and a reception. The insignia of the eternal come within the ken of the temporal, the spiritual is translated into the physical.

34 Echoing the familiar formula about faith seeking an understanding and understanding sustaining a faith. This dictum bears heavily on the nature of 'authority' earlier discussed.

35 As part of his grim description of the forbidding face of Egdon Heath in his native Dorset, a landscape of sinister intent, apt to Hardy's mood of nature's indifference to man and likely enmity to boot.

36 As Berkeley said of things: 'Their being is to be perceived'. Cf. Ecclesiastes 3.11.

8   Versions of Vocabulary

1 Also a right internal currency of a faith's language is crucial to its spiritual integrity and intellectual honesty, lest words either miscarry or grow hackneyed. While it is true that rite and symbol can convey and seal meaning and/or silently receive it, only words can tell it explicitly.

2 Nicholas of Cusa (1401–1464) was a scholar of many parts and wide sympathy, who knew hostility from Rome itself and, in his writings, anticipated something of the 'humanism' of the next generation. Leonardo da Vinci was a boy of twelve when he died.

3 While his impulse to reckon worthily with the Qur'an as Muslims esteemed it was genuine, he did not scruple to make careful Latin-told case for a Christian theology of the divine 'Oneness' of 'Father, Son and Holy Spirit'. *In divina natura est foecunditas* – 'love in its loving, the love-worthy love, and the united act of love' – these are 'the mind prior, the mind minded and the mind being comprehended'. Three are one circle denoted, as 'circle, centre, diameter and circumference'. There was no doubt of the acumen he brought to his Islamic interests and to Jewry and their Judaism.

4 Dictionaries are liable to use tautology or to fall back on phrases which are less than satisfactory when, in discourse, we need a single word for due clarity.

5 Samuel Johnson's *English Dictionary*, produced between 1747 and 1755, was a work of great industry and some degree of bias. Edward W. Lane (1801–1876) worked on his monumental *Arabic–English Dictionary* for eleven years until two years before his death.

6 Daniel Defoe: *Robinson Crusoe*, 1719, London ed. 1965, pp. 218–19.

7 It is in line with the characteristic of Muslim thought to care more for the reality of Allah as 'imperative' for ethics than 'indicative' for theology. Let the 'query' interest pass into the 'prayer/worship' practice where 'interrogatives' have what alone matters. This was expressed, with too little intellectual care, when Fazlur-Rahman declared: 'The Qur'an is no treatise about God and His nature: His existence for the Qur'an is strictly functional.' *Major Themes of the Qur'an*, Chicago, 1980, p. 1. Its business is about 'man and his behaviour'. It seems odd to have Allah thought of as 'functional', given so much in the Qur'an about the human trust as both 'risk' and 'privilege', and God's engagement with human conscience and will as necessary arbiters of an intelligent, grateful response, and also negligent of the repeated rubric about 'the divine Names' and their recital.

8 In a memorable contribution to thought on 'inter-thought' about world religions, Wilfred Cantwell Smith called urgent attention to the distinction on which he insisted between religious faith and religious belief. His concern was well-taken and resembled, in some measure, Martin Buber's distinction between 'trust in' and 'credence that', though Buber distorted *pistis* and *emunah* in the terms by which he distinguished between them. Smith's thesis was in his *The Meaning and End of Religion*, New York, 1964 and *Belief and History*, Charlottesville, 1977. Can there be authentic 'trust in' without some degree of 'belief that'?

9 There was a similar dimension in the famous (infamous) *riddah* in the brief Caliphate of Abu Bakr, when some 'renegers' from Islam assumed that Muhammad's demise had freed them from their pledged allegiance to him and that no 'doctrinal' *confessio* carried it forward to his successor presiding over a community of faith.

10 Surahs 6.91, 22.74 and 39.67 make this highly significant comment on unworthy (i.e. pagan) concepts of, or assumptions about, Allah. The gram-

< 179 >

matical form of verb and its own noun with the meaning of 'reckon', 'assess', 'weigh' and 'measure' – together with the adjective *Al-Qadir* – might be said to capture the entire business of theology in 'doing justice' to God, alike in thought and worship, in mind and heart. Its implications are miles away from the notion that Islam has been, or can be, indifferent to its theological tasks, by falling back on sheer dogmatism or neglecting to think, in the name of law alone as our concern. The verses raise the urgent question: 'How do we test what our ideas are?'

11　It is pointless to wonder whether in some way this triad of nouns, with one, singular subject, echoes in any way the Christian theme of divine 'trinity', except to say that three descriptives are no violation of inherent unity.

12　The passage follows closely the paraphrase used by C. H. Dodd in his monumental commentary of the Fourth Gospel. C. H. Dodd: *Interpretation of the Fourth Gospel*, Cambridge, 1954 and *Historical Tradition in the Fourth Gospel*, Cambridge, 1963.

13　*Theotokos*, 'Mother of God', does not occur in the New Testament. It is an unhappy matter that its prominence in Christian vocabulary is most current in those expressions of 'Orthodox' (in its double sense) Christianity that are physically closest to the Muslim context. 'Mother of God', just as 'King of the Jews' has the precious, valid sense in which it can be said, present in the utterly impossible sense with which it can never be meant.

14　Using 'negotiate' in its strict sense – not of driving a bargain – but of laying aside sloth (*otium*), allowing perplexity its honest place and recruiting meaning from its very negation, using the obstacle as a stepping stone. 'Negotiate' means that in an adverse world we can never merely 'proclaim'.

15　It is necessary to link 'faith' and 'theology' here inasmuch as Christian faith is inherently theological, i.e. it belongs with, and only proceeds from, a trust in God according to its confidence as to that 'God in 'Christ', via the conviction that having 'Christ' as divine clue is the God-given, God-telling act-in-character. If this seems a 'circularity' it is because it cannot be otherwise. Or, more simply put, 'it takes God to disclose God' – which only formulates 'the Word made flesh'; Christianity being – here throughout – theological faith as the key to all else.

16　This, with the immediate sequence: 'keep yourselves from idols' is almost, time-wise, the concluding – and conclusive – passage in the New Testament.

17　'Final' is not to forget or ignore the brief and precarious recovery under the Hasmoneans but the sense that had once been under David and Solomon, which was never recovered; the significance of 'exile' left its indelible mark on the psyche until the advent of 20th century Zionism.

18　When theology tells of 'the pre-existence of Christ' it cannot require some concept of a 'physicality' somehow abiding from outside time, otherwise no 'incarnation' ever happened. The Eternal, entering time, must do so 'at a time'. The pre-existence of Christ means that what – in its time – came to be Jesus the Christ was in no way 'innovative' but expressive of what was eternally so in the nature of God. The sense of its 'coming to pass' equates with its incidence in time.

19　The same applies to the translation 'Men of goodwill' in the Christmas form

< 180 >

and elsewhere – not some Dickensian *bonhomie* but a congruence of the human and the divine, effectuating one purpose in the harmony of means and end.

20 There is no doubt that, for example, a work of art, being 'love-begotten', is an object of love. The analogy of art or drama or music here is crucial to help shut out crude notions of physical paternity and to help focus the inherently 'trinitarian' sequence of mind in movement, measure and meaning.

21 Which is only to say that by which identity is recognized is that by which it exists, as happens with a 'character' in a play so that a 'what' is a 'who'.

22 For they had become acquainted with Jesus, according to the Synoptic Gospels, in the very different terms of fishermen recruited to be itinerant preachers.

23 William Shakespeare: *Twelfth Night*, Act 3, Scene 1, lines 12–13, perhaps recalling his father's trade as glove-maker, 'cheveral' being stretch-able leather – hence 'cheveralized' theology.

24 Horace Bushnell: *The Vicarious Sacrifice*, New York, 1871, pp. 112, 113 and 69.

25 *Ibid.*, p. 73.

26 *Ibid.*, p. 85 and pp. 75–7: ' . . . fulfilling in every particular the Christly terms of sacrifice'.

27 Robert Browning: *Collected Poems*, Oxford, 1940, 'Saul', Stanza xxvii, p. 231. A much loved theme, it recurs again in 'The Ring and the Book', his long classic.

28 The Greek term *harpagmos* denotes a status, rank, or dignity so prized or coveted as never to be relinquished, but rather 'let go' from such jealous 'grasp' the better to fulfil its meaning. Divine status as Messiah was of this self-foregoing *qua* self-fulfilling quality. 'Misprision' is a legal term which means a culpable failure from outside to value, appreciate and duly recognize given reality. Theologies may do the same.

29 It is thus a deep moral principle and no mere ritual dictum. Only by discerning handling does vocabulary yield its point to comprehension. Otherwise much goes astray in mere citation.

30 Hymns have sometimes used unrealistically devout language on this theme as, for example

> Here I rest for ever viewing
> Mercy poured in streams of blood,
> Precious drops my soul bedewing
> Plead and claim my peace with God.

31 Herman Melville: *Moby Dick*, New York, 1854, in Chapter xlv, 'The Affidavit', 1930 ed., p. 205: 'For God's sake, be economical with your lamps and candles! Not a gallon you burn but at least one drop of man's blood was spilled for it.' Likewise 'the price of coal' was registered in grim mining tragedies. Prices are paid *for* that are never paid *to* a vendor.

31 The Greek word is *exegesato*, variously rendered as 'declared him', 'made him known' in line with the preceding clause 'in the bosom of the Father' or 'nearest to the Father's heart – such was the task of 'the intimate expositor'.

< 181 >

9   *The Necessary Ministries of Doubt*

1   Herbert Butterfield: *Christianity and History*, London, 1949, p. 146. He was Vice-Chancellor at Cambridge and wrote on *The Whig Interpretation of History* and *The Origins of Modern Science*. He probed the nature of historical knowledge, the drama of 'a risky universe', given the factor of human nature and the inter-relation of theological belief and the human story. His parting 'principle' had its evident paradox.

2   The Vulgate has *arguet mundum de peccato*, to translate the Greek *elegxei*. It is significant that 'conviction' in English has the same double sense of 'being convinced' and 'being convicted'. *Arguo* has the sense of 'making clear' and, thus, also of refuting and reproving. 'Expose' and 'expound' do well for the double activity of the Holy Spirit as understood in this Gospel. Neither cancels, but only requires, the other.

3   Inasmuch as 'My Lord and my God' captures the theology of Christhood as personal *confessio*. The word 'first' here must leave room for a credal process already underway by the time of the authorship of this Gospel – a process evident in the Pauline formula 'Our Lord Jesus Christ' used in any sequence of the nouns, and 'It is a faithful saying.'

4   See, for example, A. E. Harvey: *Jesus on Trial, A Study in the Fourth Gospel*, London, 1976.

5   G. H. C. MacGregor: *The Gospel of John*, London, 1938, p. 298. The inner quotation is from E. F. Scott: *The Fourth Gospel, Its Purpose and Theology*.

6   It is sad that the word 'theologian' should be often confined to scholars with treatises, whereas it ought to mean the self in pursuit and possession of love and knowledge divinely had. Cf. Chapter 6.

7   The stance often suggested in current 'dialogue' as the way through an openness to others' truth for an unyielding commitment to one's own. But such 'privatizing' of belief and believing cannot well mean an abeyance of their public relevance – a relevance the more crucial when there are serious incompatibilities in beliefs with the claims of common good and public welfare. There are so many dangerous ways of 'being religious'. To co-exist well we must somehow co-inhabit our worlds. Inner integrity has to be outwardly salutary.

8   See, for example, the carefully documented study of its mind-set in Stephen Sizer: *Christian Zionism, Road-Map to Armageddon?*, Leicester, 2004.

9   Hosea 1.8: 'I am not the "I AM" you think I am' is in direct disavowal of the formula in Exodus 3.14 in the pledge at Moses' commissioning and of the Exodus datum as to YAHWEH's being 'their God and they his people'.

10   As in Isaiah 41.1, 4 and 5, 49.1, 51.5, 60.9 and 66.19. What 'Isles' could a landlocked prophet have in mind – Hormuz down the Gulf, or those that gave name to *Al-Jaza'ir* (Algiers) off the North African shore? Or was it that, for Ezekiel, the commerce of Tyre that brought them into ken? Or were they the 'miniatures' of all territory, some Hebraic Hesperides?

11   Psalm 137. This reversal of direction is the central fact of the New Testament, personally symbolized by the Christian Jewishness of the Apostle Paul, its supreme exemplar. See below.

12   Notably in the sundry passages where Muhammad is personally addressed

< 182 >

and where his very persona is crucial to the deliverances he received. This is remarkably so, despite the traditional view that these were totally apart from any mental or volitional part of his own, either in their incidence or their content. See fuller discussion in my: *Muhammad in the Qur'an, The Task and the Text*, London, 2001. Divine authorship need not, and did not, exclude the 'messenger-necessity' to which the *Shahadah* witnesses. 'We have sent it down upon your heart' says Surah 46.194 cf. 42.24 and 2.97.

13   Thus Fazlur Rahman remarks: 'The aim of the Qur'an is man and his behaviour, not God'. It 'is no treatise about God and His nature: His existence, for the Qur'an, is strictly functional' as the giver of guidance and 'merciful justice'. *Major Themes of the Qur'an*, Chicago, 1980, pp. 3 and 1, as noted earlier.

14   Perhaps the most celebrated of Muslim 'agnostics' was the poet recluse Abu-l-'Ala al-Ma'arri (973–1058) whose blindness and his reputation enabled him to elude reprisals while remaining avowedly a vigorous exponent of religious doubt. See: *The Tragic in Islam*, London, 2004, pp. 178–92.

15   Notably in respect of the role of the human Muhammad in the recipience of the Qur'an (see note 12), the reading of 'the Night Journey and *Mi'raj*', the impulse to the Hijrah and the Jewish or Christian factors in its origins.

16   Cf. 2 Corinthians 11.28 where Paul ends a long catalogue of his love's expenditures with 'the care of all the churches' as weighing upon him 'daily'. The pastoral tradition goes back, via the 'shepherd' analogy, to Isaiah 43.24 with its bold attribution of 'carrying Israel as a burden' to YAHWEH Himself': 'You have made me to serve by your sins'.

17   Could it be that the Emmaus narrative, in Luke 24.13, which continues to the Ascension in one single day, is really a compression of a much longer, slower education of the apostles in these two features of their task and meaning, namely the steady custody of 'the Scriptures' *and* the liturgy in 'bread and wine'?

18   That commerce, in an earlier age, is vividly described in the vehement terms of Ezekiel's charge against Tyre in Chapter 27. It is an impressive catalogue of wares from the 'ends of the earth'. Tyre's ships had masts from Lebanon and linen sails from Egypt. Shipping was thus an apt analogy for the 'foreign parts' from which – by rigorous sanction of diet – Jewry must be self-excluded. When Peter arrived in Cornelius' Caesarea did he recall his 'Messianic' words at the other Caesarea (Philippi) so recent in his story, though so different now in his comprehension?

19   Though with conditions about laws entirely within their readiness. It is noteworthy that when Peter, in Acts 15.11 reported on the Cornelius encounter, he said that he realized that 'Gentiles were admissible even as Jews', that is, the Gospel was not an exclusively Jewish entity, opened to non-Jews out of generosity, but an inherently inclusive one which had its matrix in Jewish 'covenant'. The point concerned us earlier.

20   It was in the nature of the Christian faith that it could only be realized as open to all races after the Passion of Jesus, though its being universal of reach was earlier mirrored in, for example, parables about Samaritans and the readiness of welcome for Rome's taxgathers as (?) 'renegade Jews'.

< 183 >

21 For these, however slow of wit and sense, nevertheless had a point. Idolatries exist of far more heinous measure than those suspect in the terms of 1 Corinthians, and it is well to give them no quarter.

22 There is so much more we need to know about that 1st century world, so Mediterranean-tied and its purview so stinted. The closure of the Canon by the late 3rd century was no doubt meant to foreclose doctrinally dubious sources. 'Sufficient' – the term Anglicans use – is from the geographical cultural angle a very generous one to apply. Consider too the long necessity of 'Tradition'.

23 For postures of 'authority', ecclesiastical, papal or academic will coincide with concepts of 'truth'. How the latter is served and commended will determine the worth and temper of the other.

24 It is surprising how, in some New Testament scholarship, this point – and its many evidences – have been either ignored or denied.

25 Karl Barth: *Evangelical Theology: An Introduction*, trans. Gromer Soley, Edinburgh, 1979, p. 131. He underlined the word *ashamed*.

26 William Shakespeare: *3 King Henry VI*, Act 4, Scene 2, lines 7–9.

27 The precedent about 'idol meats' in the Corinthian Church would seem to fit closely the current dilemma in the Anglican Communion over the legitimacy of homosexual activity in Christian living and/or within Holy Orders. There are close parallels – those who must repudiate such liberty and those who insist their conscience freely allows it. There is a similar sequel in accusations of 'weaker brethren' on the one hand and of treacherous libertines on the other. Yet, in either case, each 'to his own master stands or falls', and what warrants 'judging a brother' (Romans 14.3–6)? Can that Pauline principle concede, in this homosexual issue, a like tolerance of acute difference on the grounds that both parties obey their conscience under God in genuine sincerity?

If so, however, that will not lessen as the task of – in this case – those 'diehard weaker brethren' to be the more urgent in keeping alive the radical question whether homosexual intercourse can ever be compatible with the incarnational truth of the body, and all its usages, as 'the temple of the Holy Spirit'. The more liberty is conceded, the more its interrogation must persist, but always with the corollary of Romans 14.4 about 'judging God's servant'.

28 Alfred Lord Tennyson: *Poetical Works*, London, 1994 ed., p. 161. In a long poem of 130 three-line stanzas, the mood deepens in 1833 with *In Memoriam A. H. H.* where, in stanza cxxiii he wrote:
That which we invoke to bless
Our dearest faith, our ghastliest doubt . . .
I found him not in world or sun . . .
I heard a voice: 'Believe no more'
And heard an ever-breaking shore
That tumbled in the Godless deep.

29 R. S. Thomas: *No Truce with the Furies*, Newcastle, 1995, p. 14. 'The Lost', ('exiles within our own country').

30 *Ibid.*, 'Incarnations', p. 35.

31 The poem, surely never meant to become a hymn, told his deeply private

< 184 >

thoughts amid the mists of the Tyrrhenian Sea as he returned from near death in Tunisia (from which he was rescued by a devoted servant) as the final episode of an 'eastern tour'. He was still busy with the – for him – vexed question of Anglican authority and the meaning of 'apostolical succession'. His mood was deeply introspective. It is doubtful whether his cast of mind was not, indeed, 'ever thus'. There was also his career at issue.

32 The point of religious self-seeking and self-deluding is frequent in the novels and character studies of Iris Murdoch. See also her *The Sovereignty of Good*, London, 1970, p. 71.

33 It is intriguing that the same Latin root which takes us to 'the confessional' also tells the theme and substance of belief.

34 See: A. M. Hadfield, *Charles Williams: An Exploration of his Life and Work*, Oxford, 1965, p. 35, quoting Williams' 'Office Hymn for the Feast of St. Thomas Didymus, Apostle and Sceptic'. The poem has a second stanza which runs:

> Yet no wise dare we falter
> In our world – hear us so!
> We stand before Thine altar
> Denying that we know,
> Confess Thee 'ere Thou sever
> Us from Thy household true,
> Lord God, confess we never
> Knowing not, swore we knew.

35 According to 2 Timothy 1.12 which, even if from another hand, speaks as from his heart. What he had 'committed' to Christ was none other than the trust Christ had committed to him, of which he wrote in 1 Corinthians 9.17 and 2 Timothy 1.12. The distinction between *what* and *who*, while crucial, is not of course absolute. As with 'love', some measure of identity, character, discernible 'desirability', is elemental but they only find their worthiness in being recognized and saluted by the response that answers them in personal kind.

10 *Expediences of Politics*

1 Like the clause 'buried . . . ' mention of Pontius Pilate was held important, to underline the actuality, the historicity, of Jesus' crucifixion – this in the face of recurrent Docetic, and other, scepticisms about its 'reality'. For these, doubting how the divine could ever 'suffer', and 'suffer' such depths of humiliation, surmised that the Cross must, somehow, have been only 'in the realm of seeming', or only a 'charade'. Naming the regime 'under' which it happened meant its real 'event-status', as with 'and was buried'.

2 Cf. John 1.29 and 37. The terms in which, proleptically, the two disciples were 'introduced' to Jesus – as the Johannine perspective has it. The will to crucify was not, essentially, at the door of Romans and Jews. They merely happened to be around, as contemporaries. The deed was/is inclusively human.

3 These being the motivating factors. On this reading of Judas' 'kiss' as a gesture of final abandonment by Judas of his hopes of Jesus in zealot terms see my: *Faith at Suicide*, Brighton & Portland, 2005, Chapter 6.

< 185 >

4   See M. Saghir H. Ma'sumi: *Imam Razi's 'Ilm al'Akhlaq*, Eng. trans. Islamabad, 1969, p. 250. Al-Razi (1149–1209) wrote the ethical work here translated, with the title: 'The Book of Soul and Spirit: An Exposition of their Faculties'.

5   If coining a word is allowed, on the pattern of 'enmesh' or 'entwine'. The political order has its due liability for the discipline of common good, with courts and penalties to enforce it. 'Police' and 'politics' have obviously close linkage. The onus on the Christian citizen *qua* church is not to usurp this power, still less to recruit for its own – thus coercive – interest, but to bear strenuously on its will to justice and compassion in such measures. See below.

6   However exclusive to divine origin revealed law may be understood to be (and so 'theocratic'), its implementation – and its reading – will always lie in human hands and wills. 'Theocracy' then is never a viable word for what actually happens.

7   That Hijrah into a power-dimension set a permanent seal on the nature of Islam – hence its place as the start of its calendar. Nevertheless what is essentially definitive of Islam was, and is, that Meccan (only preached) message for which sake alone that Hijrah transpired.

8   Seeing that the State is always to be tributary to ends beyond its own, while the means it employs for them must always be the vigilant care of the Christian conscience, private and corporate.

9   One has to say 'differently' in that the Islamic had the entire Scriptural sanction eternalized, as it were, in its defining Qur'an, whereas the definitive New Testament text was effectively finalized – and totally composed – more than two and a half centuries prior to Constantine and is totally innocent of his 'ecclesiasticalism'.

10 In Matthew 5.46–47 Jesus bids his hearers break free from the old tradition that reserved the *Shalom* greeting from Jewish lips to Jewish ears alone and reinforced the point by noting God's undiscriminating 'rain' on all and sundry. The Greek word *teleios* is not 'Perfect as your Father . . . ' but 'inclusive'.

11 That such a measure of 'de-privileging' the Church should have been dubbed 'national apostasy' would have been quite outrageous for less blinkered minds. The preacher also linked it oddly with Samuel's assurance (in 1 Samuel 12.23) that he 'would not cease to pray' for his people over their ardour to acquire and be set under a king!

12 He had deliberately brought the Roman 'eagles', the imperial banners, into the city under cover of darkness, assuming that, if they were not thus visible, the assured Jewish uprising against their offensive, blaspheming presence would be cheated of its reasons. Not so, and after a humiliating stand-off, Pilate had to yield to them.

13 The Roman term 'Friend of Caesar' seems to have been only a mere allusion to an assumed amity. Or may it have been a more 'official' title denoting some intimacy?

14 The passage in John 18.33–38 – explored in Chapter 8 – on the exchanges between Pilate and Jesus is a classic example of the miscarriage of words. 'King is your word' (i.e. 'not mine') Jesus has to reply, if he is not to assent to Pilate's Roman meaning in it. Yet he will not deny the 'kingness' that is his. But how does he convey into utter ignorance what he needs it to say?

< 186 >

15 Using the word in the strict sense of 'disjoined' or 'not integral' and certainly not domineering.

16 If it is scrupulously 'co-existent' and not 'exclusively bent', some ongoing 'establishment' of Christian faith does proper justice to the vital possession of history. More importantly, it cherishes for all the significance of what its deliberate abolition would dangerously imply, i.e. a statehood becoming its own conscience-less self as states are liable to do. The negative implications of what may be positively arguable are not to be ignored. Such is history.

17 Paul's phrase in Galatians 4.25 may well cover both the Judaic and Islamic, where the issue belongs.

18 At the core of the matter was the Messianic meaning and the relation of 'Messiah' to YAHWEH. Just as in his handling of the Sabbath – and other occasions of his ' . . . but I say to you . . . ' – Jesus appealed to his inner sense of vocation as pointing to a Messianic fulfilment in the sheer light of how his day-to-day ministry was leading. See: 'Jesus in his Christ Experience', in: '*The Education of Christian Faith*, Brighton & Portland, 2000, pp. 3–20.

19 'Stemming from the love *of* God' – all the New Testament understands – and not simply from our love to God, as in the ancient double form of the love commandment. Through the significance of Jesus in life and in the Cross, the active love of God towards us becomes, as it never had been before – its eternity apart – within human ken and experience. As such, it brought a responsive impulse, a self-surrender in its own terms. As 'Command', love to God remained but could now be obeyed in more than mere observing of a precept.

20 Meaning by 'prerogative' a capacity proper to its nature, a legitimacy duly belonging to a task.

21 As addressing the autonomy of the self inside the meaning of the privilege in our creaturehood and the human dignity in and for a Gospel that intends our freedom in the very shape of its authority. 'Where the Spirit of the Lord is there is liberty' (2 Corinthians 3.17) tells what can only be reciprocal between truth and its love, grace and its welcome.

22 The age-long Islamic Caliphate came to a dire end in 1924 and, despite several efforts, has never been revived. Turkey abolished it in the context of Ataturk's 'secular' mind. There were elements in the Arab Revolt that were unhappy about the Caliphate's being in 'Ottoman' hands rather than Arab. That ethnic factor, among others, currently troubles the *Ummah* ideal of a single, world-wide Muslim hegemony. Though the Caliphate finds no mention in the Qur'an, there is no doubt of the centrality of political power and its exercise in the realization of Islam as religion.

23 This, in 1 John 4.18, might be paraphrased: 'love that has reached its full quality of inclusiveness is thereby freed from the fear that is ever apprehensive, whether of being vulnerable, or broken, or deserted'. For love lives and serves in its own lovedness in God.

24 The phrase in Revelation 6.16 is at the heart of New Testament paradox. Literally, the saying would be quite incongruous. The supreme judgment on sin and wrong is made in the sovereignty of the love that suffers to redeem. 'The face . . . on the throne' had worn the 'crown of thorns'. For 'as is His majesty, so is His mercy'.

< 187 >

11   *An Honest Will to Faith*

1   The issue, in terms of words and meanings, was broached in Chapter 8. Here it lies more deeply in the philosophical problem of 'meaning', when we are discontent with the sheer observational empiricism of the sciences.

2   William James: *Selected Papers on Philosophy*, London ed., 1907, 'The Will to Believe', pp. 99–124, originally published in 1897.

3   *Ibid.*, p. 100. William James (1842–1910) taught famously at Harvard.

4   *Ibid.*, p. 101, adding: perhaps dubiously – in the nonchalance of some – 'there is some believing tendency wherever there is a willingness to act at all'.

5   Either way, there is a verdict (the word meaning both a view as to truth and a decision given). Either we posit benediction or malediction in our reception of the world and our experience of its procedures. Then our heart-verdict (in line with either in the intellect) will be either a 'blessing' or a 'cursing'. There is no neutrality around the moral case, because there is entire 'neutrality' about how the material-physical order functions. See below on 'the secular'.

6   The philosophical issue in note 5 thus becomes the theological question of the goodness or 'malignity' of the 'God' whom any theology, as such, must 'esteem' or 'disesteem'. Cf. the discussion of the reach of 'divine unity' in Chapter 3.

7   It is a sad thing that the meaning of *paracletos* and its kindred verb *parakaleo* has been lost in the popular current sense of an armchair and cushions. 'To call alongside' in need or hope, suggesting dependence, leads on to a resulting gift of adequacy thereby. There is a scene in the Bayeux Tapestry where Bishop Odo is shown 'comforting his troops' with a prodding spear to urge them on.

8   In that neither bread nor wine 'arrive' to be such except by dint of long, patient and skilful human care – a care, however, which could never avail to produce them, if the natural order, its chemistry, its reactions, its sun and soil, were other than they co-operating are.

9   Thomas Traherne: *Centuries, Poems and Thanksgivings*, ed. H. M. Margoliouth, Oxford, 1968, Vol. 2, p. 156, 'Amendment', and Thomas Traherne: *Centuries*, Oxford, 1960, Century 1, 29, cf. also 25, 27 and 28.

10   In this very context, Thomas Traherne writes in: *The Way to Blessedness*, or: *Christian Ethicks*, ed. M. Bottrall, London, 1962, p. 51: 'He that would not be a stranger to the universe, an alien to felicity, and a foreigner to himself, must know God to be an infinite Benefactor, all eternity full of treasures, the world itself the beginning of gifts, and his own soul the possessor of all, in communion with the Deity.' Must not many a burdened spirit rather feel 'a stranger to the universe' (how should one be otherwise?), an alien to felicity, and certainly a 'foreigner to himself'. In the following sentence, Traherne adds: 'The business of religion is complacency with God' – exactly, except that Traherne is using 'complacency' in its 17th century sense of 'delight'.

11   The physical associations of 'begotten' have long confused and distorted the meaning here. The analogy from music or literature has always been, as it were, 'trinitarian' – the original and devising (deriving) mind, the concrete

< 188 >

expression or presentation, and – thirdly – the impact and influence, the whence and where and whither of all meaning.

12 Some ideas of divine omnipotence have divined that forgiveness, from God, must be like some wave of a wand. That there is a costliness about forgiveness is rooted in any sound moral theism as well as in the nature of human guilt.

13 William Shakespeare: *Macbeth*, Act 2, Scene 3, line 123. The two sons of the king, Duncan, murdered by Macbeth, in the immediate horror of the discovery. 'Foul and fair a day' is a refrain in the play. It *might* be applied to the perception of Good Friday as the climatic expression of the foulness of human wrong and the Passion of divine suffering.

14 William Wordsworth: *Poetical Works*, ed. T. Hutchinson, Oxford, 1905, p. 492. 'Ode to Duty'.

15 Robert Browning: *Poetical Works*, Oxford, 1941, 'Bishop Blougram's Apology', p. 444, lines 627–9.

16 Lovely lines and to be spoken by one of three hired murderers in wait for Banquo whom Macbeth has commissioned them to kill. *Op. cit.* note 13, Act 3, Scene 3, lines 5–7.

17 Or where we look for Him, depending on how the psalm is read. When the psalmist in the famous 23rd declares: 'I will always be in the house of the Lord', it would seem that he is referring to the good earth as his landscape spread 'before him' with its 'green pastures' and 'running waters', rather than to a heavenly destiny of immortality.

18 Hence, surely, the constant connection in the New Testament between love and knowledge, in respect of God and Christ. The impulsiveness of love must not be mistaken for its blindness. It responds with the abandon all faithful lovers know, because it has the credentials by which alone it is kindled. Yet that 'abandon' – in terms of fidelity and passionate compassion – is only its language of trust.

19 Perhaps it is fair, against the background of this whole chapter, to wonder why, for so long, modern scientists have decried and scorned the notion of a 'geocentric' universe and an 'anthropocentric' earth. They were right in respect of vast immensity on the one hand and sheer brevity with the microcosmic on the other. But who 'tells' the vastness how amazingly vast it is? A vastness of which it is utterly unaware without us? Whence did any Hubble telescope take off to explore infinitude unless from this single planet, where alone resided the cunning to produce and send it? (If far elsewhere there are similar creaturehoods, their being there, if proven, in no way infringes our own.) If we are rendered entirely 'dwarfed' by a universe so enormous and daunting, it is one we alone have measured. There is no need for us to be cowed or minimized by immensity – an immensity all oblivious of its own magnitude until *we* enlighten it, enlightening an entity all incapable of self-discovery without us. If the negligible microcosm is in a macrocosm the reverse is the other truth. The sun continues to 'rise and set' and 'run its circuit course', when scientifically we know well enough it does no such thing. On scouting the 'geocentric' and the 'anthrocentric' see, for example: Richard Tarnas: *The Passion of the Western Mind: Understanding the Ideas that Have Shaped our world View*, New York and

< 189 >

London, 1991. The poet, G. M. Hopkins, had the right point tersely when he wrote:

> The earth and heaven, so little known,
> Are measured outward from my breast.
> I am the midst of every zone
> And justify the East and West.

> *The Major Works*, ed. C. Phillips, Oxford, 2002, p. 77.

12   *The Wounded Name and Its Kindred Servants*

1   William Shakespeare: *Hamlet*, Act 5, Scene 2, lines 196–7. Shakespeare was thinking of the calumny and the reproach which would vilify him if the real story stayed untold. Thus the words are apt for all studied in Chapters 1 and 4 about the blameworthiness of God. These words apply here, however, to how the truly 'wounded Name' is divinely there in Jesus crucified, though 'standing unknown' among so many as the true 'thus it was' concerning God as love.

2   'The place of the Name' was, for psalmist and prophet, the very title of Jerusalem, while Exodus 3.10 assured Moses that the Exodus was the place where YAHWEH would be known by that Name, written into lived experience and apt for knowing in no other way. See: *Semitism: The Whence and Whither*, Brighton & Portland, 2004, pp. 7–23.

3   The term in four New Testament passages is formed from *makros* (far distant) used in Luke 15.13 of that willful destination, and *thumos* (mind). The father's 'reach' in the story is that of bearing the pain of that 'distance' in such compassion that the wanderer can visualize an unchanged home to which he can retrace his way.

4   The point here is much more than the famous Kantian 'categorical imperative' held to necessitate the existence of God as its ground and sanction. That 'practical reason' has to be enriched by the deeper elements of emotion, reverence and love, in our experience of being in trust with values we in no way originate. A classic study here is that of W. R. Sorley: *Moral Values and the Idea of God*, Cambridge, 1921.

5   A mystique in which Shakespeare and the Elizabethans loved to indulge – the 'divinity that doth hedge a king'. Hence the cult of the 'Royal' adjective to grace military regiments, an art academy and a society for the protection of birds. What might its presence add or its absence withhold?

6   Shakespeare in *Henry V* gave a notable example in having his 'royal Harry' go disguised and anonymous among his troops in the dark night before Agincourt, conversing round a camp-fire – in sharp contrast to the French nobility lolling in elegant tents discussing their admirable horses. Which is 'royal'? Assessments must decide (see Act 4 Prologue and Sc. 1). Or, as the great Sufi poet, Jalal al-Din Rumi has it in his Mathnawi, 'Through love the King is made a slave', ii.1462.

7   Robert Browning: *Poetical Works*, Oxford, 1940, p. 226, in 'Saul' finds in David's love for the stricken king a sure clue to a greater capacity in God for the like. In context he meant human love as never 'surpassing' the divine in

< 190 >

generosity. Here the divine is never 'surpassed' by the reality of human wrong in its ever being beyond response.

8   That 'God is Muslim' or 'God is Christian' would be utterly pretentious in the abstract (though that 'God is Jewish' is a corollary of Judaism). Yet the whole argument here is that the 'necessity' that makes us Christian derives from the God of our theology.

9   Those two words in Matthew's Passion narrative (27.37) in their stark brevity could well enshrine the whole reality of the Cross – 'this person, this place'. The grim factuality of the soldiers' watch in its uncertain length is one with the interpreting vigil of all Christian theology.

10 To speak of 'experience' – being a thing of time – as 'God's' can only be within the meaning of the Incarnation. What can be 'vicarious' in the nature of response always belongs with the 'vulnerable'. Only in 'bearing' is there ever 'bearing away', as John 1.29 has it in the double sense of the Greek verb *airon*. See R. S. Thomas: *No Truce with the Furies*, Newcastle, 1995, p. 42, published after *Collected Poems, 1945–1990*.

11 The biographical point is fairly made. It could well be that his insanity resulted from the intensity of his fervour and the sheer egoism of his tumultuous mind, in which he dramatized his own pioneering 'wisdom'. It is necessary also to remember how prone he was to physical frailty. His eleven silent years in lunacy required the 'long-suffering' in his sister his philosophy decried. Cf. Inroduction, note 15.

12 See *The Antichrist*, section 24, p. 153.

13 This is a happier version of his meaning than 'the super-man'. There was a loadedness about Nietzsche's aphorisms that popular conclusions often mistook.

14 In the sense that its meanings gain from the very radical clarity with which they are disowned and scorned.

15 Christian martyrology was often near to suicidal in the deliberate wish to die. See a study in: G. W. Bowerstock: *Martyrdom and Rome*, Cambridge, 1995, and, differently, in my: *Faith at Suicide: Violent Religion and Human Despair*, Brighton & Portland, 2005, pp. 52–9.

16 Algernon Swinburne in 'Hymn to Proserpine', see: *Selected Poems*, ed. L. M. Findlay, Manchester, 1982, pp. 57–61.

17 See: Patrick Pearse: *Plays, Stories, Poems*, Dublin, 1980, p. 340, and Ruth D. Edwards: *Patrick Pearse: The Triumph of Failure*, London, 1977.

18 His public preaching was only part of his mission. Education of disciples was the other. It is well to keep in mind that part of 'his trial', of what beset him, was the sheer diversity among those disciples (zealots with publicans) and the confusions over why they were 'with him' in varieties of Messianic hope.

19 That surely has always been the required sense and not the puzzlement about ever being led into temptation. In popular Messianic hope was the thought of antecedent 'woes' which must needs be at 'maximum' since, if more came after alleged Messianic event, that event would be disproved as final. Hence the idea of dire troubles prior to the climax, the longing not to undergo them or, otherwise, not be overwhelmed by them ('Deliver us from the evil'). We might paraphrase now: 'Do not let evil so do its worst that we succumb but

< 191 >

ever deliver us from it.' There is no doubt that this clause fully confirms the Messianic meaning of the entire prayer.

20   George Herbert: *The English Poems*, ed. C. A. Patrides, London, 1974, p. 193.

21   'Lamb' and 'throne' here would be meaningless if 'Lamb' was read in some literal 'born of a sheep' sense. The paradox only means, if 'Lamb' (initial capital 'L') is known in the full sense of a self-giving love in sacrificial bearing of wrong as the way of its forgiveness. To speak of 'the Lamb of God' is to know this inherent quality as the truth of Christian theology. It is in no way told by analogies from Temple sacrifice or even from the story of Abraham, where he and his 'Isaac' are merely obeying some command and in no way comprehendingly coping with an evil situation for its redemption. The 'Lamb' language has been much misread in preaching. We come closer to its authentic meaning in the biography of Jeremiah who read his prophetic vocation as something that made him 'sacrificial' in responding to it.

< 192 >

INDEX OF NAMES, TERMS AND PHRASES

< 193 >

< 194 >

< 195 >

< 196 >

< 197 >

< 198 >

< 199 >

< 200 >

< 201 >

BIBLICAL REFERENCES

Hebrew Bible

Genesis
1.12	141
3.5	40

Exodus
3.10	152
3.10–14	55, 174, 182, 190
23.9	136

Leviticus
19.18	136
25.5	136

Numbers
6.24–26	176

Deuteronomy
7.7	58

Judges
11.24	57

Job
1.6	100
38.7	100

Psalms
2.7	102
8 all	4
23 all	189
27.13	140
35.27	164, 173
63.5	149
80.17	100
103.13	103
122.7	173
130.1	4
137 all	182
139 all	3, 123
144.3	102

Proverbs
18.10	152

Ecclesiastes
3.11	94, 178
12.6	178

Isaiah
1.5	65
18.8	69
41.1–5	182
43.24	152, 183
48.15	173
49.1	182
51.5	182
53 all	64, 68, 164
60.9	182
63.9	152
66.19	182

Jeremiah
15.17	67

Hosea
1.8	182

Amos
9.7	67

Zechariah
4.6	65, 114
8.23	63, 114

Malachi
1.6	103

New Testament

Matthew
5.46–47	186
11.28–30	157
16.13–15	67
27.37	191
27.63–65	177

Mark
6.20	67
12.37	67

Luke
10.34	151
22.28	65, 160
24.35	34, 117

< 203 >

QURANIC REFERENCES